State-building in the Western Balkans

The Western Balkans have seen rapid changes since the end of the violent conflicts in the 1990s. The EU has been one of the main drivers for change, focusing on the political, economic and social transformation of the region to prepare the countries for membership in the Union. EU enlargement has never before been this complex and inter-connected with processes of state-building and democratization. It can be argued that the EU is actively involved in state-building. By focusing on a number of case studies, it will be demonstrated how complex the transformation towards independent statehood and modern democratic governance has been (and continues to be) for most Western Balkan states. While some chapters focus explicitly on the role of the EU in these transformative procedures, others discuss the role of outside influences on state-building, democratization and independent governance more implicitly. The picture painted is one of multiple and inter-connected alterations that have long-term consequences for the political systems of the region.

This book was published as a special issue of *Nationalities Papers*.

Soeren Keil is Lecturer in International Relations at Canterbury Christ Church, UK. His research focuses on the political systems of the post-Yugoslav states, in particular forms of territorial and non-territorial autonomy. He is the author of *Multinational Federalism in Bosnia and Herzegovina* (Ashgate, 2013) and numerous articles on the political development of the former Yugoslav states and the role of the European Union in the region.

The Association for the Study of Nationalities
www.nationalities.org

Edited by
Karl Cordell, *University of Plymouth*
Florian Bieber, *University of Kent, Canterbury*
Stefan Wolff, *University of Nottingham*

The books in this series focus on the dynamics and interactions of significant minority and majority nationalisms in the context of globalisation and their social, political and economic causes and consequences. Each book is focused on an important topic drawn from the rigorously peer-reviewed articles published in *Nationalities Papers* and *Ethnopolitics*, and includes authoritative theoretical reflection and empirical analysis by some of the most widely recognized experts in the world.

Nationalities Papers

Conflict in South-Eastern Europe at the End of the Twentieth Century
A "Scholars' Initiative" assesses some of the controversies
Edited by Thomas Emmert and Charles Ingrao

Identities, Nations and Politics After Communism
Edited by Roger E. Kanet

Crimes of State Past and Present
Government-Sponsored Atrocities and International Legal Responses
Edited by David M. Crowe

The Communist Quest for National Legitimacy in Europe, 1918–1989
Edited by Martin Mevius

The Comparative Approach to National Movements
Miroslav Hroch and Nationalism Studies
Edited by Alexander Maxwell

State-building in the Western Balkans
European Approaches to Democratization
Edited by Soeren Keil

Ethnopolitics

Gambling on Humanitarian Intervention
Edited by Timothy W. Crawford and Alan J. Kuperman

Ethnopolitics of Elections
Edited by Florian Bieber and Stefan Wolff

Internationalized State-building after Violent Conflict
Bosnia Ten Years after Dayton
Edited by Marc Weller and Stefan Wolff

Governance in Ethnically Mixed Cities
Edited by Sherrill Stroschein

Transnationalism in the Balkans
Edited by Denisa Kostovicova and Vesna Bojicic-Dzelilovic

Cultural Autonomy in Contemporary Europe
Edited by David J. Smith and Karl Cordell

EU Conflict Management
Edited by James Hughes

Ethnicity and Religion
Intersections and Comparisons
*Edited by Joseph Ruane and
 Jennifer Todd*

Migration and Divided Societies
Edited by Chris Gilligan and Susan Ball

State-building in the Western Balkans
European Approaches to Democratization

Edited by
Soeren Keil

LONDON AND NEW YORK

First published 2014 by Routledge

2 Park Square, Milton Park, Abingdon, Oxfordshire OX14 4RN
711 Third Avenue, New York, NY 10017

Routledge is an imprint of the Taylor & Francis Group, an informa business

First issued in paperback 2018

Copyright © 2014 Association for the Study of Nationalities

All rights reserved. No part of this book may be reprinted or reproduced or utilised in any form or by any electronic, mechanical, or other means, now known or hereafter invented, including photocopying and recording, or in any information storage or retrieval system, without permission in writing from the publishers.

Notice:
Product or corporate names may be trademarks or registered trademarks, and are used only for identification and explanation without intent to infringe.

British Library Cataloguing in Publication Data
A catalogue record for this book is available from the British Library

ISBN13: 978-0-415-72073-1 (hbk)
ISBN13: 978-1-138-37752-3 (pbk)

Typeset in Times New Roman
by Taylor & Francis Books

Publisher's Note
The publisher accepts responsibility for any inconsistencies that may have arisen during the conversion of this book from journal articles to book chapters, namely the possible inclusion of journal terminology.

Disclaimer
Every effort has been made to contact copyright holders for their permission to reprint material in this book. The publishers would be grateful to hear from any copyright holder who is not here acknowledged and will undertake to rectify any errors or omissions in future editions of this book.

Contents

Citation Information	ix
1. Introduction: Europeanization, state-building and democratization in the Western Balkans *Soeren Keil*	1
2. International statebuilding as contentious politics: the case of post conflict Bosnia and Herzegovina *Outi Keranen*	12
3. The OSCE Mission in Bosnia and Herzegovina: Testing the limits of ownership *Valery Perry and Soeren Keil*	29
4. "Quadratic nexus" and the process of democratization and state-building in Albania and Kosovo: a comparison *Gëzim Krasniqi*	53
5. Cutting the mists of the Black Mountain: *Cleavages in Montenegro's divide over statehood and identity* *Jelena Dzankic*	70
6. The role of the EU in promoting good governance in Macedonia: towards efficiency and effectiveness or deliberative democracy? *Marija Risteska*	89
7. Another "strategic accession"? The EU and Serbia (2000–2010) *Bernhard Stahl*	105
8. EU Member State-Building in the Western Balkans: (Prolonged) EU-protectorates or new model of sustainable enlargement? Conclusion *Jens Woelk*	127
Index	141

Citation Information

The chapters in this book were originally published in *Nationalities Papers*, volume 41, issue 3 (May 2013). When citing this material, please use the original page numbering for each article, as follows:

Chapter 1
Europeanization, state-building and democratization in the Western Balkans
Soeren Keil
Nationalities Papers, volume 41, issue 3 (May 2013) pp. 343–353

Chapter 2
International statebuilding as contentious politics: the case of post conflict Bosnia and Herzegovina
Outi Keranen
Nationalities Papers, volume 41, issue 3 (May 2013) pp. 354–370

Chapter 3
The OSCE Mission in Bosnia and Herzegovina: Testing the limits of ownership
Valery Perry and Soeren Keil
Nationalities Papers, volume 41, issue 3 (May 2013) pp. 371–394

Chapter 4
"Quadratic nexus" and the process of democratization and state-building in Albania and Kosovo: a comparison
Gëzim Krasniqi
Nationalities Papers, volume 41, issue 3 (May 2013) pp. 395–411

Chapter 5
Cutting the mists of the Black Mountain: Cleavages in Montenegro's divide over statehood and identity
Jelena Dzankic
Nationalities Papers, volume 41, issue 3 (May 2013) pp. 412–430

Chapter 6
The role of the EU in promoting good governance in Macedonia: towards efficiency and effectiveness or deliberative democracy?
Marija Risteska
Nationalities Papers, volume 41, issue 3 (May 2013) pp. 431–446

CITATION INFORMATION

Chapter 7
Another "strategic accession"? The EU and Serbia (2000–2010)
Bernhard Stahl
Nationalities Papers, volume 41, issue 3 (May 2013) pp. 447–468

Chapter 8
EU Member State-Building in the Western Balkans: (Prolonged) EU-protectorates or new model of sustainable enlargement? Conclusion
Jens Woelk
Nationalities Papers, volume 41, issue 3 (May 2013) pp. 469–482

Please direct any queries you may have about the citations to clsuk.permissions@cengage.com

INTRODUCTION

Europeanization, state-building and democratization in the Western Balkans

Soeren Keil

Applied Social Sciences, Canterbury Christ Church University, UK

The Western Balkans have seen rapid changes since the end of the violent conflicts in the 1990s. The European Union (EU) has been one of the main drivers for change, focusing on the political, economic and social transformation of the region to prepare the countries for membership in the Union. This introduction to the special issue will clarify the key terms and their interaction in the Western Balkans. EU enlargement has never before been this complex and inter-connected with processes of state-building and democratization. The focus on conditionality as the main tool of the EU in the region has had positive and negative effects. It can be argued that the EU is actively involved in state-building processes and therefore the term *EU Member State Building* will be used to explain the engagement of the Union with the countries in the region. This paper will discuss the concept of EU Member State Building, its potential and its pitfalls. It will be demonstrated that the stabilization of the region is unlikely to take place without an active role for the EU; however, the current approach has reached its limits and it is time to think about alternative options to integrate the Western Balkans into European structures.

Introduction

There is general consensus among political elites and academics that the countries in the Western Balkans[1] undergo complex transformations and witness far-reaching changes to their political, social and economic systems. This special issue will assess these complicated processes from the perspectives of Europeanization, state-building and democratization. What will be demonstrated is that while each country faces some unique historical legacies and current problems to deal with, there are three general trends that can be observed. First, all countries of the Western Balkans aspire to membership in the European Union (EU). They are part of the EU's Stabilization and Association Process (SAP) and as such have to implement the *acquis communautaire* of the EU. This Europeanization process in itself will lead to far-reaching changes in the countries' political, social and economic systems. Second, all states in the Western Balkans have weak state structures and some of them, such as Bosnia and Kosovo, are contested in their very existence as independent states. Consequently it can be argued that the establishment of stateness, meaning efficient governance institutions, full control over the state's territory and good neighborly relations with other states in the region, remains a key challenge. To address some of the fundamental weaknesses in these states, important reforms will have to be implemented to ensure democratic decision-making, the rule of law, the protection of minorities and the establishment of an efficient economic and social system. Finally, all states in the Western Balkans are young democracies. While democracy is deeply-rooted in some of them such as Croatia, other countries are still undergoing important steps towards consolidating democratic structures. Challenges such as the enforcement of the rule of law, the fight against corruption in the bureaucracy and the establishment of cooperative patterns between government and opposition remain. As the contributions to this special issue will demonstrate, overcoming these weaknesses in democratic governance will be a long-term process and require deep changes to the political system and even the political culture.

This introduction will first offer a definition of the key terms of Europeanization, state-building and democratization and will discuss these processes in the context of the Western Balkans. In part two it will be demonstrated how these transformations are connected and that we can talk about an *EU Member State Building* process in the region. Finally, part three will introduce the papers of this special issue and summarize their main arguments in the context of *EU Member State Building*. The majority of papers in this special issue have been presented at the UACES annual conference 2011 in Cambridge, UK. This also underlines how important it is to study the integration of the Western Balkans into the EU as an essential part of European Studies and therefore demonstrates the transition of a region that used to be studied in conflict resolution classes and in courses that focused on international intervention. The main theme of this special issue is the recognition that the Western Balkans are part of Europe and that their destiny lies in the EU's hands. The challenge for the region is no longer about peace-building but about a process of preparation for membership in European structures. The integration of the Western Balkans into the EU has the potential to become the single most successful foreign policy achievement of the Union. In its importance it is probably comparable to overcoming the century-old conflicts between Germany and France that stood at the beginning of the European integration process. Ending the violence in the Western Balkans, establishing efficient and modern democratic states and integrating these states into the EU are massive tasks. However, considering the possible alternatives of long-term instability it is certainly a task worthwhile.

Definition of terms

Before we will be able to analyze the complex process of EU Member State Building in the Western Balkans and its main characteristics and challenges, it is important to clarify the most important definitions used by the authors of this special issue.

When describing the process of Europeanization, the most common definition refers to a

> Process of a) construction, b) diffusion and c) institutionalization of formal and informal rules, procedures, policy paradigms, styles, 'ways of doing things', and shared beliefs and norms which are first defined and consolidated in the EU policy process and then incorporated in the logic of domestic (national and subnational) discourse, political structures and public choices. (Radaelli 2006, 30)

Europeanization in this context is understood as the influence of the EU on its Member States' political, economic and social systems (Quaglia et al. 2007). It is argued that the EU as a political system impacts on its Member States because decisions taken at a European level can have a long-term effect on each individual Member State (Hix 2005). The best example of the impact of Europeanization in its classic understanding is the introduction of a new currency, the Euro, as a result of the Maastricht Treaty.

However, the countries of the Western Balkans are not Member States of the EU. Nevertheless, they are affected by important changes as a result of decisions taken in Brussels. Because they are part of the accession process they have to implement the *acquis communautaire*, the EU's legal foundation, and they have to reform their political and economic systems to comply with the Copenhagen Criteria, which specify the conditions for membership in the Union. Therefore, as Schimmelpfennig and Sedelmeier (2005a, 2005b) have demonstrated, the EU can have a massive impact on countries before they join the Union. The process of integration into the Union therefore results in the implementation of a massive amount of EU laws, regulations and directives, changes to the bureaucracy and far-reaching changes to constitutional norms on citizenship, voting rights, property rights and the creation of a legal basis for the transfer of sovereignty to the EU (Claes 2007).

When talking about "Europeanization, South East European style," it has been pointed out that this is an externally-driven, coercive and increasingly demanding process (Anastasakis 2005, 82). Belloni (2009, 317) has argued that the "Balkans have changed Europe and the EU as much as the EU is currently trying to change its southeastern neighbours." He concludes that the Europeanization of the countries in the former Yugoslavia should focus on "the coherence of [European] policy towards the region, focus less on a Europeanized political elite and more on citizens and civil society organizations, and carefully deploy incentives and rewards to sustain the reform process that is already under way" (2009, 314).

The European integration of this region is complex and a long-term process. It is multi-layered and the EU itself faces completely new challenges in the region. Florian Bieber (2011) has demonstrated that there are a number of minimalist states in the region, "which barely fulfill functions generally associated with states" (1784). Bieber argues that the state structures that were created after the end of violence in Bosnia, Kosovo and the state union of Serbia and Montenegro were aimed at resolving the conflicts but were unable to establish an efficient monopoly of the use of force, democratic decision-making capacities and embedded statehood (1785–1790). States that are unable to perform basic state functions such as providing security, ensuring a basic level of social welfare and providing political incentives for economic growth are the result of the violent break-up of the former Yugoslavia. The focus of EU integration in the Western Balkans therefore lies on state-building to overcome the results of the violent break-up of Yugoslavia, which aims at rebuilding fundamental governance structures such as political institutions, civil societies and economic and welfare systems. The focus of state-building lies on the reconstruction of whole countries and societies, including their democratization and the establishment of a functional civil society (Etzioni 2009, 102). The EU therefore becomes an actor in the state-building process in the Western Balkans. Through the process of Europeanization it is hoped that the EU will use its influence and the final incentive of membership to promote the establishment of efficient state structures and administrations that are capable of coping with the pressures of membership in the Union. However, it has been discussed that external state-building has had only limited success in the past (Paris 2004; Sisk and Paris 2007; Ghani and Lockhart 2009). Chandler (2009, 3) argues that "international statebuilding intervention is necessary but not sufficient." Europeanization as the process of the preparation of the countries in the Western Balkans for their membership in the EU therefore focuses on the establishment of efficient state structures, including the reconstruction of economic and welfare systems after violent conflicts in the region. The carrot of membership in the EU is used to motivate political elites in these countries to implement important reforms to strengthen state capacity and enhance democratic decision-making. In fact, democratization is a further feature of

Europeanization in the region. The first Copenhagen Criterion focuses on democratic governance, minority protection and the rule of law.[2] Democratization in this context refers to the establishment and strengthening of democratic governance. This includes free and fair elections, a professional parliamentary service, cooperation between government and opposition, civil society input into government activities and legislation and the establishment of *Rechtsstaatlichkeit* (rule of law). Scholars of democratization have focused on the establishment of political institutions, civil society and a changing political culture in which election results are respected, conflicts are solved by political and legal means and the judiciary is independent from political influence (Linz and Stepan 1996; Diamond 1999, 2008; Merkel 2004). What is clear at this point is that the process of state-building is necessarily connected to democratization in the Western Balkans, because the establishment and strengthening of democratic governance remains a fundamental principle of external (and internal) state-building and consolidation in the region. The Europeanization of the Western Balkans refers to a process in which the EU supports the implementation of European standards (defined by the EU's conditionality) in the Western Balkans. Because of the authoritarian past and the violent break-up of Yugoslavia, democratization and state-building are fundamental elements of this Europeanization. The EU, in other words, is building states which can eventually join the Union.

EU Member State Building

The above discussion demonstrates that the countries in the Western Balkans undergo a complicated transformation. They are deeply embedded in the process of EU integration via the SAP, which focuses not only on the Copenhagen Criteria but also on regional cooperation and reconciliation. All countries with the exception of Kosovo have signed Stabilization and Association Agreements (SAA) with the EU over the last years, which legally bind them into a process of political and economic integration. In addition, Croatia, Macedonia, Montenegro and Serbia have received candidate status and Croatia has concluded EU accession negotiations in 2011. The European Commission has recently suggested that Croatia should join the EU in July 2013,[3] and it has suggested membership negotiations for Macedonia,[4] while official negotiations started earlier in 2012 with Montenegro.

The Europeanization of the Western Balkans is a process that focuses on stabilizing and reforming the political and economic systems in these countries by encouraging local elites to implement "European standards." At the same it is envisaged that the process will help to overcome the legacies of the recent past and encourage regional cooperation, reconciliation and result in cross-border synergies. To some extent this process has been very successful and since the end of violence in Kosovo in 1999 and in Macedonia in 2000 there has been no major eruption of violence in the region with the exception of the riots in Kosovo in 2004. Furthermore, the states in the Western Balkans have become stabilized and with the exception of Bosnia and Kosovo are not contested as such anymore. Important forums of regional cooperation have been created, first through the Stability Pact for South Eastern Europe and its successor the Regional Cooperation Council, but also in important other areas such as energy and security.

The Europeanization of the region focuses on active state-building and democratization. In contrast to the earlier enlargement rounds in 2004 and 2007, which saw 12 Central and Eastern European States join the Union, new challenges have forced the EU and its Member States to outline new criteria and new methods for the integration process. Because most of the Western Balkans countries are post-conflict societies,[5] the integration process necessarily needed to address some of the legacies of these conflicts, in particular economic reconstruction, political institution-building, reconciliation and regional cooperation. Furthermore, all states in the region with the exception of Albania have declared their independence from Yugoslavia and some of them, such as Bosnia and Kosovo, have never been independent before. Others, such as Croatia and Serbia, have never been fully democratic polities before and have never existed as independent states in their current borders. Weak statehood and weak democratic institutions are therefore characteristic of the region. The existence of semi-authoritarian regimes in Croatia and Serbia until 2000 (Zakošek 2008) and the outbreak of violence in Macedonia in 2000 demonstrate that these political systems were far from consolidated in the first years after the break-up of Yugoslavia.

The process of EU Member State Building is multi-layered. It started in 1999, when the European Council defined the SAP and added cooperation with the ICTY and regional co-operation as additional conditions for all countries in the Western Balkans. While the European perspective for the countries of the region has been upheld by the European Council in the Feira Meeting (June 2000) and in Thessaloniki (June 2003), the need for reform in the region remained a constant and ever-visible condition. The conclusion of Thessaloniki therefore reads:

> During the last four years, the European Union's policy of Stabilisation and Association has contributed critically to progress achieved throughout the region in promoting stability and in bringing the countries closer to the Union. It now needs to be strengthened and enriched with elements from the enlargement process, so that it can better meet the new challenges, as the countries move from stabilisation and reconstruction to sustainable development, association and integration into European structures. The Union's thus enriched policy of Stabilisation and Association, including the Stabilisation and Association Agreements, will constitute the overall framework for the European course of the Western Balkan countries, all the way to their future accession. (EU Commission, *The Thessaloniki Agenda for the Western Balkans*)

The process is clearly defined: the countries of the Western Balkans want to join the EU and the EU is willing to accept them, if they fulfill the conditions. The conditions, defined by the EU without any input from the potential candidate countries, have however been specified further. Not only did the EU attempt to overcome the results and the legacies of the (most recent) past by focusing on the co-operation with the ICTY as a form of retributive justice (without encouraging local forms of reconciliation), but also regional co-operation became a way of encouraging the states of the former Yugoslavia to overcome their recent violent past and to model the EU in miniature. It is consequently not surprising that the main thing regional co-operation has resulted in is a free trade agreement among the countries of the region and some co-operation in energy, security and police matters. However, the lack of joint negotiations with the EU (as occurred in Eastern Europe) means that the incentives for true regional co-operation are low. In fact, the border dispute between Croatia and Slovenia threatened Croatian accession at a point where membership negotiations were nearly completed. Furthermore, regional co-operation has not resulted in long-term co-operation and synergies that supported joint projects to move EU integration forward. Inter-state relations remain volatile, as the situation in Northern Kosovo demonstrates.

Furthermore, over the last ten years conditionality has become even further qualified and specified. The EU refers continuously to other organizations in their progress reports and adopts their legal framework as part of the EU's conditionality. In that respect the Progress Report for Bosnia mentions the decision of the European Court of Human Rights in the Finci/Sejdic case and connects the resolution of this case to Bosnia's progress in EU integration. The Venice Commission is another institution which has been mentioned numerous times over the last years. Their recommendations become part of the EU's reform suggestions. The International Criminal Court also features prominently in most country progress reports, because most countries have signed bilateral agreements with the USA which forbid the prosecution and transferal of US citizens. In many respects it is easy to understand the EU's reliance on other institutions and their guidelines. On the one side it has to be mentioned that EU conditionality is very vague and even the Copenhagen Criteria are political rather than technical, leaving a lot of room for interpretation. On the other side, there has been a trend in EU enlargement to specify general conditions by referring to more specific policies of other organizations. This occurred most openly in the case of Eastern Europe, when the countries in East and Central Europe had to implement the standard minority rights suggestions of the OSCE, and the High Commissioner on National Minorities became a key actor in minority rights legislation.

Specifying conditionality as such therefore has been common practice in EU enlargement before and so has the reliance on other institutions; what however is new in the Western Balkans is the direct intervention mechanisms for the EU when its conditionality is not met. These direct intervention practices occur on three levels. First, the EU can intervene directly in the political process, as is the case in Bosnia through the High Representative and the EU Special Representative, which were united in one position until 2011. The EU Police Mission and a small military mission mean that the EU is also directly involved in questions of internal (and external) security as well as security sector reform. In Kosovo, the EU is involved in the appointment of the International Civilian Representative, who oversees the democratization process in the country and has had a right to veto legislation. Furthermore, the EU's rule of law mission EULEX has intervened in internal investigation and local court cases. In Macedonia, the EU Special Representative has become the main moderator between Macedonian and Albanian parties and remains the main mediator in case of conflict.

Second, the EU can support certain parties, laws, actions and persons directly. The elections in Serbia in 2008 were heavily influenced by the EU's support for President Tadić directly in the Presidential election, and for his Democratic Party (DS) in the following parliamentary elections. The elections were won by Tadić and the DS, and consequently Serbia's EU integration progressed at high speed. The EU made it clear that an electoral outcome not in its favor would result in a slowdown and potential reverse of the EU integration process, as can be witnessed in Serbia since the electoral success of Tomislav Nikolić and the formation of a new government without the DS. Similarly, the EU continues to support openly moderate parties in Bosnia, although with less success than in the case of Serbia.

Finally, the EU can threaten to block further progress in the EU enlargement process or to stop financial assistance. Chandler (2010) has pointed out that in the fragile societies of the Western Balkans it does not matter if the EU intervenes directly or threatens to withhold some funds: both result in a crisis of local democracy and illegitimate pressure on democratically elected officials. He argues that EU conditionality has focused not on formal democratic principles but on governance and "administrative practices and policy choices of governments" (Chandler 2007, 596). The EU, in other words, has focused much more on *policy-output* rather than on the organizational principles of the *polity* itself. This is a clear shift from the conditionality applied in Eastern and Central Europe and is commonly connected to colonialism, international trusteeship or state-building rather than enlargement. It is in this interference in the internal affairs of independent states, and the specific application of Brussels-designed solutions to the region, that the reference to the European Raj finds its relevant application (Knaus and Martin 2003).

EU Member State Building therefore qualifies as a new model of enlargement. It comes, however, with a number of negative side-effects. For one, there is the obvious problem of democratic justification of extensive EU intervention in the internal affairs of sovereign states (even if these states have declared to join the EU). It might be justified to argue that potential and real candidate countries have already announced that they are happy to pool some of their sovereignty to Brussels; however, they certainly have not declared that they are happy with Brussels' involvement in sensitive policy areas. We should imagine, for example, that the EU would tell Italy that its police has failed in the fight against organized crime (which probably it has) and that it therefore needs to reform its police units according to principles put together by officials of the European Commission. We can imagine the outcry that would occur and how Italy would defend its right to decide on the organization of its police units. Yet, Bosnian politicians were forced to agree on an EU-designed reform of the police. The Bosnian police reform also highlights another negative effect of EU Member State Building. The EU has no common practices on policing, and the attempt to design a new police structure for Bosnia failed and caused a massive political crisis in the country in 2008. Because the EU focuses more on policy, it is more likely that the EU will focus on areas where there are no European standards and consequently its conditionality and reform suggestions might conflict not only with local traditions, but also with practices in some EU Member States. The Copenhagen Criteria outline basic structural conditions that countries have to fulfill before joining the EU. When these Criteria were established n 1993 they were kept very general purposely to accommodate the institutional, economic, societal and legal differences among the current and future Member States. By shifting the focus from these general structures towards more in-depth policy suggestions, EU conditionality attempts to fake a unity in European policies which does not exist. Fundamentally, the EU is not a state and many policy areas remain in the domain of the Member States, which consequently will result in policy output. However, the different legal and political cultures in Europe have always been seen as a value rather than a problem, not least by the founding fathers of the EU. By focusing on specific policies in its conditionality towards the Western Balkans, the EU pretends that diversity itself is not a value anymore, since "European standards" are the norm that needs to be fulfilled. There is thirdly the negative side effect that the EU claims to act on behalf of the citizens of the countries, yet their voice and their concerns are not addressed through EU Member State Building. If anything, they become more anachronistic with the EU, their governments and politics in general, which can be very dangerous in a region where nationalism is still a strong force. If the EU wants to engage more actively in the region and motivate the local politicians to implement important reforms, which are desperately needed, then it should support citizens' initiatives, local NGOs and those parties that form around social and political issues other than nationalism. The core criticism of EU Member State Building, however, has to be the fact that it is not building Member States. It is creating new dependencies, establishing new dominant party systems and encouraging new veto players, which will make EU integration more complex and time-consuming in the future. The reason why Eastern enlargement went relatively smoothly is because there was a general consensus among the citizens and the elites on the advantages of membership in the EU. It was seen as the next logical step after many countries gained their full (ideological) independence after 1989. In the Western Balkans such a consensus remains missing. While generally a majority of citizens support EU integration in all countries, most of them do so conditionally. Serbs are willing to sacrifice EU integration if it means keeping Kosovo, while politicians of the Republika Srpska in Bosnia have made it clear that their first priority is to protect the Serbs in Bosnia. At the same time, Kosovo's progress will depend on a settlement between Albanians and Serbs in Kosovo and between Kosovo and Serbia on the status of the former Serbian province. Macedonian politicians want to join under the condition that the country will enter the Union under its constitutional name of Republic of Macedonia, a demand heavily contested and vetoed by Greece. It comes as no surprise that Montenegro has made the most advances in EU integration over the last five years. The country enjoys relative prosperity due to tourism and Foreign Direct Investment (FDI). While the governing party DPS and the opposition agree on little, EU integration is accepted by them as the only option to ensure Montenegro's continued economic development and its future as a tiny state in South-East Europe. Montenegro's success in EU integration therefore is the result of two lucky combinations: firstly the status of the country as such is not contested either internally or externally. Secondly, while opposition and government are polarized and disagree on fundamental issues such as NATO membership, they nevertheless agree on the goal of EU integration. What this means for the EU is that the creation of a general consensus on EU integration is of fundamental importance in the process of EU Member State Building. This means addressing conflicts and state weakness quickly and motivating local elites, but in particular citizens, to support EU-related reforms. This includes openly pushing for a constitutional reform in Bosnia, putting pressure on Serbia and Kosovo to come to a joint agreement and influencing both Macedonia and Greece to come to a joint agreement. In the light of the current financial crisis it seems as if the EU is in a particularly good position to influence Greece's negative stance. The EU and its Member States should make it clear that there will be no progress in integration if these status questions are not resolved in mutual agreement. At the same time it should be pointed out that those actors that are seen as particularly destructive to a solution should be punished, for example by limiting their financial support from the EU or by isolating them and fostering new coalitions. The key remains a focus on civil society and those parties that address that focus on economic and political development. The EU should shift its focus away from political elites to local leaders, NGO representatives and indeed local citizens and support their effects to overcome the past and work together for a better (European) future.

Structure of this special issue

The papers in this special issue all address different elements of EU Member State Building: some more directly, such as Gezim Krasniqi's comparison of state and nation-building in Kosovo and Albania, and some more indirectly like Jelena Dzankic, who looks at the internal and external factors that contributed to the development of the Montenegrin party system. What all papers have in common is their focus on Europeanization, State-Building and Democratization in the Western Balkans. The authors all agree that the EU has had and continues to have a massive influence on the political development in the region. Nevertheless – and this is the message of the contributors – it is also important to take the internal developments in the region into account, something that has not yet been understood fully in Brussels. Focusing on internal dynamics in party interaction and obstruction, Outi Keranen demonstrates how even the best attempts to implement the Dayton Peace Agreement by international actors have been resisted by different parties in Bosnia. She describes how different projects of state-building have undermined the Bosnian state and continue to contest the legal existence of Bosnia and Herzegovina. As described above, this questioning of the status has resulted in heavy EU intervention, but the EU has been unable to solve the crisis, despite continued lip-service to Bosnian unity. What is needed is a new agreement on the Bosnian state, a constitutional reform that includes all actors and brings together the different demands by ensuring the creation of a functioning state and the protection of the different peoples in Bosnia at the same time. That both are not impossible can be learnt from Spain, Belgium, Canada and India. Valery Perry and Soeren Keil demonstrate how some of the ideas of the OSCE have had a positive impact on Bosnia, but also demonstrate the unwillingness of key Bosnian actors to change and contribute to the reform process. They argue that the weakness of the OSCE lies in the fact that its implementation powers were limited and that it often did not receive the support of other international organizations in Bosnia, such as the Office of the High Representative. They nevertheless conclude that external actors can have an influence if they work together with local officials and if they have the power to implement deep changes even against the resistance of local obstructers. Gezim Krasniqi discusses the role of minorities and external actors in the state-building and democratization projects in Albania and Kosovo. He demonstrates that historical experiences and the relationship with the kin-state play a key role for the different attitudes of the Greek minority in Albania and the Serb minority in Kosovo. What remains strikingly important, however, is the need for willingness among the minority and majority population to live together and work together in the common state, which both claim to be their home. In particular, in relation to Kosovo Krasniqi demonstrates how international actors have influenced the state-building and democratization project and he picks up on some of the criticisms of EU Member State Building which have been discussed in the previous section. Once again it becomes obvious that it can only be the EU and its representatives that bring Kosovo Albanians and Serbs as well as Kosovo and Serbia together and solve the complex issue of Kosovo's status. The disunity among European countries on the Kosovo issues contributes to the escalation of the conflict and European ignorance can easily create the next frozen conflict. Jelena Dzankic's paper analyses the development of identity and party politics in Montenegro since the break-up of Yugoslavia at the beginning of the 1990s. She demonstrates how identification patterns have changed and how the split of the DPS has resulted in a massive reconfiguration of identity and party politics in Montenegro. She particularly focuses on the internal factors that have led to the changes and demonstrates that while there is a deep split between the opposition and ruling parties, Montenegro as such is not contested as an independent country anymore, despite the creation of a party system along ethno-national lines. Marija Risteska discusses the role of the EU in good governance promotion in Macedonia with her contribution. She comes to the conclusion that good governance is an essential element of EU conditionality; however, the EU continues to focus on short-term policy changes rather than long-term structural and cultural changes. This results in a lack of deep-rooted reforms and there is little change in the actual administrative practices in Macedonia. We can see how EU Member State Building tries to change policy rather than polity and instead of focusing on democratic and legal structures in the administration and the government apparatus, the EU focuses on efficiency and effectiveness of administrative processes. The EU's limited impact on good governance in Macedonia demonstrates the limits of EU Member State Building and indeed can be seen as a classic example of how EU policies fail to prepare the candidate for membership. Bernhard Stahl looks at the relationship between the EU and Serbia. He comes to the conclusion that there is a "civilizatory conflict" between these two actors. He attributes this in particular to the dominance of the national discourse in Serbian politics and the EU's character as a post-modern (indeed post-nation state) political system. The different approaches and perspectives cannot be overcome by simply imposing the EU's will, but will ultimately have to lead to a cultural change in Serbia as well. Following the logic of argument presented above, the EU should focus on establishing democratic and liberal structures in Serbia's political, cultural and economic system and therefore contribute to its inclusion in the European market. Over time the European discourse will become more important than the nationalist discourse and old structures can change. This indeed will need time, passion and a lot of financial and political resources, but it is certainly a worthwhile exercise if we only imagine the alternative and a return of nationalist anti-democratic forces in Serbia. Finally, Jens Woelk summarizes all papers, by discussing their contextual contributions to the current debate on EU Member State Building and by looking for joint themes and further research questions.

This special issue hopes to demonstrate how important a renewed discussion on the EU's engagement with the Western Balkans is and why the current situation is potentially unsustainable. In the midst of the EU's financial crisis, it is important to remind EU officials and politicians that their promise of membership is still worth some leverage in the Western Balkans, but their current ignorance and "enlargement-fatigue" contribute to further alienation between the EU and the Western Balkan countries. While Croatia will join the EU in 2013, it should not take decades until the other countries of the region follow. While the local approach to EU integration needs to change as well, since too many elites profit from the current status-quo, it is the EU that continues to have the support of the majority of the population of the Western Balkan countries. Using this leverage wisely means that the integration of the Western Balkans into European structures does not have to be decades away.

Notes

1. The term "countries of the Western Balkans" refers to the former Yugoslav Republics of Croatia, Bosnia and Herzegovina, Serbia, Macedonia and Montenegro (minus Slovenia, which joined the EU in 2004). It also includes Kosovo and Albania. I will use the terms "Western Balkans," the former Yugoslavia and Southeastern Europe to describe these countries.
2. These criteria can be seen at: http://ec.europa.eu/enlargement/policy/conditions-membership/index_en.htm (05 February 2013).
3. See the European Commission's Opinion on the Application for Accession to the European Union by the Republic of Croatia. (European Commission *Opinion on the Application for Accession*).
4. See the Progress Reports for Montenegro (European Commission Montenegro 2011 Progress Report) and Macedonia (European Commission Former Yugoslav Republic of Macedonia 2011 Progress Report).
5. This certainly applies to Croatia, Bosnia and Herzegovina, Kosovo and Serbia. Montenegro was also part of the Yugoslav involvement in the Croatian, Bosnian and Kosovo War and the violence in Macedonia did not end in a civil war because the EU and NATO intervened early. Albania has also seen numerous violent clashes in the 1990s and the breakdown of the so-called pyramid scheme ended in de-facto anarchy and violence between different social groups in Albania.

References

Anastasakis, Othon. 2005. "The Europeanization of the Balkans." *Brown Journal of World Affairs* 12: 77–88.
Belloni, Roberto. 2009. "European Integration and the Western Balkans: Lessons, Prospects and Obstacles." *Journal of Balkan and Near Eastern Studies* 11: 313–331.
Bieber, Florian. 2011. "Building Impossible States? State-Building Strategies and EU Membership in the Western Balkans." *Europe-Asia Studies* 63: 1783–1802.
Chandler, David. 2007. "EU Statebuilding: Securing the Liberal Peace Through EU Enlargement." *Global Society* 21: 593–607.
Chandler, David. 2009. "Introduction." In *Statebuilding and Intervention. Policies, Practices and Paradigms*, edited by David Chandler. 1–14. London: Routledge.

Chandler, David. 2010. "The EU and Southeastern Europe: the Rise of Post-Liberal Governance." *Third World Quarterly* 31: 69–85.
Claes, Monica. 2007. "The Europeanization of National Constitutions in the Constitutionalization of Europe: Some Observations Against the Background of the Constitutional Experience of the EU-15." *Croatian Yearbook of European Law and Policy* 3: 1–38.
Diamond, Larry. 1999. *Developing Democracy: Toward Consolidation*. Baltimore: John Hopkins University Press.
Diamond, Larry. 2008. *The Spirit of Democracy: The Struggle to Build Free Societies Throughout the World*. New York: Times Books.
Etzioni, Amitai. 2009. "Reconstruction: An Agenda." In *Statebuilding and Intervention. Policies, Practices and Paradigms*, edited by David Chandler, 101–121. London: Routledge.
European Commission. *Former Yugoslav Republic of Macedonia 2011 Progress Report*. SEC (2011) 1203 final. Brussels, 12 October 2011. Web. 06 December 2011. http://ec.europa.eu/enlargement/pdf/key_documents/2011/package/mk_rapport_2011_en.pdf.
European Commission. Montenegro 2011 Progress Report. SEC (2011) 1204 final. Brussels, 12 October 2011. Web. 06 December 2011. http://ec.europa.eu/enlargement/pdf/key_documents/2011/package/mn_rapport_2011_en.pdf.
European Commission. *Opinion on the Application for Accession to the European Union by the Republic of Croatia*. COM (2011) 667 final. Brussels, 12 October 2011. Web. 06 December 2011. http://ec.europa.eu/enlargement/pdf/key_documents/2011/package/hr_opinion_2011_en.pdf.
European Commission. *The Thessaloniki Agenda for the Western Balkans*. Annex A. Thessaloniki, 16 June 2003. Web. 23 January 2012. http://ec.europa.eu/enlargement/enlargement_process/accession_process/how_does_a_country_join_the_eu/sap/thessaloniki_agenda_en.htm.
Ghani, Ashraf, and Clare Lockhart. 2009. *Fixing Failed States*. Oxford: Oxford University Press.
Hix, Simon. 2005. *The Political System of the European Union*. 2nd ed. Basingstoke: Palgrave.
Knaus, Gerald, and Felix Martin. 2003. "Travails of the European Raj- Lessons from Bosnia and Herzegovina." *Journal of Democracy* 14: 60–74.
Linz, Juan J., and Alfred Stepan. 1996. *Problems of Democratic Transition and Consolidation. Southern Europe, Southern America and Post- Communist Europe*. Baltimore: The John Hopkins University Press.
Merkel, Wolfgang. 2004. "Embedded and Defective Democracies." *Democratization* 11: 49–75.
Paris, Roland. 2004. *At War's End: Building Peace After Civil Conflict*. Cambridge: Cambridge University Press.
Quaglia, Lucia, Neuvonen, Mari, Miyakoshi, Machiko and Michelle Cini. 2007. "Europeanization." In *European Union Politics*, edited by Michelle Cini. 405–420. 2nd ed. Oxford: Oxford University Press.
Radaelli, Claudio M. 2006. "Europeanization: Solution or Problem?." In *Palgrave Advances in European Union Studies*, edited by Michelle Cini and Angela Bourne, 56–76. Basingstoke: Palgrave.
Schimmelpfennig, Frank, and Ulrich Sedelmeier, eds. 2005a. *The Europeanization of Central and Eastern Europe*. New York: Cornell University Press.
Schimmelpfennig, Frank, and Ulrich Sedelmeier, eds. 2005b. *The Politics of European Union Enlargement*. London: Routledge.
Sisk, Timothey, and Roland Paris. 2007. *Managing Contradictions: The Inherent Dilemmas of Postwar Statebuilding*. International Peace Academy/Research Partnership on Postwar Statebuilding. Web. 05 December 2011. http://www.ipinst.org/media/pdf/publications/iparpps.pdf.
Zakošek, Nenad. 2008. "Democratization, State-building and War: The Cases of Serbia and Croatia." *Democratization* 15: 588–610.

International statebuilding as contentious politics: the case of post conflict Bosnia and Herzegovina

Outi Keranen

Department of International Relations, London School of Economics and Political Science, United Kingdom

The post-conflict space in Bosnia and Herzegovina has been marked by a multiplicity of statebuilding projects: in addition to the much-analyzed internationally-led statebuilding process, parallel Bosniak, Bosnian Serb and Bosnian Croat statebuilding trajectories exist. They seek to undermine and challenge the international statebuilding venture by appropriating and adapting the liberal statebuilding processes. This is carried out through the institutions and processes of governance put in place by international statebuilders to subvert the statebuilding trajectory. Focusing on the local appropriation of processes and institutions of governance, the paper maps out the repertoires of contention entailing boycotts, walk-outs, protests and refusals to co-operate in an attempt to explain and understand how local contention vis-à-vis the international statebuilding trajectory is carried out.

Points of departure

Statebuilding, nation-building and democratization are contentious processes. While this certainly has been the case in terms of historical state formation, it also applies to contemporary states engaged in such processes. In addition to being contentious, many of today's statebuilding and democratization trajectories have a distinct international dimension. This is due to the West's increasing concern over the political organization and stability of weak or peripheral states manifested in the global governance agenda. The perceived solution to the dangers of weak statehood has been the paradigm of statebuilding that denotes not only the technical aspect of constructing the institutional infrastructure of the state but also extensive social-engineering so as to build subjects for modern liberal states. Whilst the international statebuilding agenda and practices are endorsed by many in local societies, they are also encountered by local, often alternative, statebuilding agendas in the local spaces. These parallel statebuilding trajectories frequently engage, for a variety of reasons, in resisting the wholesale social, political and economic change envisaged by the international statebuilding agencies[1]. In an attempt to explore the hybridity that marks post-conflict spaces (Mac Ginty 2011), this paper centres on local practices of contention acted out in the institutions and processes of governance, set up by the international statebuilding agencies. These acts of resistance are explored through the case study of post-conflict peacebuilding and statebuilding in Bosnia and Herzegovina (hereafter Bosnia), focusing on the first 15 years of the process (1995–2010). Bosnia provides a compelling case of extensive and prolonged social and political engineering, resiliently contested by many locals in Bosnia. The essay reflects upon some initial findings on the alternative local statebuilding agendas and the ways in which they seek to re-negotiate and appropriate the internationally-led statebuilding processes. Analyzed through interactions between the internal and external statebuilders, statebuilding is understood here as a pattern of relations and interactions that determine the form and course of the process. This casts doubt on the top-to-bottom models of statebuilding where hegemonic international policies are imposed upon passive local subjects. Indeed, the analysis suggests that local statebuilding agencies appropriate elements of "liberal peace"[2] (Richmond 2006). While the procedural aspects of international statebuilding – meant to provide the infrastructure for functioning and efficient state – are employed to resist the internationally-led statebuilding process, international statebuilding discourses on democracy, human rights and local ownership are adopted by local actors in order to mobilize and justify such resistance. Local contestation arises partly from the alternative statebuilding agendas of the Bosniaks, Bosnian Serbs and Bosnian Croats, but is also generated by the nature of the international statebuilding which is perceived locally either as non-democratic and "neo-colonial" or ineffective and half-hearted. In practice the contentious local performances – boycotts, walk-outs, demonstrations and protests – operate at different levels of governance. While at the central level the functioning of the joint institutions based on principles of power-sharing are regularly hindered, at the municipal level bureaucratic means of undermining the international statebuilding process are employed. International statebuilders counter local acts of contention largely by means of coercion (whether political or military), capital (aid) and commitment (supporting local "moderates").

It is the interactions between the international statebuilding practices entailing coercion, capital and commitment on the one hand and local contentious practices on the other that are of interest to this analysis. Indeed, the paper tentatively suggests that these interactions have led to a statebuilding process in Bosnia that is constantly being shaped, negotiated and redefined.

While local actors endorsing and promoting the international agenda have been researched (Belloni 2001; Helms 2003; Burde 2004), local agencies challenging the process have elicited less attention. Research on "spoilers" of peace (Stedman 1997; Zahar 2010) is useful in this regard; yet, it suffers from the overtly political and subjective framing of spoilers within the framework of liberal statebuilding (Newman and Richmond 2006). Understanding local resistance to the international statebuilding in terms of personal aggrandizement by the few reduces the complex socio-political space into an image of a lawless borderland incapable of governing itself (Duffield 2001). As Pouligny puts it, the realisation that local non-compliance may have a more varied range of ultimate goals as opposed to those suggested by research on "spoilers" or "other bad guys" reveals the limits of an analysis informed by game theory (2006, 217). The central assertion put forth here is that local contestation of the international statebuilding consists of practices and narratives stemming from an amalgam of national and personal interest, of ethnic manipulation and genuine post-war inter-ethnic grievance. Drawing on the cultural strand of contentious politics research, the local resistance to the international statebuilding trajectory is conceptualized as a form of contentious claim-making; it is public, collective action entailing the making of claims that bear on other groups' interests (McAdam, Tarrow and Tilly 2001). While various forms of contentious politics can be identified, for instance social movements and protest groups, the contention witnessed in Bosnia centres on ethno-national networks that hold positions of power in the society and share a common worldview, while coordinating contentious claim-making based on ethnic and/or nationalist demands. A few words are also in order with regards to operationalizing contention. For a majority of the contentious politics scholars, contentious politics refers to public and episodic making of claims, involving a government, that affects the target's interests, if realized (McAdam, Tarrow and Tilly 2001; Tilly 2008; Tilly and Tarrow 2007). Drawing on this conceptualization, contentious politics in the context of Bosnia thus denotes the claimant–object relationship between local and international actors. As this paper tells a story of internationalized contention, the level of analysis is on the international sphere and consequently, the focus of the analysis is on the contentious dynamics between the international and local statebuilders[3]. Local practices and discourses aimed at making demands, undermining, challenging or outright rejecting international agencies' (primarily the Office of the High Representative, OHR) policies or rhetoric are considered here as contentious practices. The analysis draws on the contentious politics literature using political opportunity structures, mobilizing structures and framing as the conceptual framework through which to understand local contention and address the "how" question of such resistance. Political opportunity structures refer to the "consistent – but not necessarily formal or permanent – dimensions of the political environment that provide incentives for people to undertake collective action by affecting their expectations for success or failure" (Tarrow 1994, 189). Mobilizing structures, on the other hand, denote the formal organizational means as well as informal networks available to actors engaged in contention (McAdam, Tarrow and Tilly, 2001, 16). Finally, frames, as understood here, are "metaphors, symbolic representations and cognitive cues" (McAdam, McCarthy and Zald 1996, 262) that provide interpretations of problems, understand such issues in a meaningful way and suggest possible solutions.

Statebuilding agendas

Before proceeding with the analysis, it is useful to briefly outline the various statebuilding agendas. A word of caution is in order here; statebuilding projects are by no means monoliths and significant internal variance does occur. While it is clear that the "international community" contains substantially differing points of view on how to go about reconstructing Bosnia, also the local statebuilding agendas entail divergence, generally between moderate and extreme elements. Nevertheless, it is possible to establish the broad outlines of the various statebuilding projects. The Bosniak statebuilding agenda, for instance, aims for a state with strong central authority; such a vision of the Bosnian state coincides with the Bosniak interests as they are assumed to be the largest ethnic group in Bosnia. The Bosniak self-understanding and consequently, the statebuilding practice and discourse are intertwined with a narrative of victimhood. The Bosniaks view themselves as the victims of the previous war and the genocidal politics of Serbia and the Bosnian Serbs. The Bosnian Serb statebuilding vision, in turn, has graduated from the initial refusal to accept the Dayton Peace Accord (DPA) to the fierce protection of the entity, Republika Srpska (RS), granted to the Bosnian Serbs in Dayton. While considerable internal disagreements between moderates and hardliners over the status of the RS are still a common place, any attempts to centralize the country's governance have been met with resistance from Banja Luka. The Bosnian Croat views on Bosnian statehood vary geographically between Croats living in multi-ethnic Central Bosnian areas and their counterparts living in more ethnically homogeneous western Herzegovina. While the former were largely conditioned by the experience and necessity of living amidst other nationalities, the latter had a more narrow experience of multi-ethnicity (International Crisis Group 1998a, 2). Yet, the majority of the Croats in Bosnia regard the structure of the country, which left Croats without an entity of their own, as highly problematic. The Croat statebuilding agenda, whether in its more moderate or hard-line version, thus advocates a change to the current set-up of the country ranging from calls for a Croat-entity to the reorganization of the country's governance in line with economic regions. The Croat statebuilding project has sought to challenge and undermine aspects of international statebuilding that are seen to further centralize the state or directly threaten the parallel structures (banks, schools, utility companies, etc.) that the Croat community has succeeded in maintaining in Croat-dominated areas. It is also useful to briefly flag out certain elements of the international involvement in post-Dayton Bosnia[4]. In addition to the range of technical tasks (demobilization and de-arming of combatants, de-mining, organizing elections and so on), the most important political objectives of the international community immediately after the war were the creation of democratic institutions, promoting human rights, advancing refugee returns and capturing war criminals. The initial international involvement was marked by internal tensions between differing policy lines; while the Americans emphasized the military aspects of the peace agreement guided by the desire to "get in heavy and get out quick" (Wheeler 2008), the Europeans argued that the civilian elements were the key to sustainable peace (Holbrooke 1999; Bildt 1998). Despite the initial differences, all the international actors involved shared the conviction that Bosnia should remain a single state within the framework of the DPA. Many internationals were also convinced that the pre-war multi-ethnic character of Bosnia could – and should – be restored ("New Bosnia Mediator"). This was based on the idea that creating mono-ethnic states would go against the European ideal of pluralism, let alone set a dangerous precedent for other parts of the world (Neville-Jones 2010). Indeed, the irreversibility of the DPA became the mantra directing not only the OHR's[5] involvement, but of the international community as a whole. Actions that sought to challenge the international statebuilding strategies were thus interpreted as "anti-Dayton" behaviour. Not only did such behaviour break the terms of the peace agreement, but it was also tantamount to irresponsible behaviour by the political elites who betrayed the trust of the electorate ("Envoy: Bosnia's Officials"). In the course of the statebuilding project, however, particularly the Euro-American position has gradually shifted away from the inviolability of the DPA towards a more centralized model of governance. The international statebuilding efforts began to address the problem that is considered to be at the core of the slow statebuilding process; the structure of the country as set in Dayton. According to this line of thinking, mechanisms designed for the protection of the constituent peoples' rights (for instance the entity vote giving veto rights to the three constituent groups) have enabled effective local contestation and obstructed the process. It follows, therefore, that the Constitution of the country based on the DPA should be reformed in order to make more progress possible. In line with such thinking, the international community established a variety of state level institutions, such as the State Border Service, the Court of Bosnia and Herzegovina, state-level customs agency and state-level justice and defence ministries. In many ways this recalibration of policy represents a paradox as it has often been the RS – the strongest supporter of the DPA, even if not the state, that gave them their entity – that is accused of "anti-Dayton" behaviour; the centralization efforts carried out by certain parts of the international community could easily be interpreted as such. The contestation that such actions have generated in the RS has been mobilized largely through the framing of centralization attempts as a threat to the existence of Serbs in Bosnia.

The above implies that in order to understand the increasingly strained relationship between the internal and external statebuilders it is necessary to try to tease out patterns and changes in the international involvement in Bosnia. This is so as the nature of the international community's involvement in the post-conflict development creates the political opportunity structures within which local actors operate. This analysis suggests that a change in the approach of certain international actors has considerably contributed to the escalation of local contestation. In this regard the attempt to reform the constitution set out in Dayton has become one of the primary sources of local contestation. Reflecting the shift from peacebuilding to statebuilding in the late 1990s, the international approach to rebuilding Bosnia has prioritized stable and efficient statehood as necessitated by the Euro-Atlantic integration. According to this line of policy, "the DPA is not the ceiling but the floor" ("A Decade On") and thus should be changed in order to strengthen the functioning of the country's central institutions. Particularly the Bosnian Serbs have regarded such attempts as a threat to the survival of the RS. The shift in the international approach has also given an extended lease of life to the Bosniak dream of the centralized state; consequently, the Bosniak statebuilding project has taken an unyielding stance in negotiations between local actors and opposed any international statebuilding policies that do not result in a fully centralized state. Coupled with the above change in the Euro-American policy, the qualitative reduction in the statebuilding instruments available to the international statebuilders in Bosnia, namely the OHR, also merits attention. While the dramatic reduction in the international military strength provides a limitation to the physical force, during the recent years the OHR has begun to lose its most valuable statebuilding instrument, its international as well as local credibility and legitimacy. In recent years much of the local co-operation has waned; while the international community in general and the OHR in particular are regarded as having played a valuable role immediately after the war, more than a decade after the conflict it is no longer perceived as having a legitimate role in the country.

Local contentious repertoire: boycotts, walk-outs and protests

The remainder of this paper focuses on the contentious performances and the dynamic between the internal and external actors. Due to space constraints the analysis focuses on some of the key episodes of contention; namely the 1999 Poplašen/Brčko crisis and the 2001 Croat self-rule campaign. Much of the analysis centres on the Bosnian Serb and Bosnian Croat practices; this is due to the fact that relatively little Bosniak contestation operates through the institutions and processes of governance as the functioning of the joint institutions is generally in their interest. An exception is Mostar, discussed later on, where Bosniaks have actively used the city's administrative structures to undermine the efforts to unify the town. Perhaps the most frequent episodes of blocking the functioning of the state level institutions and processes take place at the joint institutions of governance. This is enabled by the power-sharing system of governance which grants each national group a veto over decisions perceived as threats to their respective national interests. A recent example of this was the blocking of the extension of foreign judges mandates by the Bosnian Serb politicians. The Peace Implementation Council (PIC), tasked with monitoring the implementation of the DPA, declared in 2009 that the Bosnian authorities had failed to provide the Court and Prosecutor's Office the financial means to recruit national judges and prosecutors to replace their international counterparts (OHR 14 December 2009). Bosnian Serbs challenged the call for extension of the mandate as unconstitutional and reiterated that all international judges should withdraw from Bosnia ("Bosnian Serb PM"). RS officials consequently used the Bosnian Parliament and the entity voting mechanism to block the adoption of the legislation relating to the international judiciary. This led to the High Representative using the Bonn powers to impose the law, thus extending the mandate of international judges by three years.

Beyond this example, boycotts, walk-outs and refusals to cooperate have featured regularly in the repertoire of contentious practices, particularly in the immediate years after the war. The inauguration of the new Bosnian Parliament in 1996 began with Bosnian Serb boycott, demonstrating an effective way of undermining the externally-led statebuilding process. Indeed, both Bosnian Serbs and Croats have engaged in a number of further boycotts over the arrest of war crimes indictees, Western interference in the internal politics (particularly in relation to the RS) as well as OHR-imposed changes in the rules of the political game in the Bosnia[6].

One of the most serious threats to the international community's statebuilding process came in 1999 when Bosnian Serbs staged a boycott of the joint institutions in response to the dual crisis of the dismissal of the RS President by the OHR and the decision on the Brčko district. Nikola Poplašen, regarded as a Serb hard-liner bent on non-cooperation with the international community, was dismissed from office after attempting to sideline his moderate political rivals in the RS, who were supported by the internationals in Bosnia. Following a debate in the RS National Assembly, the decision was passed to declare Poplašen's dismissal as unconstitutional ("Bosnian Serb Lawmakers"). Poplašen himself framed the dismissal as an affront to international legal and democratic norms, let alone to the DPA and the Constitution of the country. In a letter to the OHR, Poplašen likened himself to the High Representative as a guarantor of peace and stability in the region, committed to the democratic development and prosperity of his people. He noted that "if peace, stability and economic prosperity in this region are our common goal, then there should be agreements, cooperation and mutual respect and not boycotts, ultimatums and threats" ("President Criticizes Envoy's").

The status of the strategically important town of Brčko was left undecided in the 1995 peace negotiations, as the parties were unable to agree on the fate of the territory. In 1999, coinciding with the Poplašen crisis, the Brčko Arbitration Tribunal awarded the district a special status which meant that neither the Federation nor the RS has exclusive jurisdiction over the area. The Serbs particularly were disillusioned by the decision as they had cooperated with the international community in introducing multi-ethnic policing and local administration with the expectation that Brčko would become part of the RS to ensure the territorial continuity (International Crisis Group 1999a). Again, the Bosnian Serb lawmakers rejected the Brčko decision and adopted a resolution calling for Serb officials to interrupt their participation in the joint Bosnian institutions. The Brčko decision was framed as a verdict that in effect "annulled" the DPA; the Serb member of the Presidency suggests that the Brčko decision would result "not only to a division of RS into two separate parts but real danger for the fate of the DPA" ("Foreigner's Rulings Challenged"). While SRS officials engaged in a seven-month long boycott of the joint and entity level government institutions and Poplašen refused to leave the job, anti-international community protests were organized in the Eastern RS. As the International Crisis Group reports, with little public debate in the media – controlled largely by the political elites – on the two issues, Serb hardliners found it easy to mobilize the people (1999a). Radical factions of the Serb political party machinery – particularly that of the SRS – provided the structures for mobilizing people to protest against the international statebuilders. In an attempt to cash in on the view shared by many in the Serb community that the international community was biased against them, the SRS took advantage of its organizational readiness to organize public meetings and protest rallies (International Crisis Group 1999a, 6). Moreover, media controlled by Serb parties was also used to mobilize and organize protests against the international community; for instance in Brčko the Serb-controlled radio urged all Serbs to take part in demonstrations against the Poplašen and Brčko decisions

("Bosnia: Radio Urges"). Protesters in the RS threw stones at international officials and attacked US peacekeepers. Extremists in the Serb community also planted bombs in the OHR Banja Luka office and at a US military office in Bijeljina. The protesters distributed leaflets in Banja Luka urging Serbs to rise against the High Representative, and attack "the occupiers with clubs, stones and petrol bombs" and "to be ready to use automatic weapons" ("Bosnia Serbs Call"). The OHR responded to the contention discursively by rejecting the authority of the RS National Assembly and by decertification of Poplašen, together with the declaration of non-cooperation with any RS government containing Poplašen's SRS party. Shortly after the contentious episode, the NATO-led bombing of Kosovo complicated the relationship between the RS and the international community further. While the NATO bombing of Kosovo created a serious strife within the international community as Moscow condemned the actions, it also gave Serb secessionists the basis for demanding a redrawing of borders. Yet, the RS remained largely peaceful during the NATO air raids on Kosovo chiefly due to the presence of a moderate Prime Minister and ally of the international statebuilders, Milorad Dodik, who secured substantial international aid in exchange for a non-confrontational stance during the Kosovo campaign (International Crisis Group 1999b, 9). Capital and commitment, as strategies of international statebuilders, thus ensured order in the country.

Although the Poplašen/Brčko crisis was eventually averted, contentious interactions between the international statebuilders and the RS reached another highpoint few years later. Seen as the main source of protection of war criminals and resistance to minority returnees, the OHR sought to centralize the local police forces. The watershed moment in the process that was systematically rejected by the RS came in 2005 when the OHR decided to link police reform with the EU integration. Police reform, in other words, became a precondition for the signing of the Stabilization Association Agreement, a first step on the accession path. As Ashdown notes in his memoirs, "I rang Chris Patten in late October and asked if he could weigh in as Commissioner and say that these reforms were required if BiH wanted to join Europe" (2007, 249). This illustrates the arbitrary nature of the international statebuilding trajectory; while centralized police forces are a rarity elsewhere in Europe (Parish 2007, 19), it became a precondition for Bosnia's accession in order to force through the reform that was subjected to resilient local resistance. This linking of police reform to the signing of the SAA became highly problematic from the point of view of the OHR; the EU maintained that the accession process was a voluntary one and thus the OHR could not use its Bonn powers to impose the police reform (Parish 2007). Given that the designs to centralize the police were threatening the autonomy of the Serb entity, the RS yet again resisted the process. The OHR finally set a deadline for agreeing on the police reform. When the deadline passed and no agreement was reached, the OHR engaged in a further process of centralizing the state so as to discipline the obstructing Serbs; as the ICG reports the centralizing process was designed as "a shock and awe" display of the OHR's authority and its ability to deal with local resistance (International Crisis Group 2009, 12). With no local consultation, the High Representative altered the way in which the state level executive and legislative bodies functioned and in essence made it more difficult for national groups to use their veto powers to protect their national interests. This plunged the Bosnian Serbs and the OHR into a further cycle of contestation. Sensing a divide in the international community, Banja Luka mobilized Moscow's support and Russia duly condemned the OHR's actions[7]. Framing it as an unconstitutional and illegal decree, Serbs organized mass anti-OHR demonstrations in the RS, while the President of the Republic resigned. In the face of the pressure, the EU and the OHR were forced to negotiate with Banja

Luka. Eventually, the OHR was forced to accept a watered down agreement bearing little resemblance to the original police reform as a face saving compromise. The attempts to reform the police were not only unnecessary and too far-reaching, but also came at the time when the status of Kosovo was a potentially destabilizing issue (International Crisis Group 2009, 14). As many commentators have aptly pointed out, this marked the beginning of the decline in the OHR's credibility (McMahon & Western 2009; Parish 2007). The case is also indicative of how international intervention has produced contention, rather than merely acting in response to it.

Dreams of self-rule: the "Croat" question

While Bosnian Croat contestation of the internationally-led statebuilding can be traced back to the establishment of the European Union administration in Mostar in 1994, one of the most substantial Croat challenges to the post-war process came in the early 2000s with the self-rule campaign. It began with the creation of formal mobilizing structures, the Croat National Congress and the Croat Peoples' Assembly, in 2000 (initiated by the nationalist HDZ party together with smaller Croat parties) which enabled dissemination of information by issuing declarations as well as framing the issues at hand (that is, the Croat status in Bosnia) and actors involved. Other points of mobilization, such as the Association of Croatian Military Invalids of the Homeland War (HVIDRA) as well as the Croat elite-controlled banks also played a role in terms of support and financial resources. These formal structures played a crucial role in the tumultuous period in early 2000 which witnessed various episodes of contentious actions. The starting point was the November 2000 elections which were accompanied by a referendum on Croat rights, deemed illegal by the Organization for Security and Co-operation in Europe (OSCE). The referendum, supported by organizations such as HVIDRA (Bojičić-Dželilović 2004, 13), centred on the question whether the Croats in Bosnia should have their own political, educational, cultural and scientific institutions on Bosnian territory and reportedly the overwhelming majority of the voters answered favourably (Bieber 2001, 2). In addition to organizing the referendum, representatives of the main Croat party, HDZ, initiated a boycott of the joint institutions as a protest against the change in the electoral law. The OHR responded in turn by removing Croat-held seats from Cantonal Assemblies. Moreover, the OHR and the OSCE continued to downplay the Croat National Congress by asserting that "everybody has the right to meet but whatever they come up with has no legal weight and is not legally binding..." ("OSCE and OHR about"). The international responses undoubtedly reinforced the confrontational dynamic whereby the international decertification of the Croat protests added to the Croats' sense of undemocratic imposition of international will and disenfranchisement (HDZ BiH Official).

The turbulent relations culminated in the Croat attempt to establish self-rule in Herzegovina in 2001 by relying on parallel state structures in the Croat-controlled territories. Guided by the injustice frame claiming that "the OSCE and the international community turned the Federation into a Bosniak entity" ("OHR BiH Media" 28 February 2001c), an alliance of Croat nationalist parties, the Croat National Congress, voted for the creation of an Inter-Cantonal Council tasked to protect Croat interests and with the establishment of parallel Croat institutions which were envisaged to have the final authority on all Croat matters in Bosnia [8]. The Croat members of the Federal Army walked out as a demonstration of loyalty to the Croat National Congress. The Croat self-rule was premised on the establishment of a presidency, legislative council and entity and cantonal parliaments, as well as on its own system of taxation. Croat national insignia and Coat of

Arms were deployed in an act of contesting the Bosnian state symbols. Again, formal organizations such as the Inter-Cantonal Council, the Headquarters for the Protection of Identity and Croat National Interests and HVIDRA, as well as the Catholic Church served as mobilizing structures through which injustice frames relating to the status of Croats in Bosnia were channelled and support for the action obtained. HVIDRA organized the withdrawal of the Croat faction from the Federal army, in addition to organizing anti-international community rallies and protests, and even warned the Bosnian Croat politicians not to yield to international demands (Bojičić-Dželilović 2004, 13). The Headquarters for the Protection of Identity and Interests of Croat People, founded in Vitez in March 2001, issued regular statements during the self-rule attempt. The organization offered its support to the Inter-Cantonal Council and demanded that all Croat army personnel leave the Federation army. In reinforcing the Croat self-image of victimhood, the organization appealed to the Croat public by noting that "we also call the Croat people to not allow the tearing of the Croat being, and to stand by us and all others who strive towards the equality of the Croat people in BiH" ("OHR BiH Media" 28 March 2001d). While allegations surrounding the directing of illegal government funds to the Bosnian Catholic Church by Croat politicians have surfaced, Bosnian Croat priests from the Catholic Church took part in meetings of organizations involved in the self-rule attempt and publicly condemned the international community's behaviour towards Bosnian Croats which "takes equality away from Croats" ("OHR BiH Media" 14 December 2000b)[9]. In addition to lending support for the contentious actions and seeking to discursively mobilize Croats for the cause, some Catholic priests also used religious services to reinforce the injustice frames which constructed the Croats as the victims and blamed the international community. Whereas the above structures and institutions sought to mobilize support through discursive frames and the organization of walk-outs and protests, the Croat elite controlled Hercegovačka Bank provided financial means for the self-rule attempt (Bieber 2001, 2).

According to an international investigation, the bank had previously operated as a funding source for high ranking Bosnian Croat war crime indictees as well as campaigns to change the Bosnian Constitution to suit Croat interests. During the 2001 self-rule attempt, army officials withdrawn from the Federal Army were paid from the funds held by the bank (OHR 16 December 2002). When SFOR troops raided the bank in April 2001, large scale demonstrations and riots erupted, resulting in international investigators being taken hostage. Again, HVIDRA was behind the organization of the violent demonstrations (Bojičić-Dželilović 2004). The OHR responded to the Croat contention by coercive means. Dismissals of the self-rule leadership as well as travel bans were initiated. In addition, the HDZ and other politicians involved in the action were framed by the OHR as having betrayed the Croat population in Bosnia with irresponsible actions. The elites, according to the OHR, were distinctly unconcerned by the well-being of their constituents; they were engaged in criminal and corrupt activities that were to benefit a few at the expense of the wider Croat community. Hence, no basis for negotiation between the HDZ and the OHR existed (OHR 7 March 2001a). In this framing of the Croat contention, the OHR represented itself as the true friend of the Croat people and as such, tasked itself to save the population from the predatory elites. In many ways the contentious action taken by the Croats in an attempt to gain autonomy, widened the opportunities for the international statebuilders to deal forcefully with the obstructionist HDZ. Given the flagrant defiance of the DPA as well as the Washington Agreement of 1994, which had forced the Croats to share the Federation with the Bosniak majority, the OHR found it easy to justify the severe sanctions it imposed upon the leaders of the self-rule campaign.

Contention at local level institutions

The principal theme that emerges from the above discussion is the complexity of the local–international dynamic. Statebuilding, as viewed through contentious politics, is a continuous process of negotiation which leads into compromised outcomes. Political opportunities condition the emergence of contestation and the repertoires deployed, while local agencies engage in framing that legitimizes and mobilizes contestation vis-à-vis international statebuilders. International actors respond to contestation which often generates further local contestation. Such logic is not limited to the level of central state institutions; institutions of governance have served as vehicles of contentious politics also at the entity level. Particularly noteworthy in this regard is the law on referendum in the RS, regarded as a direct violation of the DPA by international officials in Bosnia. Although the law does not allude to specific questions a referendum might pose, the notion of referendum in the Serb discourse has generally referred to either measures taken by the OHR or the entity's status within Bosnia. Initially decreed in 1993 and amended in 2010, the law makes results of referenda legally binding for institutions of the RS. It has become, particularly in recent years, the sine qua non of Serb resistance to international impositions or attempts to reform the constitution. This has prompted further confrontation not only between the local groups but also between the international community and the RS. It is also at the cantonal level where most of the Bosniak resistance operates. Particularly in Mostar Bosniaks have engaged in the blocking of decision-making and boycotting meetings. This was the case when the OHR introduced the Mostar Statute that sought to unify the town: during the preparation process of the reform, the main Bosniak party in Mostar, SDA, boycotted the Commission tasked to write the Statute. The resistance was framed as an opposition to the attempts to turn Mostar into a Croat city and weaken the institutional guarantees for other groups' rights by the OHR. Following the eventual failure of both Bosniaks and Croats to ratify the Statute, the OHR imposed the decision.

Also the cantonal level institutions, many of which are mono-ethnic, have been used to contest aspects of the externally-led statebuilding. This is particularly the case when it comes to resisting refugee return. The reversal of the effects of ethnic cleansing during the war through refugee return has been one of the key pillars in the international mission in Bosnia. As declared in annex VII of the DPA, "The early return of refugees and displaced persons is an important objective of the settlement of the conflict in Bosnia and Herzegovina" (Dayton Peace Accord para. 1). This was seen as a way to compensate the human rights violations that occurred during the war as well as to reverse the effects of ethnic cleansing. Local contestation of such international policy is largely driven by the desire of the majority national group in the area to maintain the status quo. Local municipalities have challenged the policy by engaging in "large scale and orchestrated" practices such as issuing looting permits relating to houses owned by returnees, encouraging occupation of returnees' properties and returns by members of their own nationality, refusing to evict illegal occupants of properties, illegal reallocations of land to the representatives of the majority nationality and delays and refusals in implementing laws to protect returnees, not to mention violent demonstrations against returnees (OHR 8 September 2000a). In Croat-dominated areas a vital part of the organizational network that mobilizes and maintains contention has been business interests whose control over the economy has been an efficient way to block minority returns and encourage Croat majority returns. According to the ICG, Croatian companies linked to the nationalist political structures in Zagreb invested heavily in the Croat-controlled Cantons in Bosnia, thus incentivizing majority returns by offering employment to Bosnian Croats (International Crisis Group 1998b, 4). One of Croatia's leading wood-processing companies, Finvest, became an overwhelmingly dominant economic player in the Croat-controlled Canton 10 by gradually taking over economic functions performed previously by other companies, for instance a saw mill that used to employ over 2,000 workers before the war. Particularly in the northern parts of the Canton the whole economy became dependent on the company, which had close links with the main Croat party, the HDZ (International Crisis Group 1998b, 8). Similar cases of economic and employment discrimination have been reported in relation to other companies in Bosnia, such as the Croat-controlled Aluminij in Mostar and the Serb-owned Ljubija iron mine (Amnesty International 2006). Indeed, it is the nationalist party structures, in collaboration with certain commercial interests, that form the core of the mobilizing structures through which the resistance against the international community's aim of repatriating refugees is performed. Moreover, the media has played an important role in framing minority returns as a threat to the majority and mobilizing support for the cause. Particularly in the immediate years after the war, the media were successful in creating an atmosphere of hostility to returnees (International Crisis Group 1997, 2).

The international community has responded to local contention directed against the refugee returns with a combination of coercion and capital. The political form of coercion, primarily the dismissals of elected office holders who have administratively blocked return, represent a regular version of international attempts to deal with the contentious actions. Yet, the use of capital in dis-incentivizing disruptions of returns has been the main tool in the international statebuilding toolkit. This has meant that substantial aid flows have been directed to stimulate refugee returns. The US government, for instance, launched a $70 million reintegration and stabilization program of local communities, aimed at facilitating the return of 100,000 individuals belonging to minority groups (Human Rights Watch 2001). In 2002, €23.5 million from the €71.9 million of EU funding to the country was directed to the return process (Reliefweb 27 February 2011). The attempt to provide incentives for the implementation of returns by means of capital is also accompanied by the withdrawal of aid where local officials have not collaborated with the international community's vision of a multi-ethnic Bosnia; the aforementioned US government initiative left three local administrations (Prijedor, Pale and Foca) out of the financial aid package. The correlation between local implementation of refugee return and financial aid has also been contracted into the Stabilization and Association Process; in order to progress towards EU membership and the associated financial gains, the Bosnian authorities are expected to "ensure that the refugee return is properly funded and fully operational" (EC Council Decision 18 February 2008). While concerns over the local contention of refugee return featured prominently in the international agenda in the early years of the statebuilding process, such concerns have been somewhat overshadowed in recent years by urgent issues such as the Constitutional reform. In many ways, the administrative contention operating in the municipal level has been successful; while considerable numbers of refugees and displaced persons have returned to their pre-war towns and villages, the ethnic makeup of the country has not been reversed to match that of the pre-war years. From the estimated 2 million Bosnians that were internally displaced or became refugees due to the conflict, by 2010 approximately 500,000 have returned to their places of origin. Many of those returns, particularly to areas currently occupied by other national groups, have been of temporary nature in order to sell or exchange properties (United Nations Refugee Agency 31 December 2010).

Framing contestation

In an attempt to explore local practices of contestation beyond the institutions of governance, it is pertinent to briefly explore the symbolic and discursive realm of local resistance. The argument put forth here suggests that exclusive symbols of nationhood as well as discursive legitimization of contentious practices are salient features in the maintenance of alternative statebuilding projects and resistant identities. An integral part in the process of reproducing meaning and interpreting reality are symbols of identity and belonging. In post-Dayton Bosnia the use of separate flags, coat of arms, language and script (Torsti 2004), re-naming public spaces (Robinson et al. 2001) as well as separate national holidays have cemented the exclusive identities and sites of loyalty and consequently, the alternative, local statebuilding agendas. The externally-sponsored attempts to create at least some degree of overarching Bosnian "state identity", such as the common flag and national holidays, have found little resonance beyond the Bosniak community. Instead, most of the Serbs and some of the Croats in Bosnia continue to fly alternative flags and celebrate their respective holidays. The separate symbols convey meanings and ideals of "Bosniakness", "Bosnian Croatness" or "Bosnian Serbness" and have enabled the respective statebuilding elites to simplify and frame the complexities of the post-war reality and the international involvement. While symbols have played an important role in maintaining parallel statebuilding projects, appropriated international statebuilding discourses have rationalized contentious actions, thus legitimizing them. The mechanism of framing is particularly useful in this regard as it draws attention to the ways in which the prevailing interpretations of externally-led statebuilding process are problematized and alternative understandings of the situation produced. Crucially, this reinterpretation entails "diagnostic" frames which identify problems and allocate blame as well as "prognostic" frames that propose solutions to the problems (Benford and Snow 2000, 615). The adoption of global statebuilding discourses has allowed an articulated and coherent narrative that justifies resistant actions; in this regard the discourses of human rights, democracy and local ownership have been particularly salient.

While human rights have formed the cornerstone of international statebuilding agendas in general and in Bosnia in particular, all the three national groups have based their contestation of the international statebuilding on the need to protect the human rights of their respective groups. Much of Bosnian Croat resistance – such as opposition to the changes in the election law and the self-rule campaign – is based on the framing of the Croat status as a minority group rather than a constituent nation. The injustice frame (Benford and Snow 2000, 615) seeking to amplify the victimization of the group, articulated particularly by nationalist political parties as well as certain representatives of the Catholic Church, posits that "the basic postulates of democracy and rights of the Croat people in BiH have been violated" ("OHR BiH Media" 10 April 2001b). For their Serb counterparts, namely interest groups representing the veterans and victims of the war, resistance is framed as a necessary action resulting from international statebuilding practices that jeopardize the basic rights of Bosnian Serbs by seeking to centralize the state. Particularly the OHR has been framed as a force bent on "acting towards the RS and Serb people in BiH is a discriminatory way" ("OHR BiH Media" 16 December 2004). Giving empirical resonance to the Serb narrative is the perceived anti-Serb bias of the Hague Tribunal and the focus of the OHR's disciplinary actions disproportionately on the RS. At the same time, in the Bosniak statebuilding discourse the very existence of the dysfunctional governance structure violates the rights of the primary victims of the war. While the diagnostic frames of all the three groups frame international statebuilding as a violation of their respective human rights, the prognostic frames propose different solutions. Whereas the Bosnian Serb and Croat frames see the decentralized nature of the state as the only solution to guarantee the human rights of everyone and thus the strengthening of the central state as a threat, the Bosniak frame draws on moral responsibility of the international community to right the wrongs suffered by the Bosniaks during the war and thus create a strong, Bosniak-led Bosnian state (Silajdžić 2008).

In the same way that ideas of human rights discourses have been "localized", democracy has featured regularly in the local narratives of resistance. Needless to say, in the international statebuilding discourse democracy is the key peacebuilding and statebuilding instrument. However, the contradictions in the international democratization practice – imposition of democracy by non-democratic means – have been exploited by local agencies seeking to challenge the international presence. All the local statebuilding discourses frequently represent international involvement as non-democratic and/or oppressive and foreground the detrimental consequences of such statebuilding practice to the country's future. While the RS has framed the OHR as an "occupier" ("Bosnian Serb Leader") that stifles democracy and is in fact an affront to international law, Bosnian Croat narratives have highlighted the violation of democratic norms that the country's current organization enables. This, according to the Croat discourse, has led to underrepresentation of Croats in the country's institutions. Although the presence of international statebuilders has generally coincided with the Bosniak statebuilding agenda, Bosniak discourses have criticized the lack of international will to force through statebuilding reforms. The above discourses have allowed local politicians from all parties to represent themselves as the champions of democracy. Intertwined in the Serb narratives of democracy are ideas of local ownership. An example of yet another narrative borrowed from the international statebuilding lexicon, the RS has challenged the international presence in the country by noting that particularly the OHR has become the problem, rather than the solution: "time has come", as the RS Prime Minister Dodik noted, to give the "people of Bosnia and Herzegovina and their democratically elected leaders…full responsibility for their future" (Dodik 2009). As the above discursive appropriations imply, local agencies frequently challenge international statebuilding efforts on their own terms and in doing so, seek to authorize and rationalize acts of contestation vis-à-vis the international statebuilding project. Practices of contestation, in turn, allow the local statebuilding agencies to engage in re-negotiating the parameters of the internationally-led statebuilding trajectory as they slow down and impede the process.

Concluding thoughts

This analysis has reflected on the initial findings on the contentious dynamic between internal and external statebuilders in post-Dayton Bosnia. In what can be characterized as "hybrid peace", the institutional and procedural elements of the international statebuilding have been subverted and appropriated by local agencies for the demands of their respective statebuilding agendas. This is done through the deployment of mobilizing structures such as the organizational capabilities of political parties as well as religious and commercial entities. Disseminated by media controlled by actors engaged in contention vis-à-vis the international statebuilders, politicians, political activists and members of clergy among others have framed internationally-led statebuilding efforts as detrimental to the interests and, indeed, the very survival of their respective groups. While undoubtedly the Dayton Peace Agreement has created a political system which in itself acts as an overarching opportunity structure for subverting the statebuilding process, also the international discourses employed to legitimize the international intervention provide opportunities for local statebuilding agencies. Particularly the narratives of democratization, human rights and local ownership, underpinned by universalist tendencies, are adopted in local space to challenge the international statebuilding that regularly compromises the norms it declares to be advancing. Moreover, changes in the political opportunity structures – namely, the decline in the OHR's credibility, the shift in the international attention to other conflict areas as well as growing disagreements within the international community over the statebuilding policies used – have also opened possibilities for resistance. Additionally, the impetus for changing the country's Constitution designed in Dayton advocated by certain actors in the international community has plunged the statebuilding process into a permanent crisis as changes to the Constitution are seen, particularly by the Bosnian Serbs, to have a direct impact on their status in the country. Akin to the findings of Divjak and Pugh who argue that the internationally-led neo-liberal free marketization has created opportunities for war entrepreneurs, the political dimension of the international engagement has clearly had similar ramifications (2008, 380). The peace agreement itself then, coupled with the nature of the ensuing intervention, has made it relatively easy for the local statebuilding actors to legitimize and promote their respective agendas.

In the complex dynamic of internal-external interactions, local contestation of the international statebuilding measures partly stems from – but has also contributed to – the heavy-handed international statebuilding by imposition. Paradoxically the international involvement is deemed necessary as long as "spoilers of peace" are present while at the same time the very practices of international statebuilding contribute to the existence of "spoilers". In many ways then the internal and external statebuilders maintain each other. This points to the intricate nature of the dynamic between the different statebuilders in Bosnia which is not captured adequately by "spoilers of peace" approach as it mainly focuses on managing spoiler behaviour and pays little attention to the interactions that often generate or maintain local resistance. While studies such as Barnett and Zurcher (2008) began in a more nuanced way to shed light on how the relations between the international statebuilders and local agents may contribute to the weakness of the emerging states, in-depth case studies are vital in understanding such interrelationships further. In many ways then this paper marks the beginning rather than an end of an enquiry.

Acknowledgements

The author wishes to thank Soeren Keil, Bernhard Stahl and the anonymous reviewers for valuable comments, as well as the University of London Central Research Fund and the Department of International Relations at the LSE for funding fieldwork in Bosnia in 2009 and 2010.

Notes

1. "International statebuilding agencies" refer to the principal international actors involved since the 1995 peace agreement. Those actors are the Peace Implementation Council (PIC), the Office of the High Representative (OHR), United Nations (UN), the Organization for Security and Cooperation in Europe (OSCE), the European Union (EU) as well as individual governments taking active (albeit fluctuating) interest in Bosnia such as the United States, the UK, Germany, France, Russia and Turkey.
2. Liberal peace refers to the amalgam of "peace, democracy and free market" (Richmond 2006, 292).

3. Contentious politics also operate in the domestic level, entailing non-elite claim-making directed towards municipal and state authorities. This has particularly been the case in relation to cuts in pensions and other benefits demanded by the international financial institutions in exchange for loans. While these domestic forms of contention are not the focus of this paper and cannot be discussed in detail due to space constraints, they are noteworthy in the sense that they have the potential to create unrest in Bosnia. Arguably this discontent could be harnessed by local statebuilding actors in their efforts to frame the international involvement in the country as harmful to the people.
4. For detailed and extensive studies on the international involvement in Bosnia see for instance Martina Fischer's edited volume *Peacebuilding and Civil Society in Bosnia-Herzegovina* or McMahon and Western's *Foreign Affairs* article "The death of Dayton: how to stop Bosnia from falling apart".
5. Office of the High Representative is the main implementation agency of the civilian aspects of the Dayton Peace Agreement.
6. This was particularly the case when both moderate and radical Serbs withdrew from the joint institutions of governance in 2002 in response to the OHR's change on the Law on the Council of Ministers and other changes in the structures of the central government that were seen to be detrimental to the Serb interests.
7. Russia was struggling with its own insurgency problem in the Caucasus and thus wished to see no precedents of independence set in the Balkans.
8. As shown above, parallel Croat institutions had existed since the creation of the Federation.
9. It is important to note that the Bosnian Catholic Church was split between moderates and radicals and it was mainly the more radical factions that supported the self-rule campaign.

References

"A Decade on, Bosnia Focus Shifts to Changing Peace Accords'". 2005. *Agence France Presse*. 18 November.
Amnesty International. 2006. *Bosnia and Herzegovina: Widespread discrimination blocking refugee return*. 26 2006. http://www.amnesty.org.uk/news_details.asp?NewsID=16770
Ashdown, Paddy. 2007. *Swords and Ploughshares: Bringing Peace to the 21st Century*. London: Weidenfeld and Nicolson.
Barnett, Michael, and Christoph Zurcher. 2008. "The Peacebuilder's Contract: How External State-Building Reinforces Weak Statehood." In *The Dilemmas of Statebuilding. Confronting the Contradictions of Post War Peace Operations*, edited by R. Paris and T. Sisk, 23–52. London: Routledge.
Belloni, Roberto. 2001. "Civil Society and Peacebuilding in Bosnia and Herzegovina." *Journal of Peace Research* 38 (2): 163–180.
Benford, Robert, and David Snow. 2000. "Framing Processes and Social Movement: An Overview and Assessment." *Annual Review of Sociology* 26 (1): 611–639.
Bieber, Florian. 2001. *Croat Self-Government in Bosnia – A Challenge for Dayton?* European Centre For Minority Issues Brief # 5. www.ecmi.de/uploads/tx_lfpubdb/brief_5.pdf
Bildt, Carl. 1998. *Peace Journey: Struggle for Peace in Bosnia*. London: Weidenfeld & Nicolson.
Bojičić-Dželilović, Vesna. 2004. *Peace on whose Terms? War Veterans' Associations in Bosnia and Hercegovina'*. Paper presented at the Paper prepared for the UNU project Spoilers of Peace Processes: Conflict Settlement and Devious Objectives.
"Bosnia: radio urges Serbs to join protest against Brcko arbitration". 1999. *BBC*. 16 March. Accessed through Nexis UK.
"Bosnia Serbs call for anti-NATO violence". 1999. *Agence France Presse*. 16 March. Accessed through Nexis UK.
"Bosnian Serb lawmakers reject international rulings". 1999. *Associated Press Worldstream*. 8 March. Accessed through Nexis UK.
"Bosnian Serb leader says Bosnia under occupation". 2009. *Associated Press Worldstream*. 23 April. Accessed via Nexus UK.
"Bosnian Serb PM Threatens Referendum Over Foreign Judges". 2009. *SRNA/BBC Monitoring Europe*. 14 December. Accessed via Nexis UK.
Burde, Dana. 2004. "Weak state, strong community? Promoting community participation in post-conflict countries." *Current Issues in Comparative Education* 6 (2): 73.

Council of the European Union. 2008. Council Decision of 18 February 2008 on the principles, priorities and conditions contained in the European Partnership with Bosnia and Herzegovina and repealing Decision 2006/55/EC. 18 February. Available at http://eur-lex.europa.eu/LexUriServ/LexUriServ.do?uri=OJ:L:2008:080:0018:01:EN:HTML

Divjak, Boris, and Michael Pugh. 2008. "The Political Economy of Corruption in Bosnia and Herzegovina." *International peacekeeping* 15 (3): 373–386.

Dodik, Milorad. 2009. "Letter to the editor: a Bosnia at peace." *The New York Times.* 21 September. http://www.nytimes.com/2009/09/22/opinion/lweb22bosnia.html

Duffield, Mark. 2001. *Global Governance and The New Wars: The Merging of Development and Security.* New York: Zed Books.

"Envoy: Bosnia's officials must shape up". 1998. *United Press International.* 9 December. Accessed through Nexis UK. European Union website "Europa". http://www.europa-eu-un.org/articles/en/article_1394_en.htm

"Foreigner's Rulings Challenged in Bosnia". 1999. *The New York Times.* 8 March. http://www.nytimes.com/1999/03/08/world/foreigner-s-rulings-challenged-in-Bosnia.html?ref=nikolapoplasen

HDZ BiH Official. 2010. Personal interview Mostar, September.

Helms, Elissa. 2003. "Women as Agents of Ethnic Reconciliation? Women's NGOs and International Intervention in Postwar Bosnia-Herzegovina." *Women's Studies International Forum* 26 (2): 15–33.

Holbrooke, Richard. 1999. *To End a War.* New York: Modern Library.

Human Rights Watch. 2001. *World Report 2001.* http://www.hrw.org/legacy/wr2k1/index.html

International Crisis Group. 1997. *Going Nowhere Fast: Refugees and Internally Displaced Persons in Bosnia and Herzegovina.* Report N°23 (May).

International Crisis Group. 1998a. *Changing Course? Implications of the Divide in Bosnian Croat Politics.* Report N° 39 (August).

International Crisis Group. 1998b. *A Hollow Promise? Return of Bosnian Serb Displaced Persons to Drvar.* Report N°29 (January).

International Crisis Group. 1999a. *Republika Srpska – Poplasen, Brcko and Kosovo: Three Crises and Out?* Report N°62 (June).

International Crisis Group. 1999b. *Republika Srpska in The Post-Kosovo Era: Collateral Damage and Transformation.* Report N°71 (July).

International Crisis Group. 2009. *Bosnia's Incomplete Transition: Between Dayton and Europe.* Report 198 (March).

Mac Ginty, Roger. 2011. *International Peacebuilding and Local Resistance: Hybrid Forms of Peace.* Basingstoke: Palgrave Macmillan.

McAdam, Doug, Sidney Tarrow, and Charles Tilly. 2001. *Dynamics of Contention.* New York: Cambridge University Press.

McAdam, Doug, John. D. McCarthy, and Mayer N. Zald. 1996. *Comparative Perspectives on Social Movements: Political Opportunities, Mobilizing Structures, and Cultural Framings.* New York: Cambridge University Press.

McMahon, Patrice. C., and Jon Western. 2009. "The Death of Dayton: How to Stop Bosnia from Falling Apart." *Foreign Affairs* 88: 69–83.

Neville-Jones, Pauline. 2010. Personal Interview. London, February.

"New Bosnia Mediator gives Himself Two Years for 'irreversible' peace". 1997. *Agence France Presse.* 2 June. Accessed through Nexis UK.

Newman, Edward, and Oliver Richmond. 2006. "Peace building and spoilers." *Conflict, Security & Development* 6 (1): 101–110.

OHR. 2000a. "Fifteen Officials Removed for Obstructing Property Law Implementation." 8 September. http://www.ohr.int/print/content_id=4030

OHR. 2000b. "BiH Media Round-Up." 14 December. http://www.ohr.int/ohr-dept/presso/bh-media-rep/round-ups/default.aspcontent_id=395

OHR. 2001a. "High Representative's Press Conference on the Dismissal of HDZ Officials." 7 March. http://www.ohr.int/ohr-dept/presso/pressb/default.aspcontent_id=3199

OHR. 2001b. "BiH Media Round-Up." 10 April. http://www.ohr.int/ohr-dept/presso/bh-media-rep/round-ups/default.aspcontent_id=469

OHR. 2001c. "BiH Media Round-Up." 28 February. http://www.ohr.int/ohr-dept/presso/bh-media-rep/round-ups/default.aspcontent_id=467

OHR. 2001d. "BiH Media Round-Up." 28 March. http://www.ohr.int/ohr-dept/presso/bh-media-rep/round-ups/default.aspcontent_id=467
OHR. 2002. "Provisional Administrator Announces Conclusions of Her Investigation." 16 December. http://www.ohr.int/other-doc/hb-padmin/default.aspcontent_id=28730.
OHR. 2004. "BiH Media Round-Up." 16 December. http://www.ohr.int/ohr-dept/presso/bh-media-rep/round-ups/default.aspcontent_id=33740
OHR. 2009. "Decision Enacting the Law on Amendments to the Law on Prosecutor's Office of Bosnia and Herzegovina." 14 December. http://www.ohr.int/decisions/judicialrdec/default.aspcontent_id=44287
"OSCE and OHR about Croat National Congress". 2000. *ONASA*. 14 December. Accessed through Nexis UK.
Parish, Matthew. T. 2007. "The Demise of the Dayton Protectorate." *Journal of intervention and statebuilding* 1 (Special Supplement):11–23.
Pouligny, Beatrice. 2006. *Peace Operations Seen from Below: UN Missions and Local People.* London: Hurst and Co.
"President Criticizes Envoy's 'Boundless Passion for Destruction of Serb Republic". 1999. *SRNA/BBC*. 8 March. Accessed through Nexis UK.
Reliefweb "European Commission adopts Euro 71.9 million programme to support Bosnia and Herzegovina." Accessed 27 February 2011. http://www.reliefweb.int/node/101775/pdf
Richmond, Oliver. 2006. "The problem of peace: understanding the 'liberal peace." *Conflict, Security & Development* 6 (3): 291–314.
Robinson, Guy M., Sten Engelstoft, and Alma Pobric. 2001. "Remaking Sarajevo: Bosnian Nationalism After the Dayton Accord." *Political Geography* 20 (2): 957–980.
Silajdžić, Haris. 2008. "Speech at the UN General Assembly." 23 September. http://www.un.org/en/ga/63/generaldebate/bosniaandherzegovina.shtml
Stedman, Stephen. J. 1997. "Spoiler Problems in Peace Processes." *International Security* 22 (2): 5–53.
Tarrow, Sidney. 1994. *Power in Social Movements.* Cambridge: Cambridge University Press.
Tilly, Charles. 2008. *Contentious Performances.* New York: Cambridge University Press.
Tilly, Charles, and Sidney Tarrow. 2007. *Contentious Politics.* Boulder: Paradigm Publishers.
Torsti, Pilvi. 2004. "History Culture and Banal Nationalism in post-War Bosnia." *South East European Politics* 5 (2/3): 142–157.
United Nations Refugee Agency in Bosnia. United Nations High Commissioner for Refugees, Representation in Bosnia and Herzegovina, Statistics Package. 2010. 31 December. http://www.internaldisplacement.org/8025708F004CE90B/(httpCountries))/C8DEEFACFF6821AD802570A7004C6A42?OpenDocument
Wheeler, Mark. 2008. Personal interview. OHR, Sarajevo, June.
Zahar, Marie-Joelle. 2010. "SRSG Mediation in Civil Wars: Revisiting the 'Spoiler' Debate." *Global Governance: A Review of Multilateralism and International Organizations* 16 (2): 265–280.

The OSCE Mission in Bosnia and Herzegovina: Testing the limits of ownership

Valery Perry[a] and Soeren Keil[b]

[a]*PILPG, Sarajevo, Bosnia and Herzegovina;* [b]*International Relations, Canterbury Christ Church University, Canterbury, UK*

This article explores the debate on local ownership in Bosnia and Herzegovina[1] by examining the limits of international community support for reform in a divided political environment in which decision-makers and politicians have little to no interest in reform themselves. After a short review of the key issues and arguments regarding ownership in BiH, the example of education reform is presented to demonstrate the role of the OSCE as an external actor in this reform sector, and the lack of any reform progress in this field in the absence of external pressure. The article closes with reflections on whether or not external organizations can make any systemic-level impact in such a hostile reform environment, and whether the OSCE can still play a constructive role in Bosnia.

Introduction

Almost 20 years after the beginning of violent hostilities that led to the dissolution of Yugoslavia and the political, economic and human crises that followed, state-building and democratization strategies in South-East Europe have been progressively less "post-war" and more "pre-Europe". The terms "European integration" and "Euro-Atlantic integration" reflect two different elements of the presumed medium- to long-term future of the Western Balkans. "European integration" is the term used to refer to the goal of prospective European Union (EU) member states – full membership in the EU. "Euro-Atlantic integration" tends to be used more in statements by American diplomats, speakers referring to NATO membership in addition to EU membership, and in statements by the Organization for Security and Cooperation in Europe (OSCE). The OSCE, with its 56 participating States, including the block of EU states, a large body of non-EU states (including many from the former Soviet Union), as well as the United States and Canada, shares a number of principles in common with the EU, but remains distinct based on its composition, security mandate and Cold War history. Support for Euro-Atlantic integration enables the OSCE – and its non-EU participants – to continue to be engaged in Bosnia and Herzegovina (BiH) even as more of BiH's future becomes seemingly embedded in a Brussels-bound trajectory.

This article will focus on the "civilian" aspect of external international organization assistance to Euro-Atlantic integration in Bosnia and Herzegovina (BiH). The aim is to look at the role of the OSCE Mission to BiH, and its role in the country's post-war, pre-integration odyssey. The OSCE Mission to BiH has been, and continues to be, the largest civilian international organization in the country. Even in 2012 the Mission had over 500 staff (approximately 15% of which are international, with the rest BiH citizens) located in 14 field offices throughout the country. While it has quite a physical presence, however, the OSCE is a quiet player, often not included in discussions about state-strengthening, state-building and democratization in prospective EU-bound countries. The OSCE neither has the "normative power" of the EU (Manners 2002), which has as its ultimate prize the accession to the Union, nor the imposition and dismissal rights of the Office of the High Representative (OHR). In fact, at a 2011 conference entitled "Exchanging Ideas on Europe 2011" (which inspired this special journal edition) a search through the dozens of papers presented finds "OSCE" in only one rather ironic context: in references to Euro-scepticism.

However, in BiH and other regions, the OSCE *has* continued to remain engaged in democratization and state-strengthening initiatives. Marc Perrin de Brichambaut, Secretary General of the OSCE from 2005–2011, has himself written:

> The OSCE has a low profile. It is no accident that its peace-building work and conflict prevention activities keep it off most people's radar screen. OSCE efforts in the areas of democratization, confidence-building and good governance take time and are anything but sensational. But the work the OSCE does in supporting post-Communist transitions, monitoring elections and mediating in some of Europe's most protracted conflicts plays an important part in keeping the peace in Europe and promoting stability. It has also been a pioneer in looking at security in a comprehensive way that links it with human rights and development policy. (2006)

In addition to being "anything but sensational", in the case of BiH a large number of the Mission's activities rely on a bottom-up approach to reform with a long-term perspective; distinctly out of the limelight in a media environment in which elite-driven politics (and bad news stories) dominate the news cycle. Its policy and programmatic trajectories over the past several years demonstrate an increasing reliance on an ownership approach to reform, whether by intent (a strategic commitment to citizen participation) or by default (an inability to engage constructively with deeply entrenched political elites).

This article seeks to ensure that the Mission *is* considered in ongoing discussions on the role of external actors in BiH's reform endeavors. The article begins with a short review of the OSCE Mission's evolving role over the past 17 years – a lengthy period of extended engagement never envisioned at the outset. This is followed by a summary of the ongoing debates on "ownership" in BiH, to acknowledge the tensions between democracy and sovereignty in a still-divided post-war state that many would define as a "frozen conflict"[2] (Biscevic 2010; Aggestam and Bjorkdahl 2011). The following section briefly looks at the single issue of education reform in order to understand the changes the Mission has had to make in working in this sector as the broader political environment in BiH has changed, particularly in the past six years. The closing section will look at the impact the Mission has had, or could still potentially have, in light of the difficult political situation in 2012, to determine whether bottom-up programmatic support can in fact translate into broader systematic political change and reform.

The OSCE Mission to BiH: comprehensive security or mission creep?

The OSCE Mission mandate has evolved based on various policy and budget decisions made over the past 17 years, with annual extension discussions falling into a fairly routine process of budget approval in which the Mission itself is not questioned, though proposed activities within the Mission have been discussed. The General Framework

Agreement for Peace (Dayton Agreement) that ended the war in 1995 specifically mandated tasks for the OSCE in Annex 1B, Article II (Regional Stabilization), Annex 3 (Elections), and Annex 6, Article XIII (Human Rights). The 5th Ministerial Council, Budapest (8 December 1995) reiterated these goals, and the BiH Budget approval (11 January 1996) reiterated the tasks noted in the Dayton Agreement. The first BiH mandate extension (through the end of 1997) on 21 November 1996, extended the Mission's mandate and called attention to the work of the Mission in elections, democracy building, human rights promotion and monitoring and regional stabilization. A second BiH mandate extension (through the end of 1998) on 11 December 1997, extended the Mission's role in elections, and also noted the Mission's work in human rights, democratization, media development and regional stabilization. Subsequently, the annual unified budget preparation and approval process has served as an opportunity for reinforcement and clarification of the Mission's mandate, as the Permanent Council requires consensus to ensure that all participating States are satisfied and in agreement with proposed plans.

The December 2001 meeting of the Peace Implementation Council (PIC) Steering Board Political Directors led to an attempt to streamline the international community's presence in BiH. This effort led to the establishment of four thematic Task Forces and the assignment of Lead Agencies to push forward on issues within these Task Forces. The OSCE was assigned a lead or co-lead role on issues related to the Property Law Implementation Plan (PLIP) and return sustainability (including education, health, pensions, social safety net, security) within the Return and Reconstruction Task Force; lead or co-lead roles in Democratization and Civil Society (elections, political parties, public campaign, youth & politics, non-governmental organizations), Defense and Security (military reform, demobilization, de-mining, and civil aviation) and Institution Monitoring (monitoring of State, Entity and District institutions) within the Institution Building Task Force; and the lead role on Human Rights (quasi-judicial institutions, legal aid/information, trial monitoring, juvenile justice reform) within the Rule of Law Task Force.

Starting with Wolfgang Petritsch's tenure as High Representative (August 1999 – May 2002), and particularly during Paddy Ashdown's term (May 2002 – January 2006), there was an increase in activities aimed at both strengthening the state and cultivating a sense of "stateness" in BiH. The OSCE Mission supported the implementation of five strategic areas included in Ashdown's "Jobs and Justice" agenda: economic reform, rule of law reform, defense reform, education reform and public administration reform. As described more below, education reform became a significant and large element of the Mission's work. The Mission's central role in election organization ended, as the process was assumed by the Central Election Commission after the adoption of the BiH Election Law in 2001 (Manning and Antic 2003). The Mission closed its media reform effort at the end of 2001, though it has since increasingly sought to engage on issues related to freedom of the media in BiH (Follow-Up Report 2010). The Mission's work in the political-military sphere continued as well with a focus on assisting BiH to meet its OSCE political military commitment, but has slimmed down as defense reform was implemented and related security issues are increasingly handled under the rubric of future possible NATO membership.[3] The Mission's "human dimension" work has more or less remained the same for the past several years, in spite of internal organizational changes, with ongoing work in democratization and governance, human rights and the rule of law, civil society and education (Perry 2005; Perry 2010).

The evolution of the Mission's focus in BiH is in many ways reflective of the evolution of approaches to post-conflict peace-building and democratization activities more generally. In the initial "heyday" of post-Cold War democratization, elections were front and center in the catalogue of democratization strategies. However, post-Dayton BiH quickly illustrated that elections were not sufficient as a democratization strategy, and needed to be supplemented by other activities including civil society promotion, institution building and local government reform.[4] There was a need for transition support activities as well as specific post-war support activities.

In addition to reflecting a more realistic approach to state-building, state-strengthening, and post-conflict democratization, this broad approach reflects the OSCE's own emphasis on *comprehensive security*. The OSCE's "three dimension" structure (political-military, economic-environmental, human dimension) therefore in itself also provides a framework for the expanded scope of the Mission to BiH.

Whose ownership?

Against this backdrop of Mission evolution, the broader context of international, external engagement was itself evolving. As international actors – countries, individual state aid agencies or international organizations – have become more involved in development, conflict prevention, peacebuilding and state strengthening efforts in the past 20 years in different trouble-spots across the globe, the word "ownership" has been increasingly bandied about. "Ownership" can mean many things, and can raise many questions. Does ownership refer to the outcome or the process? Who are the owners? Are they limited to the political elites, even in societies in which there may be a democratic deficit? What in fact is being "owned"? While infringements on local ownership might be easy to discern in a situation of outright coercion, what about "softer" forms of persuasion, which may offer a veneer of choice?[5] Another question would be if ownership is at all admirable and indeed possible in a post-conflict society like BiH, in which political elites have consistently undermined international efforts to create more functional state structures.

Simon Chesterman writes,

> the rhetoric of ownership has frequently been accompanied by an assumption that a political vacuum exists prior to the arrival of international staff. This is rarely, if ever, the case. One of these errors that is often repeated in these institutions is the conscious or unconscious assumption that, when the institutions of the state collapse or are so divided as to be dysfunctional, politics ceases to happen. In fact the control of power becomes more important than ever, for the very reason that it may be exerted through informal or incoherent means. (Chesterman 2004, 5–6)

In the realm of peacebuilding, Paris and Sisk point to the inherent paradox of foreign actors "identifying" local actors potentially capable of implementing a peace process; this mere involvement in identifying and selecting local actors as partners can defy the very principle of local ownership (Paris and Sisk 2009).

Hannah Reich views ownership in the development and peacebuilding contexts as impossible under the current structures framing international cooperation and intervention in countries, calling for changes to the relationship between external actors and the countries/parties in question in order to move towards a more cooperative partnership (Reich 2006, 7). Tim Donais, writing on ownership in the context of security sector reform, concludes that "local actors can neither be ignored, bypassed nor easily transformed", a realistic view urging flexibility and meaningful local participation in security reform processes (Donais 2009, 128). In a conference paper, Sara Hellmuller looks at ownership in peace processes, finding, for example, that in seeking "ownership", international actors may limit their coordination to political/national elites, leaving out civic actors and in turn reaffirming elites of questionable genuine legitimacy (Hellmuller 2011). What is important to highlight in this short survey is that ownership in itself is a contested concept. A proper definition of the concept of ownership depends not only on the context of the country it is applied to, but also on the policy areas. As Chesterman has pointed out,

> The language of 'ownership' is commonly used in this context [referring to political authority], but it is not clear that the term has either consistency or substance ....
> [O]wnership tends to be used figuratively – much as 'buy-in' in this context usually does not suggest an actual financial transaction – to refer in a more vague way to the relationship between stakeholders, with meanings ranging from a sense of attachment to a programme or operation to (rarely) actual controlling authority. (Chesterman 2009, 18)

In this context it is important to think about the reasons for the inclusion of local elites in state-building and democratization. The focus on reconstruction in post-conflict societies by international actors, be they states or international organizations, will ultimately only succeed if local elites identify with the process. Ownership offers a way for international actors to include local actors (politicians, civil society, refugees, former militias, etc.) into the process of state-building and reconstruction, thereby promoting legitimacy and participation. Edward Rees argues in the context of Kosovo that

> [t]he golden rule in any development activity is that the host country/organization/individual must feel a legitimate sense of ownership of the process. Ownership is ultimately about political control, and the ability of the host to participate in making political decisions about the development activity. (Rees 2005)

While this will be difficult to achieve in post-conflict and divided societies like BiH, the advantages of engaging with local elites in theory should benefit the whole state-building exercise. Local elites can be vested with authority to ensure that they feel in control of the reconstruction agenda. Donors can also ensure that local elites and civil society decide on the framework for implementation of aid projects. This should lead to more suitable projects and a more appropriate agenda focusing on the priorities of local actors rather than international ones.

It is however important to distinguish between functional and structural ownership.[6] While local actors might be involved in the implementation of projects and the allocation of aid (functional ownership), they remain nevertheless limited in the planning and implementation of a more medium and long-term strategy for state-building. An example of functional ownership can be found in the support for refugee return in BiH, which was a priority of international actors, who first implemented different projects but later handed control to local civil society organizations and local bodies. Structural ownership refers to a more deep-rooted form of engagement with local elites. It includes the involvement of local representatives in the development of policy priorities and long-term political goals. The aim of this form of ownership is to include local representatives in decision-making and long-term strategy planning (Chesterman 2009, 22). This has often focused on areas such as institution building and economic reconstruction.

In the case of education reform, which will be discussed later in this paper, it is important to focus on both aspects of ownership. Functional ownership focuses on the involvement of local elites in broad curricular design and the implementation of previously agreed targets such as the establishment of multi-ethnic schools. Structural ownership means the inclusion and, ultimately, the responsibility of BiH politicians, civil society, teachers and parents, and academics in all debates on education, including the establishment of operational policy forums for policy making (such as education ministries) and the long-term development of curricula, school books and educational concepts and frameworks.

In the BiH context, the ownership discussion began during High Representative Wolfgang Petritsch's term,[7] but gained momentum during Paddy Ashdown's tenure, most notably with a volley lobbed into the academic court by Knaus and Martin of the European Stability Initiative (ESI) (2003). What might be called the "ESI school" suggests that BiH's democratic deficit is at its core caused by the ability of BiH politicians to hide behind international actors rather than act democratically and responsibly on their own. In fact, the presence of an "international community" either actively prevents them from stepping up to the challenges of governance, or allows them to be passive, avoiding risks and responsibility. An exchange of letters in the *NATO Review* further fleshed out the parameters of the "ownership argument" as well as some contesting views (*NATO Review*, Winter, 2004). The International Crisis Group, while in the past urging aggressive international engagement in BiH and the Balkans generally, has itself assumed the ownership posture in a manner very much in line with ESI, increasingly preaching BiH (and regional) conflict resolution through the European integration process.

Others argue that ownership is impossible in the BiH political structure, citing the perfect storm of a constitutional and electoral structure that require narrow ethno-national participation and representation, the linkages between ethno-national elites and the media and religious communities, and the marginalization or exclusion of meaningful civic participation. The BiH-based Foreign Policy Initiative questions the existing legal and constitutional structure that would guarantee complete peace implementation in the absence of the OHR (*Foreign Policy Initiative*, 2011). Kurt Bassuener of the Democratization Policy Council has argued that ownership is the ideal, but will remain an impossible ideal in the current structure; external intervention through aggressive application of carrots or sticks would be required to change the playing field to allow genuine ownership to begin (Bassuener 2009; Bassuener and Weber 2010).

Ed Joseph has challenged what he calls "ownership doctrine" in an article which looks at a number of cases, including BiH. He writes, "Ownership orthodoxy, unfortunately, smothers the question as to *why* actors in distressed states fail to take ownership of their affairs" (emphasis in the original) (2007, 111). Similar to Bassuener, he looks at the potential structural barriers to real progress through ownership. "Insisting, without more, that these parties 'take ownership' of their affairs is to deny the existence of a conflict over the very terms of who, how and what ought to be the subject of ownership" (2007, 111). One can consider the Chesterman quote above in this context as well, as in the BiH environment it is fair to say that international actors did not assume there was a lack of politics, but sought to try to fundamentally *change* the politics dominating the discourse on peace implementation and accompanying reform. This debate was most vigorous in the years *before* the decline of reform progress and political dialogue since 2006, and while there is broad agreement on the diagnosis of the problems, there continues to be disagreement as to the best cure – a dose of Europe, or a more radical structural surgery.

One element of ownership which is either routinely ignored or impossibly difficult to pin down is whether or not ownership by its very nature refers primarily to international interaction with political elites, or with a broader swathe of civil society. One of the contradictions of ownership posed by Paris and Sisk relates to the role of external actors in identifying and selecting elites with whom to negotiate peace processes. This selection can significantly shape the playing field. As new political parties emerged in the late 1980s and early 1990s in BiH, the ethno-national parties consolidated more easily than non-nationally oriented parties (Pejanovic 2002), and were in a better position to be seen as interlocutors of choice by the international community. From the first moments of international discussions regarding the possible structure of a post-Yugoslav BiH, the decision to negotiate with just representatives of the three ethno-national groups, or the consideration of proposals for structural changes according to power-sharing proposals based on only three groups (consider the Cutiliero Plan), the political and subsequent structural rules of the game seem to have been irreversibly reified and established.

Some might point out that, in the case of post-war BiH, the political elites with whom the international community interacts are the democratically-elected representatives of the people; it is only natural for diplomats to deal with officials, as they stand for their citizens. But does the BiH political structure in which citizens operate and vote allow for a real choice, the development of real alternative parties and a closer correlation between what citizens want and what they get from their politicians? BiH has very limited public consultation on legislation, and presently has no provisions for citizens to bring legislative proposals to Parliament ("Implementation of Regulations" 2009)[8]. The country's electoral system is set up in a way in which there is not a single election for state office in which all BiH citizens vote for the same slate of candidates. Before and after every election in BiH, observers wonder at the difference between citizens' stated substantive interests in pre-election polls, and the seemingly contradictory election outcomes of parties and leaders who repeatedly fail to deliver. In his look at attempts to spread liberal democracy, Fareed Zakaria has harsh words for the experience of BiH:

> In counties such as Bosnia, which went to the polls within a year of the Dayton peace accords, elections only made more powerful precisely the kinds of ugly ethnic forces that have made it more difficult to build genuine liberal democracy there. The ethnic thugs stayed in power, kept the courts packed and the police well fed. The old system has stayed in place, delaying real change for years, perhaps decades. (Zakaria 2003, 155)

Paris suggests that ensuring appropriate sequencing in post-war peacebuilding, and putting institutionalization before liberalization, might yield more powerful interventions and outcomes (Paris 2004). Asim Mujkic argues that the "irrational" partnership with "reform oriented" nationalists was a "disastrous mistake", also citing Fareed Zakaria: "The greatest danger of unfettered and dysfunctional democracy is that it will discredit democracy itself ...." Zakaria 2003, 255; Fukuyama 2005; Mujkic 2008, 31).

The structure shapes the outcome; it is little wonder that the state is so functionally weak, and in fact increasingly in question.

> The lack of transparency and accountability and the dearth of the rule of law and good governance make public scrutiny a chimera. Bosnian civil society has neither the leverage nor the potential resources to perform the task handed over by the international community. (Belloni 2001, 172)

While written in 2001, Belloni's description of the way in which elites maintain the status quo is still accurate a decade later:

> By fostering community isolation, mobilization and a general feeling of insecurity, ethnic elites legitimize each other and maintain a tight grip on their constituencies. At the same time, internal dissent, as expressed by those who question the existing social order by promoting and defending the possibility of a multi-ethnic polity, is often repressed and marginalized. (Belloni 2001, 173)

The ownership debate will go on as long as there are international interventions – whether political or economic, hard or soft. Therefore, additional consideration of the impact of the OSCE in field interventions – whether Missions or negotiations – can be a useful exercise. As the OSCE Mission to BiH today has no powers of imposition, little money with which to buy or cajole support, and as a political organization is not even legally binding upon its participating States, the extent to which an ownership approach can work at either a micro- or macro-level is an interesting topic to study.

With the exception of some elements of its early role in elections, the OSCE never had executive power in BiH, and the role of ownership in the context of the Mission needs to be understood as both an outcome and part of the process of reform.

The following review will examine if a successful ownership strategy is at all possible if there is no external imposition power, and little to no domestic consensus for reform. The Mission not only had to include local elites from the outset in planning and implementation; it was nearly completely dependent upon them. It also focused on the "empowering" of key local actors, such as civil society organizations in the context of democratization, and pupils, teachers and parents in the context of education reform. The following section will discuss the impact of the OSCE in the discussion about education reform in BiH and the importance and limits of ownership during these debates. The discussion is limited to the OSCE's approach towards ownership on this issue, and therefore does not consider the strategies pursued by other organizations. This review will consider whether ownership should not only be viewed as a long-term end of international intervention, but as a means in itself in the creation of sustainable and democratic societies in post-conflict societies.

Education reform – from top-down to bottom-up

While the OSCE had addressed a number of education issues through its human rights portfolio for several years, in mid-2002 it received a mandate to begin more concerted and formalized engagement in this sector (Perry forthcoming; Perry 2003). The framework for this engagement was twofold, and largely based on the Mission's work in human rights. First, it was linked to sustainable return, which was increasingly viewed as impossible if minority returnee children were unable to attend the school in their town. Second, it was linked to the notion of youth education and cultivation of a future "successor generation", and the concerns of what this generation might look like if schooled in the divisive and exclusionary system that emerged during and after the war. While some questioned the engagement of the OSCE on this issue – it was the first time an "Education Department" was established in *any* mission[9] – in a briefing to the Peace Implementation Council by the Mission in November 2002 the political nature of the reform challenge was made clear:

> The current state of education in Bosnia and Herzegovina (BiH) represents a serious obstacle to stability, security, reconciliation, institution-building, sustainable refugee returns and economic recovery. There is a direct relationship between an effective, non-discriminatory educational system and long-term peace and security in Bosnia and Herzegovina. (OSCE 2002)

In the first years of engagement, there was considerable effort to engage high-level officials, including party officials and Ministries of Education, to reform the broader systems and structures that shaped the education reform environment. It was a political priority of the international community. Rather stunningly in retrospect, the BiH authorities presented an "Education Reform Agenda" (also referred to as "the Pledges") to the PIC on 21 November 2002, noting themselves reasons why reform was needed.[10] The pledges had been developed through six working groups in which approximately 80% of the members were BiH experts, with OHR and OSCE staff providing substantive and secretarial support as needed. The highlights of each pledge demonstrate the commitments that the BiH authorities were making at that time: (1) Access to quality education in integrated multicultural schools; (2) Provide basic education at pre-school primary and general secondary levels with modern curriculum and systems of assessment, in well managed and equipped schools; (3) Support BiH economic development through development of a modern and flexible vocational education program; (4) Raise the quality of higher education and research in BiH; (5) Ensure transparent, equitable and cost-effective use of public resources for education.

There was impressive and rapid progress at the outset. The state-level Framework Law on Primary and Secondary Education (FWL PSE) was adopted by a unanimous vote in the BiH Parliamentary Assembly in June 2003, and corresponding education laws at the Republika Srpska (RS), cantonal and Brcko levels harmonized in 2004. (The High Representative imposed harmonizing changes in Cantons 6, 8 and 10, then – and still – bastions of Croat identity politics). In doing this, BiH politicians at minimum acknowledged the principles incorporated in the Framework Law at the State level, though perhaps assuming that the education legislation – and implementation – at lower levels could always be formulated/revisited/ignored later. Further, The Ministry of Civil Affairs identified resources to set up a small Education Unit, and after several failed attempts at establishment, a Conference of Ministers of Education, bringing together the 13 MoEs, was established. In this context it can clearly be recognized that education reform focused on structural ownership at the outset. There was a wider international agenda on the re-creation of a multi-ethnic BiH society, and refugee return, post-war reconstruction and education reform all formed a part of this broader agenda. While international actors provided the broader framework and long-term goals (and significant money), it was left to local elites in the RS and the cantons to implement.

The Mission also moved to support field coordination efforts to facilitate the implementation of the May 2002 inter-entity Interim Agreement on Accommodation of Special Needs and Rights of Returnee Children, assisting in mediating numerous returnee related schooling disputes and in coordinating the drafting of the Criteria for School Names and Symbols, endorsed by the Coordination Board for the Interim Agreement in April 2004. None of these efforts was "a silver bullet"; the obstacles that followed in implementation remained daunting. However, after years in which a debate on education reform was seemingly impossible, structured mechanisms for addressing problems related to inequality were increasingly in place, to address the specific needs of returnees, but, more broadly, of all citizens.

After these fairly quick apparent successes, the reform initiative slowed for two reasons. First, experience in BiH has demonstrated that it is relatively easy to put excellent, human rights-based legal frameworks and action plans onto paper; the challenge however is to actually *implement* the needed reforms so that the *de facto* reality somewhat mirrors *de jure* legal frameworks. Basic implementation is readily and easily blocked either through political obstruction, disinterested officials or staff, or through failure to allocate funds for real change. Such practical problems became increasingly visible, particularly in the already most divided communities in the country.[11]

Second, the general political and reform environment in BiH deteriorated fairly steadily since 2006, affecting reform progress in *all* sectors. The confluence of a number of factors – including progressive disengagement in BiH affairs by the Office of the High Representative, the failure of the April package of constitutional reform, and the general elections that entrenched Milorad Dodik and Haris Silajdzic into diametrically-opposite, zero-sum negotiation postures regarding the future of BiH – led to the stalling of reform, and even some signs of reversal of reform. Regional developments, most notably Montenegro's independence referendum in 2006, and Kosovo's unilateral declaration of independence (UDI) in 2008, did not contribute to creating conditions for compromise in BiH (McMahon and Western 2009; Bassuener and Weber 2010; Chivvis 2010). While reform in BiH was never easy, it seemed to be increasingly difficult to propose reforms, as the basic goals of reform – and state-strengthening itself – were increasingly under attack.

However, against this backdrop, the Mission continued to engage in education, though increasingly working at the grassroots or expert level rather than aggressively engaging with political parties or officials; seeking side-door approaches to reform rather than barging in through the front entrance. In the absence of political commitment to reform, efforts have been made to side-step political elites by engaging directly with citizens who, quite often, note that they themselves feel excluded from the system. High-level attention from international community "principals" ended as education was preempted by other issues – police and constitutional reform, among others. What this demonstrates is that the OSCE Mission had to shift its focus from more structural forms of ownership, in which local politicians were to be empowered to implement substantial reforms, to more functional forms of ownership, in which citizens and civil society representatives became more involved in reforms that focused, on the one hand, on overcoming ethnic separation in the school system, and on the other hand on the improvement of education generally and in particular on the implementation of common European regulations in the education sector.

Further, the increasing focus on BiH's "EU future", even in the difficult political environment, left little room for a focus on education, as education is included in the *acquis communautaire* primarily in a technical sense, and certainly not in a substantive way that could address BiH's divided post-war educational structures. While delegations to BiH made continuous note of the need to end divisive practices, on the ground, high-level political attention to the continuing divisive politics of education was increasingly rare. The OSCE was invited to provide a briefing on education at a 2011 PIC meeting which attracted some interest and attention, but as of this writing, few specific actions in support of a revitalization of education reform have taken place.[12] In light of the ongoing political crisis and the fact that such education reforms are not a part of the EU accession process, the OSCE's examples of "functional ownership" have rather limited impact.[13]

In a reform environment in which progress is less a goal than simply seeking to stem the reversal of past achievements, education reform has largely stagnated, particularly in terms of efforts aimed at reducing discrimination and segregation in BiH schools. There have been no practical changes in the status of BiH's two-schools-under-one-roof since 2005, and, with the limited exception of Brčko District (Perry 2006), education broadly remains fragmented and flavored according to dominant ethnic groups in any given place. The state Education Agency envisioned by the Framework Law is minimally operational, yet has little capacity and no mechanisms to encourage – let alone enforce – shared curricular standards. The Coordination Board responsible for ensuring the rights of returnee children has done little since 2006. The Conference of Ministers of Education met only once between mid-2010 and mid-2012. New cooperative agreements between the Republika Srpska and Serbia have resulted in a situation in which there is more educational mobility between the entity and the neighboring state than within BiH.

Against this rather depressing systemic backdrop, however, the OSCE Mission continued to have education reform in its mandate, continued to have staff in support of this mandate in the field and head office, and continued to implement a range of programmatic activities. A number of programs being implemented are summarized below. This survey is by no means comprehensive; further, it is limited to Mission efforts to promote diversity and inclusion in schools – perhaps the most important element of education reform in light of human rights and mobility arguments.[14] It simply aims to demonstrate the number of reform efforts under way that seeks to make change without arousing political opposition, suggesting a strategy of incremental "stealth" reform with a (very) long-term context.

School civic bodies

In line with the OSCE's broader commitment to supporting and strengthening civil society, and in fact mainstreaming a civil society approach into work in many of its focus areas, the Mission has supported the establishment and strengthening of parent and student councils. The BiH Framework Law on Primary and Secondary Education requires that all schools have such councils, and at the beginning, the simple establishment of such councils (or the strengthening of existing similar civic bodies) was a central part of the Mission's work in the field. The theory – as with many civil society efforts – was that as more citizens became involved in their schools, the more they *themselves* would press for political reform and modernization. Mission field staff were directly involved in working with schools and providing capacity building support to students and parents to get councils up and running. Direct organization and capacity building training was stopped in 2006 – some would say prematurely – as Mission leadership questioned the capacity building approach to a broader problem that at its core is a political problem. When it later became clear that top-down reform was not on the horizon, support to school civic bodies was reintroduced. It became clear that working through civil society was one of the only available options.

In the framework of ownership, this highlights that civil society organizations, particularly parent and student councils, were seen as key "drivers of change" for the OSCE and therefore deserved more support and attention. This is both a form of functional ownership, in which these councils are motivated to press for externally established reforms, and a form of structural ownership, since it was hoped that these parent and student councils would become leading actors in a wider discussion about the quality of education in BiH and possible scenarios for change towards a better and more inclusive education system. This can also be seen by two traits within the OSCE's civil society efforts in the education sector. One was the increasing reliance on peer education and training of trainers – a methodology aimed at creating cadres of skilled persons in schools capable of continuing work in the future once the Mission eventually withdrew.[15] A second characteristic was the explicit effort to embed cross-community outreach into almost all capacity building and network activities among school civic bodies. In other words, rather than holding a training, seminar or conference for representatives from just one of BiH's ethno-national communities, events were organized to ensure participants from all communities, to provide a chance for inter-group interaction, and, hopefully, the identification of shared educational interests that could transcend the politics of delayed reform and promote a spirit of reconciliation. Within this so-called "Building Bridges" effort, student exchanges to meet and work with the "other" are organized in cooperation with schools – efforts welcomed by participants though rarely organized in the absence of the Mission or other international nudging and funding.

Curricular reform

The hottest potato in education reform is curricular reform – what children are taught. This goes to the core of exclusive identity politics, as it is rooted in subjects such as language, religion and history. One of the first curricular efforts of the international community concerned redacting hateful language from school textbooks, and ultimately supporting the development of textbooks less likely to promote a very negative view of "the other". Subsequent efforts have focused on the development of a new generation of history textbook authors and history textbooks, as well as a broader effort to develop shared curricular standards for history teaching, with some success (Karge 2008).[16] Further, a nine-year curriculum was introduced in place of the previous eight-year model.[17]

However, almost 10 years after the concerted education reform effort began there are still in effect three different ethnically defined curricula in place. There has been no political will to move forward with harmonization or modernization efforts, even when teachers and experts (from BiH and the region) have met to discuss opportunities for further work in each country, and regionally.[18] Efforts at the Mission increasingly focus on either incremental efforts to create structures for future curricular harmonization activities at the expert level (as in an ongoing three-year history curriculum reform project), development of supplemental classroom materials, or identification of trends in the teaching of other classroom subjects that would benefit from a long-term reform approach as was done with history.[19] The Mission commissioned experts to review a number of textbooks in subjects including language and literature, religion and nature and society, and to draft comprehensive assessment reports to serve as a basis for potential future curricular harmonization efforts. (It remains unclear how or whether these assessments will be used as a policy tool by the Mission to encourage policy change by the local authorities).

As another example, after a number of years supporting a BiH-wide course aimed to teach students about religions in a broad, social science-based way, more recently alternative subjects to confessional religious instruction are being developed by local experts in targeted parts of the country where there is the will to fulfill this legal requirement – one of the few possibilities in an environment in which the religious communities wield significant influence.[20] This engagement demonstrates a form of functional ownership on the issue of curricular reform, as policy discussions on long-term policy are rather limited, and in the current political environment, there is little interest among politicians and policy makers in seriously discussing meaningful curricular reform and crafting a less divisive approach to educational content. As the OSCE does not as a matter of policy seek to continue or strengthen educational policies that might further entrench divisions among children and schools, their efforts to encourage even minimal reforms that might be palatable to their domestic partners represent the art of the possible.

Index for inclusion

While the first education reform pledge referred to integrated multicultural schools, with the noted exception of schools in Brcko, public schools across BiH each have a dominant ethnic "flavor" depending on the dominant group in that location. School names and symbols, holiday celebrations and curricular and educational resources primarily reflect the dominant constituent people. This reflects the extent to which efforts to harmonize curricula and integrate students regardless of ethno-national affiliation have fallen short. Opponents of substantive reforms in the RS remind that education is an entity competency to forestall integrative reforms; opponents among Croats remind that education is a cantonal competency. As a result, the country continues to have essentially three sets of schools. Because of the lack of progress in dealing with political elites at the entity and cantonal level, it was important to shift attention to the schools themselves and change the addressor of ownership as a form of local empowerment away from the responsible educational officials in the ministries to the teachers, parents and students in the classroom.

In the absence of political will for more integrative reforms, a gentler approach has been developed. The Index for Inclusion was introduced in an effort to devolve inclusion initiatives down to schools through a self-assessment program aimed at encouraging schools to become more participatory, inclusive and open environments.[21] Schools – together with the broader school communities – receive training in how to assess their accessibility and inclusion – ranging from special needs access to participatory school civic bodies to intercultural inclusion – and then draw up multi-year plans for school improvement. Small grants are available to support school ideas and initiatives. Quite simply, this effort aims at minimizing divisive practices in schools at the school level, as it has become clear that higher-level enforcement is not likely in the current political environment. Schools in almost 40 municipalities throughout BiH elected to participate in the program, developing micro-level approaches to inclusion in their educational spaces. Many schools participating in the Index for Inclusion have developed school inclusion plans that take great steps to include children with special needs, or Roma children. Some schools and municipalities offer limited symbolic financial or material support, though the bulk of needed implementation funds come from external donors. They may at the same time fail to address the elephant in the room of non-minority constituent peoples in their midst (e.g. a Bosniak in a Serb majority area, or a Serb in a Croat majority area). This is, however, left to the participants to decide, though it can lead to strange cases of schools assessing themselves as "inclusive" in spite of being at their core structured according to one narrow ethno-national group. This is again both a form of functional ownership, in which the municipalities and schools are encouraged to develop their own preferred approach to inclusion, as well as a form of structural ownership, as there are hopes that these micro-level changes could feed into broader policy change at a higher level in the future.

National minorities

While Bosnia's schools continue to use one of three broad curricular offerings, the Mission aimed to increase the knowledge and participation of the country's "others" by supporting the development of education tools to teach about the country's 17 officially recognized national minorities. In addition to being a curricular requirement (that had simply been ignored in many cases), teaching about the "others" can provide an opportunity to discuss issues of identity, culture, difference and citizenship in an indirect way, while at the same time shedding light on the often forgotten "others" and breaking down perceptions that the country is comprised of just three groups, with little room for more complex identities. This effort combines classroom work, as schools received a first-of-its-kind workbook about BiH's national minorities (developed by a BiH textbook author in coordination with many of BiH's national minority associations), and teachers received accompanying teacher training guides on how to incorporate the materials into their lessons to discuss broader themes of cultural difference, identity and multi-cultural belonging. Schools were subsequently invited to participate in a competition to demonstrate good examples of educational efforts aimed at teaching about the country's national minorities. Well over 100 schools participated in the competition (though it is notable that no schools using the Croatian language curriculum participated). While these supplementary materials will remain at the disposal of teachers and schools throughout the country, beyond broad curricular guidance mandating that students learn about the country's national minorities, there is little incentive to use this tool robustly, as it is not a curricular requirement.

All of these examples – while summarized only briefly – share a number of features in common. First, they are all voluntary – there is no enforcement mechanism, and schools and individuals from schools participate only if they are personally interested. A strength of this approach is that the projects are not imposed, and participants (whether schools or individual students, parents or teachers) can elect whether they would like to participate. Ownership in this context becomes part of the strategy to achieve a wider reform in the educational sector, and is therefore not limited as an end. A weakness of this approach is that the self-selection process results in a situation in which the strongest and most motivated (often pro-reform) schools, officials and civic partners continue to take advantage of such opportunities, while school communities with less motivated (and often anti-reform) actors do not. Any materials developed to supplement school textbooks are exactly that – supplementary materials – meaning both that teachers have the freedom to use and consult them as they like, as well as that there is often a risk that materials not specifically referenced in the curricula will simply sit on a shelf. Schools in the RS continue to limit textbook selection to one book per class per grade; in fact many teachers have noted surprise at the range of other textbooks available, yet not available for use in their classrooms. Textbook choice is limited among schools using the Croatian-language curriculum and the Federation curriculum[22] as well, though there is somewhat more choice. Formal and systematic teacher training is spotty, meaning that while more energetic teachers may welcome the opportunity to use supplementary history or national minority materials in their lessons, it is far more common for teachers to simply stick to the strict outline in the curriculum.

Second, there is also significant room for interpretation by local participants on how they would like to implement certain elements of activities. A number of these efforts include opportunities for interested participants to apply for small grants (according to broad criteria), so they can develop relevant projects according to *their* interests and needs. The example related to the interpretation of "inclusion" noted above is relevant, as are approaches to inclusion more broadly. For some time officials in the RS have declared that allowing non-Serb children to stay home from school on days when religious holidays were celebrated was actually a sign of inclusion and appreciation of diversity; critics saw this as an example of hardening the us/them dichotomies in a school community, and a lost opportunity to teach about different religious traditions.

Third, each of these activities offers something to the participants, whether professional development, travel opportunities or funds. This provides an incentive for participation, without any sense of mandatory participation. Particularly in the absence of such "extras" from the Ministries of Education themselves, many schools and individuals find these opportunities to be personally or professionally attractive. However, long-term changes in the attitudes and particularly in the curricula will only be achieved if these activities will continue once the funds and the support of the OSCE stop. Furthermore, it can be argued that the limited number of schools participating in these projects demonstrates that while change is taking place in the BiH education system, long-term reforms of the curricula and the quality of education will require the meaningful "buy-in" of the elites in the Ministries of Education.

Finally, these engagements seek to fly under the political radar screen, avoiding possible opposition by political parties or officials who are against any efforts to break down exclusive education practices, increase opportunities for integration and inclusion and reduce (to any small extent) the ethnic exclusivity of schools in post-war BiH. They are not "sexy" enough to garnish negative media attention, and while media outlets are often invited to diversity-promoting events, they rarely attend, as good news stories are not seen as key to selling papers. As these activities are not seen as a threat, they are not openly prevented. In other words it can be summarized that engagement in education reform has been confined to the art of the possible.

The first three features noted are all firmly grounded in an ownership approach. There is nothing coercive, and in fact schools that elect to participate have a significant scope to personalize the programs to fit their needs. Observers who are against ANY external engagement could certainly find room to criticize even these "lite" reform efforts. It is fair to note that not all efforts engage local partners in *every* stage of the process. Budgetary or political concerns and priorities from the OSCE and its participating States in Vienna can affect the programmatic agenda enormously; even if an effort has 100% domestic support in a community from the beginning, if there is pressure for cuts, this happens without domestic consultation. This demonstrates the impact of the above-noted difference between functional and structural ownership. Some of the Mission efforts suffer from the same weaknesses as any civil society effort. There have been numerous reviews and assessments of the strengths and weaknesses of external civil society support efforts in BiH, all repeating a chorus of similar recommendations to build on local strengths, let local needs drive donor decisions, and build up systems rather than individuals (Smillie 2001; Pickering 2007; Belloni and Hemmer 2010; Sebastian 2010). Further, the increasing emphasis by the Mission on discrete, short-term projects and short-term quantifiable deliverables limits the scope of development and peacebuilding work.[23] Belloni refers to this "projectism", or "project mania", arguing that due to the nature of short-term projects, international agencies/donors have little potential to build up real and meaningful partnerships from the inception to the evaluation stages. He also points out the emphasis on short-term "results" rather than long-term "strategy" aimed at lasting peacebuilding (Belloni 2007). These are all reasonable observations. Multi-year projects – such as the three-year history reform effort noted above – are the exception rather than the rule.

The OSCE chose ownership as the best possible *modus operandi* for an organization with no executive mandate, few funds and a delicate political balance for an organization with 56 often very different participating States. In the absence of an executive mandate or sufficient incentives to force or strongly encourage coordination and partnership, the Mission is completely reliant on the interest in and support of the host state of BiH, and the permission of BiH officials for any of its activities. The key remaining – and still unanswered – question is whether these apolitical, micro-activities have the desired strategic political impact that led to the establishment of, and continuation of, this Mission over the past 17 years.

Is bottom-up enough?

The OSCE's Mission Statement as of mid-2011 states the following:

> The OSCE Mission to Bosnia and Herzegovina assists BiH in meeting its OSCE commitments and in progressing towards its stated goal of Euro-Atlantic integration by strengthening security and stability through completion of peace-building within the Dayton framework and developing inclusive political discourse and democratically accountable institutions that respect diversity, promote consensus and respect the rule of law. The Mission takes a comprehensive and integrated approach through its field presence, reflecting an emphasis on developing cohesive communities and on the timely identification of obstacles to progress. ("OSCE Mission to Bosnia and Herzegovina Mission Statement")

While quite broad and potentially all-encompassing, the references to peacebuilding, Dayton and "developing cohesive communities" all reflect the specific *post-war* nature of its work, as well as the conflict prevention goals of the OSCE as a whole. The reference to the Mission role to "assist" BiH clearly demonstrates that the relationship is dependent on the will, interest and motivation of BiH officials, at all levels. The Mission can *assist* BiH stakeholders in developing and implementing strategies for education reform; in meeting its human rights obligations; in strengthening the participation of citizens in public life; and in holding elected officials accountable. But assistance is no guarantee of success or progress. Ownership is consequently therefore a key element of the OSCE Mission, since "assistance" refers to a process in which BiH stakeholders remain in charge. This of course will only work properly if the stakeholders are willing to work with the OSCE and consider and accept the Mission's support, input and advice.

It would be quite easy to argue that, after 17 years of "assistance" to an environment in which such assistance may not be genuinely desired, perhaps it is time to stop even collaborative "nudging". As Outi Keranen notes in this volume, there are many in BiH who are *opposed* to the reforms being made by or requested by the international community, and who therefore engage in contentious politics to actively *subvert* the statebuilding enterprise in favor of the status quo. In his writings, Bassuener argues that such opposition makes sense, as the suggested/needed reforms to change the status quo would in fact weaken or disempower the elites who are benefiting quite substantially from the current situation (Bassuener 2009). Joseph's comments on "ownership doctrine" similarly reference the structural impediments to successful ownership, and the unresolved issues that lie at the base of the war, and of the subsequent cold peace (Joseph 2007).

However, it is possible to argue that even activities that seem to fail to gain broader systemic "traction" can play a role in the big, long-term picture of democratic consolidation. The majority of civil society participants in events organized by the Mission do so as volunteers, on their own time, because they believe that the initiatives, meetings and activities may bring some value to them or their community. While unscientific, reflecting on post-event evaluations often distributed after Mission sponsored events, the vast majority of respondents note their interest in *more* such participatory activities, and very often note that such events are needed and would not happen in the absence of external support. If BiH civil society *were* strong enough to effectively and regularly advocate and lobby for political changes, and if the nature of BiH's democracy led elected leaders to take civic input into consideration, then it is likely that there would not be a need for a Mission to BiH, or many of the other international organizations in BiH. Few would argue that the balance of power and influence between the government and civil society is anywhere near equal at this point in time.

This raises two very important points in the discussion of ownership. First, it is important to go back to the beginning of the article, in which the question "whose ownership?" was discussed. This is a fundamental problem in BiH, because political elites have consistently avoided the implementation of suggested reforms to improve the quality of education and overcome the ethnic divides in the education system. Therefore, civil society has become the key actor for the OSCE (and for other international organizations such as the UNDP) in their quest to improve the quality of public service in the country. Second, a more fundamental issue arises out of the unwillingness of local elites to implement ANY kind of reform that would undermine their own power base and access to resources. Consequently, it is important to ask if ownership is at all possible in a divided, post-war society like Bosnia and Herzegovina. If international organizations want to be involved in state-building in these countries, it might be better to use excessive intervention for a limited amount of time to establish proper structures such as the rule of law and a functional administration, instead of focusing on incremental and weaker attempts at democratization and local ownership in a reform-hostile environment.[24]

In the current environment it is safe to say that the Mission will continue to exist for some more years, though demands for downsizing have already begun, and pressures to cut staff and programmatic spending may increasingly constrain the scope of activities. Against this backdrop, the most recent Head of Mission (an American diplomat, as is the tradition in BiH), who arrived in early autumn 2011, will have the opportunity to significantly shape the programmatic work and political vision of the institution – an opportunity that in light of the current stagnation in political reform, should not be taken lightly. Will the Mission continue its grassroots approach? Will there be pressure to increasingly do "achievable" projects, to avoid projects that have a slimmer chance of immediate, visible success? The following factors offer some initial food for thought when reflecting on a Mission moving through its teenage years, and rapidly approaching legal adulthood.

More direct political engagement

While the OSCE Mission stays informed of political dynamics, beyond the broader OSCE political commitments BiH has signed on to as a participating State, the Mission has few tools at its disposal to press for reforms that politicians might not be inclined to support. Public statements, encouragement and occasionally letters reminding officials of their obligations are the primary tools available for a Mission with limited carrots and sticks.[25] However, the Mission is potentially in an excellent position to not only seek to persuade officials and citizens of BiH's human rights and OSCE commitments, but to ensure that decision-makers in the EU, Council of Europe, NATO and key bilateral embassies have the "from the field" information that can demonstrate whether reforms are *de facto* or *de jure*, and whether they are more tangible than ink on paper and promises made.

An increasing number of shadow reports on pressing human rights concerns and issues addressed in annual EU Progress Reports, would help to ensure an additional point of view and analysis from an actor that has the tentacles in communities that the other organizations lack. More statements (preferably in conjunction with the Council of Europe, or others) calling BiH leaders to account for their actions and words (as noted in the above-noted Robbins comment) should help to provide a *counter-discourse* to the elite-driven narratives – another voice capable of showing citizens what they already know, but do not think the international community appreciates: your leaders are not telling the truth. Further, consistently and publically demonstrating support for civic voices for reform, and specifically and directly challenging officials to rise to the occasion to *respond* to citizen initiatives, can demonstrate to civil society that the international community does not view "ownership" as simply the purview of the elites, but as something to be undertaken by everyone. None of these suggestions would require executive powers or money; just a willingness to support the voices of reform that do exist, but are consistently marginalized.

Long-term goals vs. short-term fixes

Even more importantly, the OSCE should not shy away from necessary work just because there is a risk of failure. The Mission should be a political organization that uses programs to achieve its political goals; not a project-driven organization that seeks to implement projects as a traditional donor or development organization. In the absence of some unforeseen paradigm shift that would suddenly move the country's dominant political discourse away from the us-vs.-them politics of post-Dayton BiH, the country's democratic consolidation – let alone reconciliation – will take some time. While the OSCE is bound by annual 12-month budgeting and planning cycles, there must be a greater recognition that multi-year projects are needed to really seek sustainable change and long-term impact. This can be done both through more creative approaches to the annual budget, but also through lobbying participating States in Vienna to recognize that the investments made to date could be at risk if not buttressed by long-term thinking in a time of political paralysis. Current short-term project thinking makes it difficult for reform to take lasting root. Projects are not needed in the "easy to work in" areas; they are needed in the most difficult parts of the country.

There have been some moves by the Mission to focus municipal work in the more difficult and intransigent municipalities rather than the ones that are already rather reform minded; this should continue. However, less technical and tangible initiatives related to hearts and minds efforts – minority returnee integration, the substance of education including wide-scale curricular reform, and aggressive protection and promotion of human rights – require similar sustained attention in spite of the often non-quantifiable nature of project results. (One simply cannot determine whether children in a divided community distrust each other 15% less after a three-month engagement). Projects developed according to multi-year timeframes can better meet the needs of communities as well as the growing Organizational interest in impact assessment. Mission staff should to be able to develop such long-term efforts, and OSCE participating States should recognize that progress in such multi-year endeavors may not always be linear.

Commitment to OSCE standards

An effective EU-OSCE relationship is of course needed for either organization to be effective in any region of interest (Ghebali 2005; Caruso 2007; Stewart 2008). The 2003 Draft Conclusions on EU-OSCE Cooperation in Conflict Prevention, crisis management and post-conflict rehabilitation" outlines five areas of "enhanced cooperation", including fact-finding and coordination (Stewart 2006, 179–80). However, such agreements and working modalities will be incomplete until a more comprehensive EU foreign policy and strategy is increasingly harmonized and consolidated; not to mention a policy for BiH that goes beyond the seeming goal of "membership at all costs". As Soeren Keil has stated in the Introduction to this Special Issue, there is a general lack of a long-term EU strategy for the Integration of BiH as well as an unclear vision of "what Bosnia should look like" when it joins the EU. Further, the complementary yet different interests can still lead to challenges in overlap or competition (Kemp 2010). Stewart writes that, "the OSCE's ethos, interests, and practices result in a particular approach to conflict prevention. In some cases, this may be a rather different approach from the EU, an organization with wider interests and resources" (2006, 181). The Corfu Process launched in 2009 is moving forward, yet exposes the different visions among OSCE participating States regarding a European security architecture, namely concerns from Russian and several other post-Soviet states regarding OSCE human rights and democratization initiatives – and incursions – in their space (Zagorski 2011). Hoppman urges a return to the basics of comprehensive security – including an emphasis on human rights and governance – so that the OSCE can remain rooted to its "normative core" (Hoppman 2008, 79–80). It cannot be denied that in light of the country's – and the region's – eventual EU future, Brussels has a lock on top-down persuasions, incentives or standards. However, in theory more substantive coordination between the OSCE and the EU should help both organizations. More systematic, realistic and honest cooperation between the EU and the OSCE in BiH, including an open environment in which the OSCE is willing to disagree with EU assessments, clearly note the facts on the ground and suggest alternative measurements of and requirements for reform, should be the basis for a future relationship. Such an approach should help to ensure not simply future BiH membership in the EU, but the entry of an irreversibly stable and democratic country into the EU. If organizational agendas happen to diverge, this should not stop the OSCE from its commitment to long-term comprehensive security through a framework of human rights. In the case examined in this short review – education – this means a continued commitment to an inclusive education system that prepares future citizens for a shared and peaceful future rather than future social cleavages; perhaps the ultimate test of comprehensive security.

Is there an end in sight to BiH's post-Dayton peace process? At this stage, there is reason for concern that BiH could continue in its limbo of frozen conflict – neither in violent conflict nor a normal, functioning state. Future Euro-Atlantic integration *should* remain the long-term goal – not just for BiH but the region. For years the need for constitutional reform – either simply minimal compliance with a key European Court of Human Rights decision (*Case of Sejdic and Finci* 2009), or more maximalist reform to make the country somehow functional – has been increasingly acknowledged, though its possible realization seems farther away than ever (European Commission for Democracy 2004; Foreign Policy Initiative BiH 2007; Hodzic and Stojanovic 2011). However, failed attempts at such reforms can have devastating real and psychological effects. Elite agreements that fail to meet the real needs and interests of citizens "may spread disillusionment, dissatisfaction, fear and insecurity among ordinary people, which ultimately may undermine peace constituencies" (Aggestam and Bjorkdahl 2011, 4). In terms of constitutional reforms, while there are efforts among civil society to promote a broader citizen engagement in such discussions, there are strong domestic and international incentives to limit such political engagement to the elites. Similarly, considering the benefits of the current system to ruling elites, one must consider whether sufficient domestic or international incentives exist to encourage domestic ownership of reform processes; if it is rational for local elites to oppose or delay reform, without fear of significant domestic backlash or withdrawal of external support (e.g. money), then it is irrational to expect domestic political and reform priorities to change. Until the political environment and calculus in BiH changes, it is likely that the micro-level efforts being implemented throughout BiH by organizations like the OSCE will continue to make small improvements in the lives of ordinary citizens, in spite of, rather than because of, official support for progress, with functional ownership taking practical primacy over structural ownership, and targeted reform "tweaking" more prevalent than any systemic overhaul. Whether that is viewed as the naïve idealism of liberal neo-Wilsonian actors, a sort of palliative hospice care for a dying patient or a constructive long-term effort to plant seeds for future change, may largely depend on one's worldview, and will ultimately only be known with the benefit of hindsight.

Notes

1. Following the common use in the academic literature, Bosnia and Herzegovina will be shortened to "Bosnia" or "BiH". This refers to the whole territory of Bosnia and Herzegovina.
2. Secretary-General Biscevic of the Regional Cooperation Council (RCC) noted that he feared the situation in BiH was at risk of becoming a "dormant frozen conflict". The authors of this paper share the assessment that BiH can be considered as a "frozen conflict" because the major roots of the war in the first half of the 1990s have not been addressed by the Dayton Peace Agreement or the state-building project that followed. However, the frozen conflict in BiH should be distinguished from other "frozen conflicts" such as Transdnistria or Northern Cyprus, since BiH is

de facto and *de jure* one country (albeit ethnically divided) and has joint governmental institutions, which represent the country as a whole and include politicians from the three major ethnic groups, Bosniaks, Croats and Serbs.

3. In 2010 NATO granted BiH a Membership Action Plan (MAP) to assist the country in meeting terms for NATO membership.
4. The gradual expansion of Mission activities mirrors trends in development and democratization more generally. Thomas Carothers (1999) traces the development of US development assistance from the 1960s, pointing out how it in many ways mirrors the evolution in thinking about democratization strategies in the 1980s and 1990s.
5. For example, if a country wishes to be in the Council of Europe, or NATO, it must meet certain terms and conditions that may not be palatable, but are worth the cost in the bigger picture.
6. On a wider discussion of different forms of ownership and their advantages and disadvantages (see Scheye and Peake 2005).
7. Petritsch, however, combined the opposing elements of heavy international intervention in the political processes with a discussion about more autonomy, independence and responsibility of local Bosnian elites (Solioz 2003).
8. In 2006, "Regulations on Consultations in Legislative Drafting" were adopted by the Council of Ministers, and an analysis of the implementation of these regulations concluded that while this opens some doors to civil society, both government officials and NGOs are poorly informed about how to use this process (Bosna i Hercegovina, Ministarstvo Pravde 2010). There is a civic effort to increase opportunities for direct democracy being led by the organization "Dosta".
9. In a sign of the changes that have occurred over the past decade, education as an issue is now quite common in OSCE programs, and openly noted on the Organization's web site along other priority areas, See OSCE official website (OSCE 2011).
10. See also a related Communiqué by the PIC Steering Board ("Communiqué" 2002).
11. For a wider discussion on obstruction by local elites in Bosnia (see Cousens 2002).
12. Following the PIC a working group comprised of the Council of Europe, EU and OSCE MBiH has been formed to consult and coordinate on an upcoming EU project related to school reconstruction. There is the potential for criteria to be established to ensure that EU funds go to schools exhibiting good practice in inclusion and integration.
13. The Annual EU Progress Report on BiH includes references to education, within the framework of economic and social rights and internal markets (education and research). However, the reviews are brief, and often do not reflect the reality on the ground. For example, the 2010 Progress Report said that the number of "two schools under one roof" had decreased, suggesting progress. In fact there has been no change since 2005. Further there are few hard requirements in the *acquis* related to the structure or content of educational structures, making less opportunity for simple reference to technical criteria or firm standards (Bosnia and Herzegovina 2010). The 2011 Progress Report of the EU also confirms this picture. It states that "Little Progress can be reported in the field of Education...Ethnic-based separation in public schools remains an issue of serious concern" (Bosnia and Herzegovina 2011).
14. The Mission also supports reform in education institutions and legislation, including work with school boards, education inspectors, school directors and bodies such as the Education Agency.
15. Peer to peer education and the training of trainers methodology is viewed as having a potential multiplier effect in an environment in which schools leaders regularly (often yearly) leave the school upon graduation, leaving potential capacity vacuums. One OSCE MBiH peer education effort focusing on strengthening student councils resulted in over 500 individual training workshops being held by student council peer trainers.
16. A second report looking at the scope of use of the new textbooks is forthcoming by the same author.
17. The 2010 Bosnia and Herzegovina 2010 EC Progress Report references the introduction of "a common, nine-year core curriculum" being introduced (p. 18). However, this is a bit misleading. The "common core curriculum" was developed through a process of pulling together all of the information being taught in the various curricula, and determining what they shared in common. It therefore does *not* include the bulk of the national subjects; nor did it constitute any newly developed and shared content. While commonality among the non-national subjects was aimed at enhancing potential mobility of students in schools across the country, leaving out the controversial identity subjects in effect continued to limit any potential mobility.

18. See for example the regional history reform initiative sponsored by the Center for Democracy and Reconciliation in Southeast Europe, at http://www.cdsee.org.
19. While history textbooks are still far from perfect, the extent to which they have improved due to the decade-plus modernization effort is visible when one looks at the quality, content and methodology of other classroom subjects.
20. The extent to which religious communities have influence in public education was visible in the spring of 2011 when the newly installed Minister of Education in Sarajevo Canton sought changes to the religious instruction offered in schools – namely making them pass/fail and optional. The outcry by the Islamic Community was significant, and in fact the reform initiative put on hold ("Bosnian Muslim Leader Criticized" 2011).
21. This approach was developed by the Center for Studies on Inclusive Education (http://www.csie.org.uk) The Index was used in the United Kingdom, and has been translated into more than 25 languages.
22. The Federation curriculum was developed by a Federation working group with the intent that the curriculum would be applied to all schools in the entity. However, only Bosniak areas/schools are implementing this, while Croat schools use their own Croatian language curriculum.
23. The OSCE annual budget process is increasingly shaped by a logframe oriented "Performance Budget Program Review" process that has a strong bias towards the short-term, the quantifiable and the apolitical; needed difficult, political, long-term work can be difficult to place within such an approach.
24. This issue points to a wider discussion of state-building vs. democratization, which has been discussed by Linz and Stepan (1996) as well as by Ghani and Lockhart (2009) and by Francis Fukuyama (2005), who all argue that "stateness" has to come before any form of democratization can be successful.
25. For example, the former Head of Mission Gary Robbins in August noted his concern about a comment by RS President Dodik that BiH is not a state, but a "state union" (echoing the words of the former relationship between Serbia and Montenegro before Montenegro held a referendum and declared independence), referencing BiH's Constitution and the Constitutional Court ("'State union' concept of Bosnia and Herzegovina has no legal basis, says Head of OSCE Mission". OSCE Mission to Bosnia and Herzegovina web site. Accessed August 11, 2011. http://www.osce.org/bih/81626).

References

Aggestam, Karin, and Annika Bjorkdahl. 2011. "Just Peace Postponed: Unending Peace Processes and Frozen Conflicts." JAD-PbP Working Paper, Lund University, January 10. Accessed September 24, 2011. http://www.lu.se/upload/LUPDF/Samhallsvetenskap/Just_and_Durable_Peace/WP_10_A4_complete_for_the_web.pdf

Bassuener, Kurt. 2009. "How to Pull Out of Bosnia–Herzegovina's Dead End: A Strategy for Success." Democratization Policy Council Briefing Paper, Sarajevo and Berlin, February 19.

Bassuener, Kurt, and Bodo Weber. 2010. "Are We There Yet? International Impatience vs. A Long-term Strategy for a Viable Bosnia." Democratization Policy Council Briefing Paper, Sarajevo and Berlin, May 31.

Belloni, Roberto. 2001. "Civil Society and Peacebuilding in Bosnia." *Journal of Peace Research* 38 (2): 163–180.

Belloni, Roberto. 2007. "Rethinking Nation-Building: The Contradictions of the Wilsonian Approach at Democracy Promotion." *Whitehead Journal of Diplomacy and International Relations* 7 (Winter/Spring): 97–109.

Belloni, R., and B. Hemmer. 2010. "Bosnia–Herzegovina: Civil Society in a Semi-Protectorate." In *Civil Society and Peacebuilding: A Critical Assessment*, edited by Thania Paffenholz, 129–152. Boulder: Lynne Rienner.

Biscevic, Hido. 2010. "Bosnia Stalemate Turning into 'Frozen Conflict'". EurActiv.com. March 2010. Accessed September 24, 2011. http://www.euractiv.com/enlargement/bosnia-stalemate-turning-frozen-conflict-news-343803

Bosna i Hercegovina, Ministarstvo Pravde. 2010. *Report on the Implementation of Regulations on Consultations in Legislative Drafting in the Institutions of Bosnia and Herzegovina.* Accessed July 5, 2011. http://www.mpr.gov.ba/ministarstvo/dokumenti/08.4%20Izvjestaj%20o%20radu%20MP%20BiH%20za%202011.pdf

Bosnia and Herzegovina 2010 Progress Report. European Commission Staff Working Document. Brussels: European Commission. Accessed November 9, 2010. http://ec.europa.eu/enlargement/pdf/key_documents/2010/package/ba_rapport_2010_en.pdf

Bosnia and Herzegovina 2011 Progress Report. European Commission. Staff Working Document. Brussels: European Commission. Accessed October 12, 2011. http://ec.europa.eu/enlargement/pdf/key_documents/2011/package/ba_rapport_2011_en.pdf

"Bosnian Muslim Leader Criticized Over Call for Protests." 2011. *Balkan Insight*, May 17. Accessed July 12, 2011. http://www.balkaninsight.com/en/article/the-head-of-bosnia-s-islamic-community-accused-of-hate-speech

Carothers, Thomas. 1999. *Aiding Democracy Abroad: The Learning Curve*. Washington, DC: Carnegie Endowment for International Peace.

Caruso, Ugo. 2007. *Interplay Between the Council of Europe, OSCE, EU and NATO, European Academy*, Bolzano: EURAC. Accessed June 3, 2011. http://www.eurac.edu/en/research/institutes/imr/Documents/ReportoninterplayWEB.pdf

Case of Sejdic and Finci v. Bosnia and Herzegovina. 2009. European Court of Human Rights, Judgment, December 22.

Chesterman, Simon. 2004. *You, The People: The United Nations, Transitional Administration and State-Building*. Oxford: Oxford University Press.

Chesterman, Simon. 2009. "Ownership in Theory and Practice: Transfer of Authority in UN Statebuilding Operations." In *Statebuilding and Intervention. Policies, Practices and Paradigms*, edited by David Chandler, 17–41. London: Routledge.

Chivvis, Christopher. 2010. "Back to the Brink in Bosnia?" *Survival: Global Politics and Strategy* 52 (1): 97–110.

"Communiqué by the PIC Steering Board." November 21, 2002. Accessed July 15, 2011. http://www.ohr.int/pic/archive.asp?sa=on

Cousens, Elizabeth. 2002. "From Missed Opportunities to Overcompensation: Implementing the Dayton Agreement on Bosnia." In *Ending Civil Wars (The Implementation of Peace Agreement)*, edited by Stephen Stedman, Donald Rothchild and Elizabeth Cousens, 531–566. London: Lynne Rienner Publishers.

Donais, Tim. 2009. "Inclusion or Exclusion? Local Ownership and Security Sector Reform." *Studies in Social Justice* 3 (1): 117–131.

European Commission for Democracy Through Law (Venice Commission). 2004. *Opinion on the Constitutional Situation in Bosnia and Herzegovina and the Powers of the High Representative*, CDL-AD (2005) 004 2, March 11, 2004.

"Follow-up Report on BiH Media and Media Regulators Under Pressure." 2010. *OSCE Mission to Bosnia and Herzegovina Report*. Accessed September 23. http://www.oscebih.org/documents/osce_bih_doc_2010092417401856eng.pdf

Foreign Policy Initiative BiH. 2007. *Governance Structures in BiH: Capacity, Ownership, EU Integration, Functioning State*. Sarajevo: Foreign Policy Initiative.

Fukuyama, Francis. 2005. "Stateness First." *Journal of Democracy* 16 (1): 84–88.

Ghani, Ashraf, and Clare Lockhart. 2009. *Fixing Failed States*. Oxford: OUP.

Ghebali, Yves. 2005. "The OSCE and European Security: Essential or Superfluous?" *St. Anne's College Europaeum Lecture*, February 18, 2005. Accessed August 30, 2011. http://www.europaeum.org/europaeum/?q=node/514

Hellmuller, Sara. 2011. "Bridging the Disconnect: Integrating Local Perspectives in Peace Processes." Paper presented at the Fourth European Conference on African Studies. Accessed July 10, 2011. http://www.nai.uu.se/ecas-4/panels/1-20/panel-20/Sara-Hellmuller-Full-paper.pdf

Hodzic, Edin, and Nenad Stojanovic. 2011. *New/Old Constitutional Engineering: Challenges and Implications of the European Court of Human Rights Decision in the Case of Sejdic & Finci v. BiH*. Sarajevo: Analitika.

Hopmann, P. Terrence. 2008. "The Future Impact of the OSCE: Business as Usual or Revitalization?" *CORE Yearbook*, 75–90. http://www.core-hamburg.de/documents/yearbook/english/08/Hopmann-en.pdf

"Implementation of Regulations on Consultation in Legislative Drafting – Actual Progress or a Dead Letter?" 2009. ACIPS Policy Brief, Sarajevo: ACIPS, May.

Joseph, Ed. 2007. "Ownership is Over-rated." *SAIS Review* 27 (2): 109–123.

Karge, Heike. 2008. *20th Century History in the Textbooks of Bosnia and Herzegovina: An Analysis of Books used for the Final Grades of Primary School*. Braunschweig, Germany: Georg Eckert Institute for International Textbook Research.

Kemp, Walter. 2010. "Issue Brief: Reaching the OSCE Summit in Astana." International Peace Institute, October. Accessed August 30, 2011. http://www.ipinst.org/index.php/publication/policy-papers/detail/300-issue-brief-reaching-the-osce-summit-in-astana.html

Knaus, Gerald, and Felix Martin. 2003. "Travails of the European Raj." *Journal of Democracy* 14 (3): 60–74.

Linz, Juan J., and Alfred Stepan. 1996. *Problems of Democratic Transition and Consolidation. Southern Europe, Southern America and Post- Communist Europe*. Baltimore: The John Hopkins University Press.

Manners, Ian. 2002. "Normative Power Europe: A Contradiction in Terms?" *Journal of Common Market Studies* 40 (2): 235–258.

Manning, Carrie, and Miljenko Antic. 2003. "The Limits of Electoral Engineering." *Journal of Democracy* 14 (3): 45–59.

McMahon, Patrice C., and Jon Western. 2009. "The Death of Dayton: How to Stop Bosnia from Falling Apart." *Foreign Affairs* 88 (5): 69–83.

Mujkic, Asim. 2008. *We, The Citizens of Ethnopolis*. Sarajevo: University of Sarajevo Human Rights Center.

OSCE. 2002. "Mission to Bosnia and Herzegovina." Briefing to the OSCE Permanent Council, November; from OSCE MBiH memo, January 18, 2005.

OSCE. 2011. "Official Web Site." Accessed July 10. http://www.osce.org/what/education

"OSCE Mission to Bosnia and Herzegovina Mission Statement," Mission web site. Accessed September 24, 2011. http://www.oscebih.org/Default.aspx?id=156&lang=EN

Paris, Roland. 2004. *At War's End: Building Peace after Civil Conflict*. Cambridge: Cambridge University Press.

Paris, Roland, and Timothy Sisk, eds. 2009. *Dilemmas of Statebuilding: Confronting the Contradictions of Postwar Peace Operations*. London: Routledge.

Pejanovic, Mirko. 2002. *Through Bosnian Eyes: The Political Memoirs of A Bosnian Serb*. Sarajevo: Sahinpasic.

Perrin de Brichambaut, Marc. 2006. "How things turned nasty for the nice guys of the OSCE." *Europe's World*. Accessed July 12, 2011. http://www.europesworld.org/NewEnglish/Home_old/Article/tabid/191/ArticleType/articleview/ArticleID/20725/language/en US/Default.aspx

Perry, Valery. 2003. "Reading, Writing and Reconciliation." *ECMI Working Paper #18*, Flensburg, Germany: ECMI. http://www.ecmi.de/uploads/tx_lfpubdb/working_paper_18.pdf

Perry, Valery. 2005. "A Decade of the Dayton Agreement and the OSCE Mission to Bosnia and Herzegovina: Reflections and Prospects." *Helsinki Monitor* 16 (4): 298–309.

Perry, Valery. 2006. "Democratic Ends, (un)Democratic Means? Reflections on Democratization Strategies in Brcko and Bosnia–Herzegovina." In *Bosnian Security After Dayton: New Perspectives*, edited by Michael Innes, 51–70. London: Routledge.

Perry, Valery. 2010. "Fifteen Years of the Human Dimension in Bosnia and Herzegovina – The Ebb and Flow of Statebuilding." *Security and Human Rights* 21 (4): 279–291.

Perry, Valery. forthcoming. "Classroom Battlegrounds for Hearts and Minds: Efforts to Reform and Transform Education in post-war Bosnia and Herzegovina." In *Civic And Uncivic Values In Bosnia-Herzegovina: The Record Since Dayton*, edited by Ola Listhaug and Sabrina P. Ramet, 225–246. Oxford: OUP.

Pickering, Paula M. 2007. *Peacebuilding in the Balkans: The View from the Ground Floor*. Ithaca: Cornell University Press.

Rees, Edward. 2005. "Public Security Management and Peace Operations. Kosovo and UNMIK: Never Land." In *After Intervention. Public Security in Post-conflict Societies: From Intervention to Sustainable Local Ownership*, edited by Anja Ebnöter and Philip Fluri, 199–232. Vienna: Bureau for Security Policy at the Austrian Ministry of Defense; National Defense Academy.

Reich, Hannah. 2006. "'Local Ownership' in Conflict Transformation Projects: Partnership, participation or Patronage?" Berghof Occasional Paper No. 27. http://reliefweb.int/sites/reliefweb.int/files/resources/CDDB393F195EC54EC125727A005937C3-Berghof-peace%20building-Sep2006.pdf

Scheye, Eric, and Gordon Peake. 2005. "Unknotting Local Ownership." In *After Intervention. Public Security in Post-conflict Societies: From Intervention to Sustainable Local Ownership*, edited by Anja Ebnöter and Philip Fluri, 235–260. Vienna: Bureau for Security Policy at the Austrian Ministry of Defense; National Defense Academy.

Sebastian, Sofia. 2010. "Assessing Democracy Assistance: Bosnia." FRIDE Project Report, May. Accessed July 12, 2011. www.fride.org/publication/775/bosnia

Smillie, Ian. 2001. "Reconstructing Bosnia, Constructing Civil Society: Disjuncture and Dilemma." *Patronage or Partnership: Local Capacity Building in Humanitarian Crises*. Bloomfield, CT: Kumarian Press/IDRC. Accessed May 8, 2011. http://books.google.at/books?id=JYqK7tD8eVcC&pg=PA25&dq=Smillie,+Ian+Reconstructing+Bosnia&hl=de&sa=X&ei=SHX9T9vVMMuk4AS0gOWUBw&redir_esc=y#v=onepage&q=Smillie%2C%20Ian%20Reconstructing%20Bosnia&f=false

Solioz, Christophe. 2003. "Quest for Sovereignty: Bosnia and Herzegovina's Challenge." *Helsinki Monitor* 14 (2): 148–160.

Stewart, Emma J. 2006. *The European Union and Conflict Prevention: Policy Evolution and Outcome*. Berlin: Lit Verlag.

Stewart, Emma J. 2008. "Restoring EU-OSCE Cooperation for Pan-European Conflict Prevention." *Contemporary Security Policy* 29 (2): 266–284.

Zagorski, Andrei. 2011. "European Security Architecture and Challenges: When Are We in 2011 As Compared to 2008? A Food for Thought Paper." European Studies Institute at MGIMO University, April. Accessed August 29, 2011. http://www.sfpa.sk/dokumenty/pozvanky/625

Zakaria, Fareed. 2003. *The Future of Freedom: Liberal Democracy at Home and Abroad*. New York: W.W. Nortan & Company.

"Quadratic nexus" and the process of democratization and state-building in Albania and Kosovo: a comparison

Gëzim Krasniqi

School of Social and Political Science, University of Edinburgh, Edinburgh, UK

This paper examines the interplay between internal and external actors in the process of democratization and state-building in Albania and Kosovo. It does so by using David J. Smith's "quadratic nexus" that links Brubaker's "triadic nexus" – nationalizing states, national minorities and external national homelands – to the institutions of an ascendant and expansive "Euro-Atlantic space". The main argument of this paper is twofold. First, it argues the nexus remains a useful framework in the study of state- and nation-building provided that it moves beyond the "civic vs. ethnic" dichotomy. Today, many states with a mixture of civic and multi-ethnic elements involve this relational nexus. Second, while comparing Albania and Kosovo, this paper argues that all the four elements of the nexus have a different impact on the process of state- and nation-building and their relationship is more conflictual in Kosovo than in Albania.

Introduction

The fall of the Berlin Wall in 1989 triggered a wave of massive political and social transformations in Eastern Europe resulting in new social and political dynamics. On the one side there was the battle for democratization and liberalization of the market, on the other the battle for enhanced rights of nations and minorities. In the latter case, both nations and national minorities saw an opportunity to improve their position within the state – the former seeking to institutionalize their domination, whereas the latter was seeking enhanced cultural rights or even autonomy. Apart from the two main actors – core nation and national minority – in the process of transformation of polities in Europe, however, external kin states as well as other external actors (be it in the form of international organizations or individual states) became heavily involved. Thus, the process of democratization and state-building in Southeast Europe involved a quadratic relationship.

This paper examines the interplay between internal and external actors in the process of democratization and state-building in Albania and Kosovo. It does so by using David J. Smith's "quadratic nexus" that links Brubaker's "triadic nexus" – nationalizing states, national minorities and external national homelands – to the institutions of an ascendant and expansive "Euro-Atlantic space". The main argument of this paper is twofold. First, it argues the nexus remains a useful framework in the study of state- and nation-building provided that it moves beyond the "civic vs. ethnic" dichotomy. Today, many states with a mixture of civic and multi-ethnic elements involve this relational nexus. Second, while comparing Albania and Kosovo, this paper argues that all the four elements of the nexus have a different impact on the process of state- and nation-building and their relationship is more conflictual in Kosovo than in Albania.

In terms of the time-frame, in the case of Albania the paper focuses on the developments since the fall of communism until the present, whereas in Kosovo it begins with the UN administration in Kosovo established in 1999, although emphasis will be put on the period after the declaration of independence in 2008.

"Quadratic nexus": depicting actors and dynamics

More than a dozen new countries appeared in the map of Europe since 1989 and in many of them various groups have been in a constant struggle for either domination or recognition of their status as a national minority. This has indulged external direct or indirect involvement of states and international organizations in those areas. An important theoretical framework used in the context of post-communist transformation and reconstruction of states in Southeast Europe (SEE) is that of the "triadic nexus" developed by Rogers Brubaker (1996, 4). Although it focuses primarily on nationalism, it depicts the process of delineating the legal framework, institutions, internal organization and institutional arrangements, legal and constitutional order, and the nature of citizenship. Brubaker's point of departure is the emergence of nationalism in the process of state-building as a progressive nationalization of the political space, which according to him, can be depicted by using a single relational nexus ("triadic nexus") that binds together three different nationalisms, which are interlocking, interactive and mutually antagonist – "nationalizing" nationalism, "homeland" nationalism and "minority" nationalism (1996, 4).

Drawing on Brubaker's theory, David J. Smith has proposed a "quadratic nexus" as a framework of analysis in the study of state-building and reconstruction, thus linking nationalizing states, national minorities and external national homelands to the institutions of an increasing web of international institutions and organizations. Certainly, the adding of the role of external actors complements Brubaker's triadic nexus for it acknowledges the increasing role of international organizations in the power struggles between minorities, kin-states and nationalizing states. In one way or another, the "quadratic nexus" is applicable in almost every case of state-building and state transformation in the Western Balkans. Due to the fact that state-building and reconstruction in post-1989 Europe was characterized by the nationalization of the political space and attempts to redefine political and national identities, which in many cases led to the eruption of conflict, the quadratic nexus offers a useful framework in the study of the tension between various actors, understood not as static concepts but as arenas of struggle for competing stances, as well as understandings of statehood and nationhood. To begin with, the Balkan region is a *par excellence* case of "mismatched" groups of people who are attached by citizenship to one polity yet by ethnic affinity to another (Brubaker 1996, 7). This creates a highly complex mosaic of national and international political actors that have a say in or influence processes of state-building.

As regards the use of this framework for the purposes of this analysis, two things need to be pointed out. First, as Brubaker makes clear, national minority, nationalizing state, and external national homeland are not fixed, static, and analytically irreducible entities but rather dynamic fields of differentiated and competing positions. Thus, as argued by Brubaker, "the triadic relation between these three 'elements' is, therefore, a *relation between relational fields;* and relations *between* the three fields are closely intertwined with relations *internal to,* and *constitutive of,* the fields" (1996, 67). Second, I subscribe to Taras Kuzio's (2001) and David J. Smith's (2002) critique of Brubaker's sharp distinction of the "nationalizing state" model from what he terms the civic state ("civic vs. ethnic" divide). In this context, as proposed by Kuzio (2001, 135), I use the concept of "nationalizing state" not as a unique experience of Eastern Europe, but rather in the context of a broader process of state and nation building that takes place in polities with a mixture of civic and multi-ethnic elements.

Comparing Albania and Kosovo

Despite differences (the recent history, political tradition, international status etc) Kosovo and Albania have many similarities. Both countries have a majority Albanian population and a minority population that does not exceed 10% of the overall population (although in Albania the percentage is even smaller). In addition, both countries have a core minority group (Greeks and Serbs respectively) that has a more prominent position within the state. Although at different stages, both countries are in a process of transition to democratic consolidation, with external actors such as the EU playing a major role in the process.

But do Albania and Kosovo represent "nationalizing states" in Brubaker's understanding of the concept? The answer is a mixed one. On the one side, both Albania and Kosovo are countries with strong ethnic majorities and many of their policies can be labeled "nationalizing". However, both countries' constitutions contain civic and multi-ethnic elements respectively and provide for inclusive citizenship, which are atypical for a classical nationalizing state. Another important element in this regard is perception. As argued by Brubaker, such a state is not one "whose representatives, authors, or agents understand and articulate it as such, but rather one that is perceived as such in the field of the national minority or the external national homeland" (1996, 63). Based on this criterion, both countries can be analyzed using the quadratic framework and the concept of nationalizing state.

In what follows, I look at these arenas of struggle and competing stances of minorities and majority first in Albania than in Kosovo.

The case of Albania

In early 1990s, even though it looked like Albania was going to remain outside the dramatic changes of 1989, history would catch up with it very soon, when in 1991 Albania's orthodox Communist system collapsed like a house of cards, leaving behind an economic disaster and a political vacuum of very high proportions (Gasteyger 2006, 213). This combined with subsequent political crises that culminated in an armed rebellion against the Berisha government in spring 1997, following the fall of the "pyramid system" – a fraudulent investment scheme. As a result, Albania's integration into the European political structures has been slow; it joined the OSCE in 1991, the CeO in 1995 and signed the Stabilization and Association Agreement with the EU in June 2006, while becoming a member of NATO in April 2008, and submitted its application for EU membership on 28 April 2009 (Krasniqi 2010c, 15).

As regards minorities in Albania, Greeks, Macedonians and Montenegrins are officially recognized as national minorities, whereas Roma and Vlachs/Aromanians are recognized as linguistic (sometimes called cultural) minorities (AHRG 2003). Both linguistic and national minorities are recognized under the Framework Convention for the Protection of National Minorities (FCNM), which entered into force in Albania in 2000 (Krasniqi 2010c, 16). Based on official statistics (CoE 2007), Albania is one of the most homogenous countries in the region (with an Albanian majority of some 98%), but minority groups often question the official state data. Results of the overall census organized in October 2011, which for the first time enabled everyone to declare (if they wished to do so) their religion and ethnicity, might provide more accurate data.

Although in smaller numbers, Albania's minority population has been historically subject to the state's nationalizing policies. Nonetheless, "[b]ecause most of the minorities were relatively small, and were no worse off and in some cases better off than most of Albanians, inter-ethnic relations did not become a source of violent conflict in Albania" (Miall 1999, 142). As regards legal status in the post-communist era, the 1991 provisional constitution, amended in 1992 and 1993 (when the Charter on Fundamental Human Rights and Freedoms was added) contained guarantees of the freedoms of speech, religion, conscience, press, and assembly (Biberaj 1999, 151). Although minorities welcomed these measures, constitutional changes did not go so far as to satisfy their demands. Moreover, in February 1992, the Albanian government took a controversial decision to ban ethnic or religious parties from standing in future elections (Bugajski 2002, 274). After protests by the CSCE, the CoE, the US, Greece and other actors, this decision was reversed (Pettifer 2001, 11). Nevertheless, since 1991, minority parties have continuously participated in elections and were part of the local and national institutions of Albania, thus making a substantial contribution to the process of democratization in their home country.

One of the most contentious issues has been minority education. As with other issues, the Greek minority has been the most persistent and demanding in this direction. After some initial reluctance, the Albanian government has granted permission and supported the opening of Greek primary and secondary language schools outside of the official "Greek minority zone"[1] such as Himara and Korça. Moreover, new departments of Greek studies have opened in the Universities of Tirana and Gjirokastra and the Albanian government has also agreed to cooperate in the building of a Greek language university in Gjirokastra funded by the Greek government (Vickers 2010, 8). More minority schools opened in the Prespa region, where a small Macedonian minority lives, as well as a Serbian school in south Albania.

Albania's first post-communist constitution was adopted only on 21 October 1998 (*Constitution of the Republic of Albania*, 22 November 1998) and it reflects the country's attempts to democratize and achieve EU membership. Its preamble and the integral text have strong civic underpinnings – they refer to the "people of Albania" rather than to an Albanian ethnic core. Article 20 of this constitution stipulates that persons belonging to national minorities exercise their ethnic, cultural, religious and linguistic rights, including the right to study and to be taught in their mother tongue, and to unite in organizations and associations for the protection of their interests and identity, in full equality before the law. Although the pressure on minorities eased substantially after the fall of communism, apart from the Greek minority, which thus far has been the most organized minority, other "minorities are either very small and have confined their activities to cultural and human rights campaigns, or have failed to overcome internal obstacles to collective action (particularly the Roma and, to a lesser extent, the Vlachs)" (Pettifer 2001, 15). In addition, shifts in the attitude towards minorities were often conditioned by the shift in power balance between the two main parties – the Democratic Party (PD) and the Socialist Party (PS), where the latter has been usually perceived as more open towards minorities. This has also had a direct bearing on Albania's relations with Greece, which under Beisha's presidency (1992–1997) were "cool and at times frosty" (ICG 2001, 9).

Greek minority in Albania

The Greek minority is the largest minority in Albania. It is concentrated mainly in the south of Albania (along the coast and the border with Greece) as well as in Tirana. Estimated to comprise around 2% of the total population of about 3.2 million, their numbers are often contested. According to the 1981 census, the Greek minority in Albania numbered some 55,000. Following the collapse of the communist regime, a substantial proportion of the Greek minority moved to Greece, and total numbers are now unclear and disputed. Greek sources claim that there are at least 200,000–250,000 Greeks living in Albania. Albanian authorities claim that this is a deliberate exaggeration that includes other categories of people, such as Orthodox Christian Albanians and the Vlach community (Bugajski 2002, 681; Vickers 2010, 1; Christopoulos 2009, 18). In fact, the Greek issue in Albania has waned and resurfaced many times in history since Albania's independence in 1912. As noted by James Pettifer,

> southern Albania and its Greek-speaking population have represented a chronic point of contention – continuing to the present – in Albania's post-independence history, manifested mainly as a territorial dispute between Albania and Greece, but also as a struggle to define a distinct Albanian ethnicity and national heritage. (2001, 5)

Education in the Greek language has historically been problematic ever since the Albanian royal regime closed down Greek language education institutions in 1933, an action that prompted Greece to take the issue at the Permanent Court of International Justice (PCIJ, *Advisory Opinion No. 26*, 6 April 1935). During communism, although primary schools and some secondary schools existed in the larger minority centers, the content of the curriculum was exclusively Albanian (Vickers 2010, 8; Pettifer 2001, 6). In general, under communism, all the residents of Albania went through the same almost unparalleled hardship due to the "bunker" mentality of the Albanian communist leadership and the unparalleled direct state control of the society, economy and politics.

Politically, the Greek minority in Albania is represented by the Democratic Union of the Greek Minority (OMONIA), which was originally established as a cultural association and later engaged in political activities (Bugajski 2002, 278). In the first multi-party elections in Albania in 1991 OMONIA won five seats in the Albanian Parliament. However, in 1992, following the enactment of legislation banning ethnic parties, the Greek community established the Union of Human Rights Party (PBDNJ), which has been part of almost every Albanian government (led by the Democratic Party or the Socialist Party). Until now, PBPNJ has remained the main political party of the Greek minority. PBPNJ has often switched coalition partners during local and national elections and has been in power in some municipalities in the south. In the elections of 2009, they made a coalition with the Socialist Party (which lost the election) thus remaining in opposition[2]. In March 2010, following PBDNJ's poor performance in the 2009 elections and its decision to remain in opposition, some members of OMONIA initiated the creation of a new political party "Greek Ethnic Minority for the Future" (MEGA).

But what are OMONIA's and PBDNJ's political demands? What have they been campaigning for all those years? Indeed, OMONIA and its electoral wing PBDNJ have often gone through serious rifts and internal debates that led to the formal emergence of a moderate and a radical wing (Pettifer 2001, 11; Bugajski 2002, 297). The predominant demand of the more moderate wing has been the creation of closer economic and cultural links with Greece (seen as the kin-state), as well as more rights in the field of education, language and self-governance for the Greek minority in Albania. However, more radical figures, supported by elements within the Greek Church, state and diaspora, have occasionally played the card of secession or *enosis* with Greece. In fact, they refer to the historical territorial claims on southern Albania by various Greek nationalist groups that claim that part of southern Albania (known to the Greeks as "Northern Epirus") belongs historically to Greece (Vickers 2010, 2). After a series of small incidents and political tensions between 1991 and 1994, in April 1994 the first armed violence broke out. An ultra-nationalist ethnic Greek militant group, known the Northern Epirus Liberation Front (MAVI), attacked a small Albanian military post, killing two soldiers. As a reaction to that, the Albanian police arrested and trialed five ethnic Greeks belonging to OMONIA who were though to have been involved in the attack (Bideleux and Jeffries 2007, 49; ICG 2001, 9).

More recently, some Greek politicians in Albania, such as the now former mayor of Himara, Vasil Bollano, have occasionally talked about the idea of an autonomous status for the Greeks in south Albania. In April 2007, Bollano made parallels to Kosovo saying that by demanding independence for "North Epirus" the Greek minority was demanding nothing more than what Albania was demanding for Kosovo. However, a constant demand coming from the representatives of the Greek minority in Albania is the one related to the wider use of the Greek language in Albania (some have even called for Greek to become the second official language). Also, they have lobbied a lot with the Albanian government, Greek state and international organizations for inclusion of ethnicity and religion in the questionnaire in the census of October 2011.

In a word, the position and attitude of the Greek minority in Albania since 1991 has been very specific and has largely been conditioned by the overall developments in the home country, political instability, changes in government etc. The transition from a human rights organization to a political party in the case of the Greek minority has been as unpredictable as Albania's transition to democracy. Internal debates have often been strong and various radical groups have surfaced. Yet PBDNJ has managed successfully to be part of the Albanian governments (left and right) for some 18 uninterrupted years. Therefore, with some exceptions, it can be said that the strategy pursued by PBDNJ has been that of cooperation and participation in the political life and system. However, in their mostly institutionalized battle for enhanced rights, the Greek minority in Albania has continuously relied on Greece and has tried to utilize the latter's direct influence as well as that through international organizations on Albania to make concessions towards the Greek minority in Albania.

External actors

After the fall of communism and Albania's opening to the world, the role of international organizations in the developments in Albania, including the issue of minorities, increased significantly. During a period of high tensions in the Albanian-Greek relations (1993–94) the OSCE's High Commissioner on National Minorities played an important role in calming the dispute and easing tensions (Miall 1999, 142). In particular, the EU had a profound transformative impact in Albania with the goal of accession to the EU serving as a motor for reforms, development and progress in Albania (Bogdani and Loughlin 2007, 221) including the adoption of more open policies towards minorities.

The involvement of various international organizations in Albania became more direct in the late 1990s, conditioned first by the collapse of the state in 1997 and then the war in Kosovo during 1998–99 and the refugee crisis that followed. In 1997, under a United Nations (UN) mandate, the European Union (EU) deployed an eight-nation force of 5,000 (known as Operation Alba) in Albania to distribute humanitarian aid and help the

Albanian authorities restore order (Pond 2006, 199). Albania's neighbors – Greece and Italy – played a great part in these help provisions. The fall of communism in Albania provided new opportunities for Greece to establish its political and economic influence in Albania and also re-connect with its ethnic kin.

Greece

Albania's relations with Greece, which encompass the status of the Albanian minority and Albanian emigrants in Greece, as well as the status of the Greek minority in Albania and its relations to Greece, has been constantly present in the political debates in Albania in the last 20 years (Krasniqi 2010c, 15). Greece does not recognize the existence of Albanians in Greece (known as Arvanites and Chams, where most of the latter were deported to Albania after the Second World War). Nonetheless, Greece's focus in its policy towards Albania has been the position of the Greek minority living there.

When it comes to the position of Greeks in Albania, Greece has been active in raising its voice in various international fora and also using its position as an economically stronger state and member of the EU to improve the position of Greeks in Albania. However, since the end of the one-party state in 1991, a large number of people from the minority population, along with other ethnic Albanians, have left Albania to take advantage of economic opportunities in Greece (Miall 1999, 142; Vickers 2010, 1). Since 1991, Greeks from Albania who move to Greece receive a "Special Identity Card of Homogeneis", which also provides for preferential treatment, in comparison to the rest of the Albanians, by both the Greek nationals and the authorities. Thus, Greeks from Albania managed almost immediately and unconditionally to receive permanent residential status in Greece, including access to work permits and special benefits for social security, health and education (Athanasiades, Zafiropoulos, and Marantzidis 2011, 8–10). Only in 2006 were the *homogeneis* from Albania allowed by the government to acquire Greek citizenship and in 2007 they started acquiring it in small numbers (Tsitselikis 2008, 7–12).

Greece has provided preferential treatment for Albanian immigrants of Greek origin. In fact, evidence shows that Greek authorities also provide the *homogeneis* identity card to a large number of Christian Orthodox Albanians as well as Vlachs who have migrated to Greece. Thus, according to reliable information from the Greek Ministry of Public Order, approximately 200,000 people (which exceeds by far the number of Greeks in Albania), were granted the status of *homogeneis* (Christopoulos 2009, 17), and most probably will soon acquire Greek citizenship. As a result of economic pressures, many Vlachs and Albanians, including Muslim Albanians who convert to Orthodoxy, claim to be Greeks to get the status of *homogeneis* and later citizenship (Vickers 2010, 1).

Yet another contentious issue in the relations between the two countries is that of the Orthodox Church of Albania, established in 1908 and recognized as Autocephalous by the Patriarchate in Istanbul in 1937. In 1993, an ethnic Greek, Anastasios Yannulatos, was appointed by the Patriarchate in Istanbul as Albania's archbishop. Fearing an eventual Hellenization of Albania's Orthodox Church, the Albanian authorities, citing the Albanian Orthodox Church constitution of 1929, demanded that the head of the Orthodox Church to be of Albanian origin or citizenship (Vickers 2010, 4). Though Yannulatos came to Albania on a provisional basis, until a suitable ethnic Albanian replacement could be found, he remains Albania's archbishop (Krasniqi 2010c, 16). The presence of Greek priests in Albania became a more contentious issue in 1993 when Albania expelled a Greek Orthodox priest amid allegations that he was involved in stirring up secessionist feelings, a move that prompted Greece to act by expelling some 30,000 Albanian immigrants (Schmidt-Neke 2009, 544; Miall 1999, 142; Bugajski 2002, 267).

Moreover, in addition to its role as a cross border advisory and intermediary for the EU's programs in Albania, Greece has used its position as an EU member to pressure Albania in relation to the Greeks in Albania on several occasions. For example, in 1994, when Albania arrested some members of OMONIA for the armed attack on a military post in Albania, Greece responded by vetoing a major European Union loan to Albania (Bideleux and Jeffries 2007, 49; Vickers 2010, 3). In a more recent case, the Greek state managed to get some important concessions, such as the permission to build monuments of fallen Greek soldiers in Albania during WWII and a maritime boundary agreement (signed in April 2009, but annulled by the Constitutional Court of Albania months later) in return for the support it gave to Albania's EU membership (namely, the ratification of Albania's Stabilization and Association Agreement with the EU by the Greek Parliament). Due to Greece's role within the EU, the former has been successful, on several occasions, in making its interests in Albania and those of the Greek minority part of the EU conditionality towards Albania.

Although in Albania the issue of national minorities did not play a major role during the system change in early 1990s, both the state of Albania and the Greek minority mobilized at later points in the face of what they perceived as threats to national unity and assimilation respectively. Albania's policies towards minorities were closely monitored by Greek elites in Albania and Greece, which proved to be increasingly sensitive to any signs of projects of nationalization. This resulted in an intersection between foreign policy and the issue of national minority which became most clear in the escalation of Greek–Albanian disputes in 1993–94 (Schmidt-Neke 2009, 544). As argued by Brubaker, national minorities' stances are also highly variable with some "favoring full cooperative participation in the institutions of the host state, including participation in coalition governments, [while] others may favor a separatist, noncooperative stance" (2009, 60). In the case of Albania, the stance of the Greek minority was mostly cooperative. As a result, the quadratic nexus was marked by tension but not permanent conflict.

The case of Kosovo[3]

Contrary to Albania which became an independent state following the demise of the Ottoman Empire in the Balkans, Kosovo was part of different state formations until 2008. After decades under Serbian rule and control, in 1999 a new chapter began for Kosovo. On 10 June 1999, the UN Security Council adopted Resolution 1244 (*UN Doc S/RES/1244*, 10 June 1999) which obliged the Federal Republic of Yugoslavia (FRY) to withdraw from Kosovo and mandated the UN to establish an international civilian presence in Kosovo in order to provide an interim administration under which the people of Kosovo would enjoy substantial autonomy within the FRY (art. 10).

Resolution 1244 vested all legislative and executive powers, including administration of the judiciary, in the hands of the Special Representative of the Secretary General (SRSG). The SRSG and the United Nations Interim Administration Mission in Kosovo (UNMIK) initiated the process of creating separate Kosovar institutions (Stahn 2001, 536), thus embarking on a process of "democratization without state" (Tansey 2007, 129). Under UN legislation, inhabitants belonging to the same ethnic or religious or linguistic group were categorized as members of "communities", whose equality before the law was guaranteed. According to UNMIK legislation, Kosovo's eight communities were Albanians, Serbs, Bosniaks, Turks, Roma, Egyptians, Ashkali and Gorans. The new Kosovar

"Provisional Institutions of Self-Government" (PISG) provided for quotas and proportional representation for smaller communities. However, despite the ethnic-neutrality and "multicultural" vision of UNMIK, de facto, what happened after 1999 was an "ethnic reversal", with Albanians and Serbs finding themselves in a reversed majority–minority relation.

"Newborn" Kosovo

Kosovo declared its independence on 17 February 2008, after a year and a half of futile negations between delegations of Kosovo and Serbia mediated by the UN Special Envoy for Kosovo, Martti Ahtisaari. Kosovo's independence derives from the "Comprehensive Proposal for the Kosovo Status Settlement" (*S/2007/168/Add.1*, 26 March 2007), known as the "Ahtisaari Plan", which proposes a supervised independence for Kosovo. Due to Serbia's refusal and the inability of the Security Council to formally endorse the plan, Kosovo declared its independence in close-coordination with its allies (the U.S.A. and EU members such as the United Kingdom, France and Germany). As a result, its independence remains both externally (by Serbia, Russia, Spain and other countries) and internally (by a part of the Serb population in Kosovo) contested.

As regards the nature of the newly declared state, Kosovo's rather modern legislation reflects the vision of international actors involved in Kosovo to build a state and society that provides for equality of all the people and groups living there. Thus, Kosovo was declared "to be a democratic, secular and multi-ethnic republic, guided by the principles of non-discrimination and protection under the law" (*Kosovo Declaration of Independence*, 17 Feb 2008) Regardless of its ethnic composition and unlike other ex-Yugoslav states, Kosovo is not defined as a national state of its titular nation, but a multi-ethnic state of all citizens, guided by principles of non-discrimination and equal protection under the law of all communities.

Such a definition of the state has important implications for the relationship between the state and various ethnic groups or communities living on its territory. In the case of Kosovo, this means that the state belongs to all its citizens, as members of their respective communities, who are equal before the law, irrespective of their numbers. In practice, this translates into a vast array of rights and protection of its non-dominant communities enshrined in the Ahtisaari Plan (Annex II), the Constitution of Kosovo (Chapter II and III) and other laws. All the constitutionally recognized communities in Kosovo are granted specific group-rights, including reserved seats in the parliament (10 for the Serb community and 10 for the rest), at least two ministerial portfolios in the government, and proportional representation, as well as quotas, on other levels of governance. Moreover, the principle of double-majority is put in place for these pieces of legislation that are of "vital interests" to communities that are not the majority.

Nonetheless, although the "Kosovar government took pains to incorporate state-of-the-art legislation on human and minority rights, and its state symbols stress the multicultural past of its inhabitants" (King 2010, 129), the reality on the ground is rather different. Return and reintegration of refugees or internally displaced people, and the integration of Serbs, especially the ones residing in northern Kosovo, in Kosovar institutions still remain contentious issues.

Kosovo Serbs

Kosovo had changed significantly after the NATO intervention in June 1999. This event had multiple consequences on the position of Serbs in Kosovo. To begin with, as the displaced Albanians returned home, many Serbs and non-Albanian residents of Kosovo left the country or were driven out into neighboring countries, or, in the worst case, were killed or went missing. According to the UNHCR, almost 200,000 Serbs and Roma left Kosovo after June 1999 (1999, 339). Indeed, many Serbs had to move from one part of Kosovo to another, thus creating various Serb-inhabited areas (known as "Serbian enclaves") all around the country, with the biggest one being in the north of Kosovo. These events inflicted new wounds and created an even bigger gap in the communication between Kosovo's two main communities – Albanians and Serbs.

In terms of the political participation, it took some time for the local Serb population to become part of the UNMIK-led Kosovar institutions. After having boycotted the first local elections in post-war Kosovo in 2000, all the Serb parties (mostly branches of parties in Serbia) and political groups in Kosovo established a single electoral list called "Coalition Return" (*Povratak*) to run for the country-wide elections in 2001. The Serb coalition polled 11.3% of the vote, winning 12 seats (supplementing the 10 set aside seats reserved for them), thus becoming the third biggest force in the Kosovo Assembly (Tansey 2007, 139). Although reluctant to fully integrate in an institutional system whose consolidation was seen as a step towards an independent Kosovo, Kosovo's Serbs nevertheless showed signs of increasing cooperation with UNMIK and within the new Kosovar institutions in the first years after the war in Kosovo. However, the improvements in interethnic relations made, reached a low point in March 2004, when violence erupted in Kosovo. This was triggered by two separate incidents: the first incident was the shooting of a Kosovo Serb youth in a village near Pristina on 15 March, which led to a blockade by Kosovo Serbs of a key road; the second incident, on 16 March, was the death of three Albanian children in the Ibar River (who, according to the Albanian media, had been chased into the river by dogs belonging to Kosovo Serbs). In reaction to the latter incident, angry mobs of Albanians directed their attacks towards the UN and the Serbs as well. The impact of the riots was huge; 19 people had been killed (8 Serbs and 11 Albanians), over 1,000 injured, some 550 homes had been burned, along with 27 monasteries and churches, and over 4,000 people were displaced (Ker-Lindsay 2009, 20).

These events had far-reaching consequences and in many ways alienated Kosovo's Serbs. As a result, most of Kosovo's Serbs would boycott Kosovo's institutions (as well as elections in autumn 2004) and turn to Belgrade, which still kept its presence in Kosovo through "parallel institutions". Despite this political boycott, Serbs kept their representation in other institutions, such as the Kosovo Police Service, Customs etc. Urged by Belgrade, the absolute majority of Kosovo Serbs boycotted the local and national elections in November 2007; instead they participated in the Serbian municipal elections organized in Kosovo on 11 May 2008 (OSCE 9). Nonetheless, a group of smaller Serb parties from Kosovo, such as the Independent Liberal Party (SLS), the Serbian Democratic Party for Kosovo and Metohija (SDS KiM) and New Democracy, participated in the elections gathering few votes (www.kqz-ks.org) and filled their reserved seats and also joined the government.

The overall political context around and after the declaration of independence of Kosovo raised new question marks and dilemmas regarding the role of Serbs in post-independence Kosovo.[4] Even those Serbs that were represented in the Kosovar parliament and government at the time of the declaration of independence were reluctant to support it. Urged on by Belgrade, after 17 February 2008, many Kosovo Serbs withdrew from the Kosovo administration. In northern Kosovo and other Kosovo Serb majority areas, the Serbian Ministry for Kosovo and Metohija promoted the establishment of parallel political structures to provide administrative services to the Kosovo Serb community (OSCE 2008, 9).

The new situation created in Kosovo after February 2008 and the issue of decentralization of power and the creation of new Serb-majority municipalities created a new division between Kosovo Serbs living north and south of the river Ibar. Immediately after independence, the Kosovar authorities initiated the creation of five new municipalities with a Serb majority and the extension of one other, in full compliance with the Ahtisaari Plan. These municipalities had to be established after the local elections of 15 November 2009, the first ones to take place in an independent Kosovo. On 15 November 2009, the Kosovo Serbs living south of Mitrovica, encouraged by Kosovo institutions, the international presence in Kosovo, as well as Serb parties and leaders from central Kosovo, defied Belgrade and turned out in significant numbers in the local elections that were to legitimize the creation of new municipalities (KIPRED 2009b, 3). The Serbs won in four municipalities, boycotted elections in three in northern Kosovo, and lost in one. In June 2010, elections were organized in another newly created municipality, where a Serb party won as well. Certainly, this was a landmark development in Kosovo.

This positive trend of Serb participation in the Kosovar institutions continued in late 2010 with the first national elections after the declaration of independence. Three Serb political groups – SLS, SDS KiM, and a citizens' initiative named the Joint Serbian List (JSL) – managed to enter parliament, gaining a total of 15 seats (www.assembly-kosova.org). The position of Serbs within Kosovar institutions was enhanced further by the fact that these parties joined forces with other minority parties in the parliament to form a coalition with two other Albanian parties. As a result, Serb representatives hold the positions of deputy-chairman of the Kosovo Assembly, deputy prime-minister, and three ministries. In addition, they are represented in the Consultative Council for Communities (with the office of the president of Kosovo), Advisory Office on Community Affairs (within the prime minister's office), Parliamentary Committee on the Rights and Interest of Communities and other institutions.

While Serbs south of Mitrovica have made a significant step towards integration into the Kosovar society and political system, Serbs north of Mitrovica have cut almost all the ties that bound them to the institutions in Pristina and have strengthened their connections with Serbia. A Kosovo Serb political elite developed there, taking influential positions in state institutions increasingly supported by Serbia, which organized local elections in Kosovo Serb areas for the first time, resulting in the re-election of the mayors of the three pre-existing municipalities of Zvecan, Zubin Potok and Leposavic and the creation of a new Mitrovica municipality (ICG 2011, 1). Although Kosovar institutions did not recognize these elections, they extended the mandate of the three mayors that were appointed in 2002 and 2004 by UNMIK and they continued to allocate a regular financial amount for the functioning of these municipalities (KIPRED 2009c, 8).

North Kosovo has in many ways become a hub of Serbs in Kosovo, an intellectual centre. It holds a university (officially called "Pristina University") which is part of Serbia's system of education. Local Serbs, who "see the North as their last stand" (ICG 2011, i), are gathered around the north Mitrovica Serb National Council, an umbrella group representing Kosovo Serbs. Apart from the continuous boycott of elections, urged by Serbia, local Serbs in the northern part of Kosovo boycotted the first overall census in Kosovo in April 2011. Tensions rose high once more in the summer of 2011 following a decision by the Kosovo government to send the Kosovo Special Police Units to seize control of the border crossings with Serbia (which were attacked and destroyed by local Serbs in February 2008) in the north in order to enforce a ban on Serbian products. This decision was met with opposition from Serbia and resistance from local Serbs who demolished and burned infrastructure there and established road barricades. Although in the EU-facilitated dialogue Kosovo and Serbia reached agreements on Kosovo customs' stamps, border crossings, civil registers and Kosovo's representation in regional meetings, tensions persist in the northern part of Kosovo as local Serbs refuse to dismantle barricades that were erected in opposition to the presence of Kosovo police and customs officers in the border points with Serbia. More recently, they have organized a referendum where the overwhelming majority voted to reject contact with independent Kosovo's institutions with Serbia, Kosovo and the international community dismissing the vote as irrelevant (*BalkanInsight* 2012).

External actors

International actors have been actively involved in Kosovo since 1999. Initially they were present through a civilian structure (UNMIK) and a military structure (KFOR), both of them assuming their mandate from the UNSC Resolution 1244. However, despite many efforts and investment, and despite the fact that UNMIK put in place a legislative framework that was supposed to transform Kosovo into a multiethnic society subject to the rule of law, Kosovo remained an ethnically divided society even after nine years of direct international rule and control (Krasniqi 2010a, 532–534).

The inability of the Security Council to endorse the Ahtisaari Plan and the unilateral character of its declaration of independence has resulted in a limited number of recognitions of Kosovo's sovereignty and independence thus far (88 as of February 2012). Kosovo's obscure legal status has resulted in a highly complex relationship with international organizations and institutions such as the UN and the EU. Neither the UN nor the EU recognizes Kosovo as a sovereign state. Yet, they are both present in Kosovo; the former through UNMIK and the latter through its Rule of Law Mission in Kosovo (EULEX) (www.eulex-kosovo.eu). Although the Ahtisaari Plan foresaw a smooth transfer of power from the UN to the EU, resulting in termination of UNMIK's mandate and an increased role for the EULEX mission and the ICO (International Civilian Office) (www.ico-kos.org) to strengthen its institutions, monitor their performance and implementation of the Ahtisaari Plan, this did not happen (Krasniqi 2010b, 25). Indeed, Kosovo invited the EU to deploy a rule of law mission in Kosovo, but because of the lack of consensus in the UN and the EU[5], EULEX was deployed in Kosovo "under the general framework of United Nations Security Resolution 1244," which conditions it to adopt a "status neutral" approach. Indeed, it took months (November 2008) for the members of the UN Security Council to approve the UN Secretary-General Ban Ki-Moon's six-point plan authorizing the EULEX mission to deploy across the entire territory of Kosovo. This situation of increased legal obscurity has complicated the matters for both the EU and UN presence in Kosovo.

As regards the role of external actors in the consolidation of the Kosovar institutions and the process of democratization, the ICO has played an important role in helping the Kosovo government to enforce minority rights standards, especially in the process of decentralization and the creation of new municipalities. As far as EULEX is concerned, despite many high expectations, during its first three years of the mandate, the EULEX Mission did not produce any significant results in the field of rule of law and fight against corruption and organized crime. Although EULEX has taken over the rule-of-law prerogatives, so far it has failed to establish Kosovo as one single legal and customs zone (Surroi 2011, 113). Nonetheless, the EU as such has played and continues to play an important role through its politics of conditionality in establishing communication between Kosovo and Serbia and improving their relations. The ongoing dialogue between Kosovo and Serbia that began in March 2011 following the adoption of an EU-Serbia resolution at the General Assembly of the UN (*A/RES/64/298*, 9 September 2010), is an example.

Serbia

Serbia's sovereignty over Kosovo was suspended on 10 June 1999 with the adoption by the UN Security Council of Resolution 1244. Nonetheless, Serbia has never ceased its activities in Kosovo, mostly through its "parallel institutions". Serbia does not recognize the independence of Kosovo and has taken various political and legal steps to challenge and even undermine it. In the external level, it has brought the issue of the legality of the declaration of independence of Kosovo before the International Court of Justice (ICJ). Internally, it has attempted to maintain and even enhance its control over the local Serbs in Kosovo, most notably in the northern part of Kosovo.

Because Serbia does not recognize Kosovo as an independent state it does not perceive itself as a kin-state of the Serb community in Kosovo. It still treats the whole of Kosovo as part of its territory. However, in practice, it never hid the fact that it wants to speak on behalf of Kosovo's Serbs and be treated as the sole representative of the Kosovo Serbs. For this purpose, the Serbian government had initially established a Serb Coordination Centre for Kosovo and later a Ministry for Kosovo. Through these institutions and other local branches in Kosovo, for years Serbia has been paying the personnel employed in Serbian elementary and secondary schools, and health centers, as well as pensioners (many of the people from these categories receive another salary from Kosovar institutions). Other projects in infrastructure were funded as well. However, despite the fact that that two thirds of Kosovo Serbs live south of the Ibar river, most of the money goes to the north of Kosovo. To sustain the Kosovo Serbs' way of life Serbia spends some €200 million annually in the North (ICG 2011, 4) As observed by KIPRED, "[t]he financial policy of Belgrade in essence shows the policy towards Kosovo Serbs north and south of river, and its aspirations to maintain the north under tight control" 2009a, 5). Many assume that Serbia's goal is to keep north Kosovo in return for the loss of the rest of the territory. In a recent statement, the Deputy Prime Minister and Interior Minister Ivica Dačić, has defended such a proposal as a solution for the Kosovo issue (*SETimes* 2011).

Despite the wide consensus among parties in Serbia that Kosovo is part of Serbia, Kosovo and, in particular, the north has become a battlefield among the ruling parties and opposition parties in Serbia for control over Kosovo's Serbs. Until mid-2008 the north was dominated by the Democratic Party of Serbia (DSS), but after the 2008 elections in Serbia and the victory of the Democratic Party (DS), the latter has increased its role and control among Serbs in Kosovo (ICG 2011, 3). The DS-led government in Belgrade, which aims for a faster EU integration, has also favored a more relaxed policy when it comes to Kosovo. Financially, this has been conditioned by the deterioration the of economic situation in Serbia. As a result, money sent to Kosovo has decreased substantially.

Serbia's position on the post-1999 developments in Kosovo has mainly gone to the detriment of integration of local Serbs in the Kosovar institutions. Both under UNMIK and after independence, Serbia has urged Serbs to boycott Kosovar institutions, thus affecting the process of democratization. As of 2009, it has actively undermined Kosovo's sovereignty by challenging it internationally as well as by tightening its control in the north. Nonetheless, as normalization of relations with Kosovo is becoming a major condition for Serbia's faster progress towards EU integration, Serbia's space for maneuver in Kosovo seems to have narrowed down substantially.

In sum, due to Kosovo's recent history of violence and ongoing legal dispute regarding its political status, the relationship between the four political fields – Kosovo, Kosovo Serbs, Serbia and the international community – has been almost constantly conflictual. In the same vein, all these political fields remain highly contested and divided internally. Although during the status negotiation process the main Albanian parties have been quite united in their stances, the present process of dialogue with Serbia and the prospects of a special status for the north of Kosovo have divided the Albanian political block. Regarding Kosovo's Serbs, their stance has been uneven, depending on the enclaves, the Serbian leaders in the enclave, as well as power politics with Belgrade. While more and more Serbs favor full cooperative participation in the Kosovar institutions, the ones in the northern part of Kosovo favor a rather separatist and noncooperative stance. The roots of this division are to be found in the violent events of June 1999 as well as 2008, which were to embed a de facto boundary along the river Ibar, effectively separating the area to the north from the rest of Kosovo. In turn, this has prompted thoughts in some quarters about the partition of Kosovo (Gow 2009, 249).

Conclusion

In this paper I have shown how minorities, nationalizing states, kin-states and other external actors, both in the cases of Kosovo and Albania, have been intertwined in a typical quadratic nexus, where the relationship is essentially relational and often conflictual. Regardless of the fact that neither Kosovo nor Albania can be classified as "ethnic" states where state ownership belongs to the core nation and where minorities are excluded from the political process and deprived of their cultural and political rights, both cases involve a quadratic relationship that can be more or less conflictual. The fact that both these two polities with strong civic (Albania) and multi-ethnic (Kosovo) underpinnings involve the quadratic nexus reinforces the argument in support of the application of the latter in a larger context of state building that goes beyond the infamous "civic vs. ethnic" divide.

In the case of Albania, the quadratic nexus re-emerged after 1991 in a new context of post-communism and transition to democracy. It was this particular context and an enhanced role of Greece, both in the capacity of the kin-state and as an EU member that have played key roles in the developments regarding the Greek minority in Albania. Although relations between Albania and Greece have improved significantly since 1991, at times théy have deteriorated as a result of the disagreements on and around the Greek minority. However, following Albania's progress towards EU membership and the already achieved NATO membership, relations between the two countries seem destined to improve. Likewise, in general, the Greek minority in Albania has been mostly cooperative in the process of democratization and state-transformation in Albania. It chose an institutional path to address its grievances and advance its agenda that seeks to improve its position. Despite occasional tensions and clashes, the relationship has been tense but not always conflictual.

In the case of Kosovo, the ongoing debates surrounding Kosovo's legal status and Serbia's refusal to recognize Kosovo create a unique situation where neither Serbia nor Kosovo can be considered to fully embody the concept of kin-state and nationalizing state respectively. However, one can depict a relational quadratic nexus there as well. The declaration of independence of Kosovo and the electoral process in 2009 and 2010 polarized the Serb community in Kosovo and also cemented the division between Serbs living south of Mitrovica, who have integrated into the Kosovar system, and those living north of Mitrovica, who have not. Many Serbs in Kosovo find themselves caught between the fires in a political battle between Pristina and Belgrade for control over them and the territory of Kosovo. Irrespective of the fact that at present the majority of Serbs in Kosovo have shown an increased intention to integrate within Kosovo, it is too early to speak of a successful process of integration and democratization of the Kosovar society. Certainly, much will depend on future developments in regard to Kosovo's sovereignty and statehood and relations between Pristina and Belgrade.

In all these developments, external actors, be they in the form of international organizations or individual states, have played a major role. Albania's relations with the EU have been largely influenced and dictated by its neighbors – Italy and Greece – that have various economic and political interests there. The EU has played its role as an anchor for economic and political reforms in Albania, which in turn have improved the position of Albania's minority groups. In the case of Kosovo, international actors – above all, the EU, the UN and the US – have been actively involved in state-building, democratization and putting in place a modern system of minority rights protection. However, disagreements on the status issue have prevented the EU and its EULEX Mission from asserting a more active role in Kosovo, especially as regards the integration of the northern part of Kosovo. Still, despite the lack of unanimity, the EU has urged both Kosovo and Serbia to be more cooperative with each other if they (especially Serbia) are to accelerate their integration into the EU. Although the February 2012 agreements paved the way for Serbia to become a candidate member (*The Economist* 2012), it remains to be seen how they are reflected in the internal situation in Kosovo.

The two cases analyzed here, nonetheless, differ in the context of minority integration with the Greek minority in Albania being more integrated than Kosovo's Serb minority. There are two main reasons that explain uneven levels of minority integration in the two countries. The first one is statehood and sovereignty. Whereas Albania is a sovereign country and has consolidated its statehood for many decades, Kosovo's sovereignty and statehood remain questioned both internally and externally. Internationally recognized and consolidated statehood and sovereignty play an important role in the process of minority integration. Being at different levels of state consolidation, Albania and Kosovo show different levels of minority integration today. Even in the case of Albania, in times of instability and political uncertainty, such as the early volatile years of Albania's statehood (1912–24), as well as the periods of 1991 and 1997, boycott and other alternative and more radical proposals came to surface from the minority representatives.

The second reason has to do with the role of kin-states. In the case of Albania, Greece does not question (at least openly) Albania's borders and has a relatively long history of political cooperation with Albania. As regards Kosovo, Serbia refuses to come to terms with the idea of an independent Kosovo. Knowing, at least hypothetically, that redrawing of borders and division along ethnic lines is still possible does not help dissenting minorities to integrate within a state.

Going back to the issue of the relational reports between various actors in this study, two points should be highlighted. These two case studies have shown how various actors observe the behavior and attitude of the other actors (even on the situations outside the given nexus) and take it into consideration while adopting their response or position. A case in point is the way in which the leaders of Albania's Greeks linked the position of Albania (acting as a kin-state) towards Kosovo to the demands of the Greek minority in Albania. But this is not always the case. For example, Greece is categorical in its denial of the existence of an Albanian non-migrant minority in Greece and on the other hand, when it comes to the Greek minority in Albania, it refers to the international standards of minority rights. Second, as shown in this paper, none of the actors is or should be treated as a monolith. Actors themselves, be it minorities, kin-states, nationalizing states or foreign states or organizations, are arenas of struggle where various political groups fight for dominance and have different perspectives on the relationship within a certain nexus. In a word, all actors have their "moderates" and "radicals".

Notes

1. Since 1921 Albania's Greek Population has been recognised as a minority living in recognised "minority zone". After the Second World War, the Albanian communists took a decision to limit the "minority zone" in southern Albania to just 99 villages thus excluding other areas with Greek population (ICG "Albania" 10).
2. Regardless of this, a Greek has been serving as Minister of Health in the Albanian government created in 2009.
3. International usage of names of towns and places is applied in this paper.
4. Although Kosovo's Serbs were represented on both sides in the negotiations mediated by Ahtisaari (Weller 198), the key actors on the process were Pristina, Belgrade and the international community.
5. Spain, Greece, Cyprus, Romania and Slovakia refuse to recognize Kosovo's independence.

References

AHRG. 2003. *Minorities: The Present and the Future*. Report of the Albanian Human Rights Group on the situation of minorities in Albania. Tirana: Kanun.
Athanasiades, Harris, Kostas Zafiropoulos, and Nikos Marantzidis. 2011. *The Limits of Political Correctness: Dual Citizenship, Governance and Education in Greece*. 1 Aug. http://www.antigone.gr/en/projects/deliverables.html
"Belgrade moves closer to Brussels." 2012. *The Economist*. 2 Mar. http://www.economist.com/blogs/easternapproaches/2012/03/serbias-eu-bid
Biberaj, Elez. 1999. *Albania in Transition: The Rocky Road to Democracy*. Boulder & Oxford: Westview.
Bideleux, Robert, and Ian Jeffries. 2007. *The Balkans: A Post-communist History*. New York: Routledge.
Bogdani, Mirela, and John Loughlin. 2007. *Albania and the European Union: The Tumultuous Journey Towards Integration and Accession*. London: I. B. Tauris.
Brubaker, Rogers. 1996. *Nationalism Reframed: Nationhood and the National Question in the New Europe*. Cambridge: Cambridge University Press.
Bugajski, Janusz. 2002. *Political Parties of Eastern Europe: A Guide to Politics in the Post-Communist Era*. London: The Centre for Strategic and International Studies.
Constitution of the Republic of Albania. 22 November 1998.
CoE, *ACFC/SR/II(2007)004/Annexes*. 2007. 18 May. http://www.coe.int/t/dghl/monitoring/minorities/3_fcnmdocs/PDF_2nd_SR_Albania_Annexes_en.pdf
Christopoulos, Dimitris. 2009. "EUDO Citizenship Observatory Country Report on Greece." *Robert Schuman Centre for Advanced Studies in collaboration with Edinburgh University Law School*. September. http://eudo-citizenship.eu/docs/CountryReports/Greece.pdf
Gasteyger, Curt. 2006. *Europe: From Division to Unification – A Documented Overview 1945–2006*. Bonn: Bundeszentrale für politische Bildung.
Gow, James. 2009. "Kosovo– The Final Frontier? From Transitional Administration to Transitional Statehood." *Journal of Intervention and Statebuilding* 3 (2): 239–257.
ICG. 2001. *Albania: State of the Nation*. ICG Balkans Report N°111.
ICG. 2011. *North Kosovo: Dual Sovereignty in Practice*. Europe Report N°211, Permanent Court of International Justice. *Advisory Opinion No. 26*. 1935. 6 Apr. http://www.worldcourts.com/pcij/eng/decisions/1935.04.06_albania.htm
Ker-Lindsay, James. 2009. *Kosovo: The Path to Contested Statehood in the Balkans*. London: I.B. Tauris.
King, Charles. 2010. *Extreme Politics. Nationalism, Violence and the End of Eastern Europe*. Oxford: Oxford University Press.

KIPRED. 2009a. *Kosovo at i Crossroad: Decentralization and the Creation of New Municipalities.* Policy Brief No. 14. Pristina: KIPRED.
KIPRED. 2009b. *Decentralization in Kosovo I: Challenges of Serb Majority Municipalities.* Policy Brief No. 15. Pristina: KIPRED.
KIPRED. 2009c. *Decentralization in Kosovo II: Challenges of Serb Majority Municipalities.* Policy Brief No. 16. Pristina: KIPRED.
Kosovo Declaration of Independence. 2008. 17 Feb. http://www.assembly-kosova.org/common/docs/Dek_Pav_e.pdf
Krasniqi, Gëzim. 2010a. "The International Community's Modus Operandi in Postwar Bosnia and Herzegovina and in Kosovo: A Critical Assessment." *Südosteuropa* 58 (4): 520–541.
Krasniqi, Gëzim. 2010b. *The Challenge of Building an Independent Citizenship Regime in a Partially Recognised State: The Case of Kosovo.* CITSEE Working Paper Series, 2010/04.
Krasniqi, Gëzim. 2010c. *Citizenship in an Emigrant Nation-state: The Case of Albania.* CITSEE Working Paper Series, 2010/13.
Kuzio, Taras. 2001. "'Nationalizing States' or Nation Building? A Critical Review of the Theoretical Literature and Empirical Evidence." *Nations and Nationalism* 7 (2): 135–154.
Miall, Hugh. 1999. "The Albanian Communities in Post-communist Transition." In *Ethnicity and Democratization in New Europe*, edited by Karl Cordell, 131–144. London: Routledge.
"Northern Serbs Vote 'No' to Kosovo." 2012. *BalkanInsight.* 16 Feb. http://www.balkaninsight.com/en/article/99-74-kosovo-serbs-say-no-to-pristina
OSCE Mission in Kosovo. 2008. *Background Report: Human Rights, Ethnic Relations and Democracy in Kosovo (Summer 2007 – Summer 2008).* http://www.osce.org/kosovo/33282
Pettifer, James. 2001. *The Greek Minority in Albania in the Aftermath of Communism.* Conflict Studies Research Centre.
Pond, Elizabeth. 2006. *Endgame in the Balkans: Regime Change, European Style.* Washington, DC: Brookings Institution Press.
Schmidt-Neke, Michael. 2009. "Albania: The Unfinished Nation State." In *Nationalism in Late and Post-Communist Europe.* Vol. 2, Nationalism in the Nation states, edited by Egbert Jahn, 522–547. Munich: Nomos.
"Serbia's Dacic Defends Idea of Kosovo Partition." 2011. *SETimes.* 19 May. http://www.setimes.com/cocoon/setimes/xhtml/en_GB/newsbriefs/setimes/newsbriefs/2011/05/19/nb-10
Smith, David J. 2002. "Framing the National Question in Central and Eastern Europe: A Quadratic Nexus?" *The Global Review of Ethnopolitics* 2 (1): 3–16.
Stahn, Carsten. 2001. "Constitution Without a State? Kosovo Under the United Nations Constitutional Framework for Self-Government." *Leiden Journal of International Law* 14 (3): 531–561.
Surroi, Veton. 2011. "The Unfinished State(s) in the Balkans and the EU: The Next Wave." In *The Western Balkans and the EU: The Hour of Europe*, edited by Jacques Rupnik, 111–120. Chaillot Papers. Paris: EU Institute for Security Studies.
Tansey, Oisin. 2007. "Democratization without a State: Democratic Regime-building in Kosovo." *Democratization* 14 (1): 129–150.
The Comprehensive Proposal for the Kosovo Status Settlement. 2007. 26 March. http://www.unosek.org/unosek/en/statusproposal.html
Tsitselikis, Constantin. 2008. "Citizenship in Greece: Present Challenges for Future Changes" [Updated version]. In *Multiple Citizenship as a Challenge to European Nation-states*, edited by Devorah Kalekin-Fishman and Pirkko Pitkänen, 145–170. Rotterdam: Sense Publishers.
UNHCR 1999. *Country Operation: Federal Republic of Yugoslavia at Glance.* http://www.unhcr.org/3e2d4d6915.pdf
United Nations General Assembly. 2010. A/RES/64/298, 9 Sep. http://www.unmikonline.org/Documents/GA64298.pdf
Vickers, Miranda. 2010. *The Greek Minority in Albania: Current Tensions.* Shrivenham: Research and Assessment Branch, Defence Academy of the United Kingdom.
Weller, Marc. 2009. *Contested Statehood: Kosovo's Struggle for Independence.* Oxford: Oxford University Press.

Cutting the mists of the Black Mountain: *Cleavages in Montenegro's divide over statehood and identity*

Jelena Dzankic

European University Institute, Florence, Italy

The two decades of Montenegro's transition that followed the disintegration of Yugoslavia were marked by the transformation of the ambitions of the ruling political elites, which pushed the republic that once sought to be a member in a federal state towards independence. The shift in the agendas of the political elites also changed the meaning of the notions of "Montenegrin" and "Serb". Hence, this paper looks at the cleavages that emerged during Montenegro's divide over statehood and identity. It asserts that elite competition in unconsolidated states prompts the emergence of ethno-cultural cleavages, which are necessary for establishing the identities of political elites and of their followers. The study first identifies the critical junctures for the emergence of functional and structural cleavages in Montenegro and associates these cleavages with the changing political context. It proceeds with an analysis of ethno-cultural cleavages, arguing that these emerged from the politicization of historical narratives. The study concludes by arguing that different types of cleavages supported the division over statehood and identity, and that as a result of the changes in identity in Montenegro, the political reinforcement of overlapping cleavages was essential in order to cement the ethno-cultural identities of the two camps.

Introduction

Statehood and nationhood has been in flux in Montenegro over the past two decades. Since 1992, Montenegro has been a republic in the Federal Republic of Yugoslavia (FRY), a member state in Serbia and Montenegro (from 2002–2006), and an independent state (from 2006 onwards). There has been a corresponding shift in people's ethnic/national identifications, largely as a result of the association of the category "Montenegrin" with independent statehood, and "Serb" with the preservation of the common state with Serbia. These dynamics are reflected in the contrasting referendum results of 1992 and 2006, as well as in the different census results of 1991 and 2003.

On 1 March 1992, when the first referendum on the independence of Montenegro was held, 95.4%[1] of voters (from a 66% turnout) opted for Montenegro to remain in a common state with the other former Yugoslav republics wishing to do so (ICG 2000, 6). At the population census conducted a year before, 61.9% of the population defined themselves as Montenegrins, 9.4% as Serbs, while the remainder were of different minorities (Federal Statistical Office 1992). Considering that in 1991, ethnic minorities boycotted the referendum, the data indicate that the majority of the people in Montenegro at the time defined themselves as "Montenegrins" and preferred a common state with Serbia to independence.

The results of the second referendum on independence in Montenegro, held on 21 May 2006, were quite different, and not just because the turnout was higher (86.5%). Independent statehood was supported by 55.5%, while the preservation of the union with Serbia was supported by 44.5% (CDT 2006 "Referendum 21/05/2006"). At the population census of 2003, 43.2% of people in Montenegro declared their national identity as "Montenegrin", while 32% professed it as "Serb" (Zavod za Statistiku Crne Gore "2003 Population Census of Montenegro"). Given that – as a result of their instrumentalization in the pre-referendum years (Bieber 2003, 11–42) – minorities supported independence in 2006, the above data indicate that the majority of the population who voted for the preservation of the common state defined themselves as "Serb", and the lion's share of the people who voted for independence identified themselves as "Montenegrins".

As an epilogue to these swift changes of identity, the most recent population census indicates that the national/ethnic identification of the population has largely stabilized, although there is still some fluidity (Zavod za Statistiku Crne Gore 2011 "2011 Population Census of Montenegro"). In 2011, 28.7% and 45% of the population declared themselves as "Serb" and "Montenegrin" respectively (Zavod za Statistiku Crne Gore 2011 "2011 Population Census of Montenegro"). The aim of this paper is to explore how ethnic/national identifications have changed as a result of the deep structural conflict that emerged during the 15 years of Montenegro's transition and how this conflict was channelled both into the political arena and into social life. In terms of the former, the main source of conflict took place in 1997. The ruling Democratic Party of Socialists (DPS), the heir of the Communist Party, split into two factions that quickly bifurcated the republic's political scene. While the DPS remained the dominant political actor in Montenegro, the opposition was formed through the coalescence of political forces around the Socialist People's Party (SNP). Initially, the conflict was over the issue of whether to support or oppose Milošević's regime, with the SNP choosing the former, and the DPS the latter. Yet, with the demise of the Milošević regime in 2000, the changing agendas of the political players offset the divide over statehood and identity in Montenegro. Gradually, the DPS became the proponent of Montenegrin independence and a separate Montenegrin ethnic identity, while the SNP promoted the common state with Serbia and a Montenegrin ethnic identity indistinct from that of the Serbs.

In examining this translation of conflict into politics, the paper focuses on the cleavages that emerged during Montenegro's divide over statehood and identity. It views cleavages in a Rokkanian fashion, which explains the formation of political parties in Western Europe (Rokkan 1970 "Citizens, Elections, Parties"; Lipset and Rokkan 1967; Rokkan 1999 "State Formation"). Hence, cleavages are representations of conflict and divisions in democratic societies, which emerge as an outcome of structural processes, such as modernization, national awakening, or state building. Yet, cleavages "freeze" conflict in major transformative moments for a polity – so called critical junctures (Mair 2001, 27–44). As such, the notion of cleavage is equally applicable to post-communist societies, which underwent comprehensive structural transformations after 1989. According to Martin (2000, 11–50), cleavages are mobilized by political actors so that they can perpetuate political divides and crystallize the party structure of the state, thus establishing clear voter alignments. This institutionalization of divisions into durable political action is possible because cleavages contain either social elements, such as class, or identitarian aspects, such as gender, race, and ethnicity (Bartolini 2005).

Building on the Rokkanian notion of the cleavage (Rokkan 1970 "Citizens, Elections, Parties"; Lipset and Rokkan 1967; Rokkan 1999 "State Formation"), this paper fosters the broader argument that in transitional societies in which the processes of state and nation building are at the core of political activity, cleavages related to ethnic/national identity become politicized. As such, they prove to be quintessential for the establishment of the identity of both political elites and of their followers. This is because elite competition for power gains salience in societies facing recovery from a negative transition[2]. If such societies have suffered from previous divides (e.g. religious, tribal, class, ethnic) as has been the case with Montenegro, these divides emerge as cleavages in the new elite competition.

In constructing this argument, the study first identifies the critical junctures in the divide over statehood and identity in Montenegro, which are essential for understanding the emergence of different cleavages in the 20 years of Montenegro's transition. The paper maintains that the 1989 "anti-bureaucratic" revolutions (ABR) and the 2000 fall of Milošević were critical junctures in which different structural (mainly ethnic) cleavages were dominant, while the 1997 split of the DPS and 2006 Montenegro's independence brought about the prevalence of functional (i.e. class, economic) cleavages. Second, the paper argues that Montenegrin political elites revived ethno-cultural narratives in order to ensure the dominance of structural over functional cleavages, thus proving that cleavages in unconsolidated states are malleable. The study concludes by relating the different types of cleavages (overlapping, cross-cutting, independent) to the development of the political landscape in Montenegro.

Critical junctures in the divide over statehood and identity

In the recent political history of Montenegro, four critical junctures can be identified – the 1989 "anti-bureaucratic" revolutions; the 1997 split of the DPS; the fall of Milošević in 2000; and the declaration of Montenegro's independence in 2006. Each of these major events "froze" an existing societal divide and reproduced it within the polity's institutional setup as an ethno-cultural (i.e. structural) and/or political (i.e. functional) cleavage. Yet, the nature of political divisions in Montenegro has led to an overlap between these two types of cleavages thus making them complementary, rather than mutually exclusive. In other words, although either structural or functional cleavages were dominant at all four critical junctures, both types of cleavages have played a role in reproducing the political struggles in Montenegro.

The replacement of one set of communist elites with the ostensibly reformist leadership at the time of the ABR, and their affiliation with Milošević's policies, ensured the continuation of Communist Party rule in Montenegro during the the disintegration of Yugoslavia in the early 1990s. The dominance of the communist heirs, who embraced Serb nationalist rhetoric, transferred ethno-religious cleavages into the political sphere. Parties with ethnic prefixes emerged, and religion became the key determinant of ethnic identity and political behaviour. At the second critical juncture, the split of the DPS in 1997, the societal division that was converted into cleavage was over the question of support or opposition to Milošević. The structural ethnic cleavages created at the time of the ABR continued to exist, but were overshadowed by these new divisions. The third critical juncture in Montenegrin politics, and the only one that was triggered externally – by the fall of Milošević in 2000 – caused the recalibration of goals of the Montenegrin political elites, which aligned into pro-independence/pro-Montenegrin and unionist/pro-Serb camps. Hence in addition to the already existing functional cleavages established at the previous critical juncture, new ethnic cleavages that differentiated Montenegrin and Serb identities resurfaced amidst struggles for political power. The final critical juncture in recent Montenegrin politics was independence in 2006, which offset another reconfiguration of the country's political scene. The cleavages that were created previously were adjoined by new functional (in this case, socio-economic) divisions, particularly with the former unionist camp that needed to adapt to the new circumstances after the resolution of the statehood issue.

In sum, the critical junctures of 1989 and 2000 were characterized by the dominance of two different structural cleavages (both with an ethnic dimension), parts of which are still an issue in the country's politics. Those of 1997 and 2006 gave rise to mostly functional (class or operational) cleavages as they were marked with the prevalence of socio-economic concerns over nationalist rhetoric and practice. A full understanding of the interplay of these cleavages is necessary for the analysis of Montenegro's divisions over statehood and identity.

Dominance of structural cleavages at critical junctures

The emergence of structural cleavages at critical junctures is often supported by an active national movement which underpinned the events that marked that juncture. In the case of Montenegro, the first structural cleavages appeared in the late 1980s. The "anti-bureaucratic" revolution, which created the conditions for Slobodan Milošević's rise to power in Serbia, also produced a set of "reformed" communist elites in Montenegro, led by Momir Bulatović and Milo Đukanović. The new Montenegrin elites remained loyal to Milošević's nationalist politics, which created social and political divisions that require explanation.

Historically, ethnic/national identity in Montenegro has been dual, which has been entrenched in the notion of the "national *homo duplex*" (Darmanović 1992, 28). That is, the categories "Serb" and "Montenegrin" were not mutually exclusive and many of the people of the Christian Orthodox faith associated themselves with both identities. This historical duality emerged during the rule of the Petrović dynasty (Roberts 2007), when Montenegro's prince-bishops used both terms to refer to their population. A form of the divide between the "Serb" and "Montenegrin" ethnic/national identity in Montenegro emerged in the period immediately preceding the creation of the Kingdom of Serbs, Croats and Slovenes and was related to the question of Montenegrin status in the new state. During 1917–18 Montenegro became an ideological and political battlefield between the proponents of unconditional unification with Serbia under the Karađorđević dynasty – the Whites – and the proponents of a union of equal members – the Greens (Rastoder 2003, 131). This dichotomy persisted throughout the following decades, until it became entrenched within the federal structures of the socialist Yugoslavia.

The Yugoslav constitutional establishment considered republics as "states although self-determination was limited by the federal constitution, phrased in such a way as to make it appear that the right had already been exercised" (Shoup 1968, 115). The decentralized Yugoslav model allowed for the flourishing of separate identities in the republics, but proclamations of extreme nationalism were sanctioned in order to avoid the interwar and World War II Yugoslav experience (Hodson, Sekulić, and Massey 1994, 1534–1558). Nevertheless, during the socialist period, identity in Montenegro was far from consolidated. In fact, the political decision to grant Montenegro the status of a republic in 1946 was aimed at smoothing the differences that existed among the population in the interwar period, and at dampening the divide between Whites and Greens. Milovan Đilas – a high ranking communist official at the time

– claimed that Montenegrins were a part of a larger corpus of Serbs, and that their history of statehood made them "the best of Serbs" (Đilas 1947, 3–4). According to Đilas, it was the status of a separate republic that should be granted to Montenegro, but not the status of a separate nation (Đilas 1947, 5). Hence, during the socialist period, there were not many explicit manifestations of a distinct Montenegrin identity (Pavlović 2003, 90–104) – and if there were any, they were considered retrograde – prompting a general consensus among the people that Montenegrins were indistinct from Serbs. These dynamics reinforced the "national *homo duplex*" in Montenegro (Darmanović 1992, 28).

Yet, the collapse of communism moved the "Montenegrin pendulum from one nexus of power to another" (Radonjić 1998, 25). Due to the influence of the media and church, Montenegrin politics developed predominantly under the umbrella of Serbian nationalism. The galvanization of the people into a movement based on Serbian nationalism is largely attributable to the conundrum surrounding identity in Montenegro described above. The fact that the elites in the first half of the 1990s did not emphasize the difference between the two counterparts of Montenegrin identity helped preserve the populist movement driven by Serbian nationalism.

At the time of the economic embargo and isolationist policies of the Federal Republic of Yugoslavia, ideas of political populism and extreme (Serbian) nationalism resonated well with the people. In the parliamentary elections of 1990 and 1992, the DPS acquired control of the absolute majority of seats in the Parliament. Since political pluralism in the republic was still nascent at this time, the former communists had a sufficient majority to control most of the Montenegrin institutions. However, the doctrine of communism was no longer the main ideological pillar of the party. Rather, the DPS was a conglomerate of politically heterogeneous elements, held together by a common wish for political survival. During the uncertainty caused by the fall of communism and the wars in the former Yugoslavia, the DPS's political survival was only possible by upholding the ethno-religious cleavages that had emerged across the region.

These cleavages continued to reproduce themselves on the Montenegrin political scene in the following years. According to Darmanović (1992), "society was constantly diverted from the important political issues the party wasn't able to solve, and at the same time homogenized through the incessant production of enemies both without (Croatian, Slovenian) and within (Muslims, Albanian, 'Montenegrin secessionists')" (28). In the Montenegrin political context, a stark difference emerged between the ruling DPS, which predominantly attracted the Christian-Orthodox majority, and the parties of ethno-religious minorities, such as Albanians, Bosniaks, and Muslims. In addition to these, two further parties emphasizing predominantly structural cleavages appeared in the republic. The Liberal Alliance of Montenegro (LSCG), a Montenegrin nationalist Movement, and the People's Party (NS), which emphasized the Serbian origins of Montenegrins, represented political players which indicated the existence of the rift among the majority of the population as well. However, due to the mesmerization of most of the population by Serbian nationalism in the early 1990s, this cleavage remained subdued until the dominant political players changed their nationalist rhetoric.

The end of the conflict in the former Yugoslavia soothed the overall political context in Montenegro, thus decreasing the level of Serb nationalism among the political elites in general. As a consequence, the critical juncture represented by the split of the DPS in 1997 yielded predominantly functional cleavages based on support of and opposition to Milošević.[3] Yet, structural cleavages re-emerged following the change of regime in Belgrade in October 2000. The two camps, which previously defined themselves through their relationship to the regime in Belgrade, became deprived of their primary meaning. The new political reality required the reinvention of their political agendas. Đukanović's DPS acquired the role of advocate of Montenegrin independence. By contrast, Bulatović's SNP came to epitomize the preservation of the common state with Serbia. As the identities of the two political camps evolved, these two wings of the former communists became two opposing poles for the Montenegrin population to identify with.

The consequence of this bifurcation of Montenegrin politics was the exacerbation of the structural cleavage among the population: that is, the differentiation between Serbs and Montenegrins, which arose from people's affiliation with unionist or pro-independence movements. This is illustrated in Table 1, which presents an overview of the first parliamentary elections after the ousting of Milošević.

If the Montenegrin parliamentary elections of 2001 are taken as the indicators of the societal division, it is notable that only 0.37% of the electorate remained neutral in the divide (CDT 2001 "Official results: Parliamentary Elections, 22 April 2001"; CDT 2002 "Official results: Parliamentary Elections, 20 October 2002"). The political players supported by that electorate were shaped by functional cleavages. One example of this is the parties concerned with the negative effects of transition, such as the loss of savings due to pyramid schemes in the early 1990s. The remaining parties revolved around two centres with slightly greater support for the independence than for the unionist cause, which is further proof of the dominance of the structural cleavages between the two camps after the removal of Milošević.

Table 1. Polarization of Montenegrin political life in April 2001[i]

Party/Coalition	Affiliation	%
Liberal Alliance of Montenegro	MNE	7.9
Serbian Radical Party "Dr Vojislav Šešelj"	YUG	1.2
Liberal Democratic Party	MNE	0.1
Party of Democratic Prosperity – Osman Redža	MNE	0.4
Democratic Alliance of Montenegro	MNE	1.0
Bosniak-Muslim Coalition in Montenegro	MNE	1.1
Party protecting the savings and social security of citizens	N/A	0.05
Together for Yugoslavia	YUG	40.8
People's Unity for Montenegro – Dr Novak Kilibarda	MNE	0.1
Democratic Union of Albanians	MNE	1.2
Yugoslav left in Montenegro	YUG	0.05
Party protecting the savings in foreign currency	N/A	0.2
"Victory is Montenegro" – Milo Đukanović	MNE	42.4
Communist and Workers' Parties – for Yugoslavia and self-management	YUG	0.5
Party of the Law of Nature	N/A	0.1
People's Socialist Party – Momir Bulatović	YUG	2.9
	Summary	
	For independence	54.14
	For Yugoslavia	45.49
	Neutral	0.37

[i]Table constructed in line with data from: Centar za Demokratsku Tranziciju, *Official results: Parliamentary Elections, 22 April 2001*. http://www.cdtmn.org/dokumenti/zvanicni-rezultati-parlamentarni-izbori-2001.pdf [accessed: 25 June 2011]

Dominance of functional cleavages at critical junctures

When concerns other than the competition between ethno-culturally diverse groups prevail in a society, functional cleavages emerge at critical junctures. This, however, does not imply that they triumph over the existing structural cleavages. Rather, they complement them, and temporarily change the dynamics of inter-group competition in the polity, as was the case in Montenegro in 1997 and 2006.

The creation of two factions within the DPS in 1997 triggered the reorganization of Montenegrin party politics. This occurred through the rapprochement of Đukanović's wing of the DPS with the anti-Milošević, yet pro-Serb, People's Party (NS), the parties of ethno-cultural minorities, such as Bosniaks and Albanians, and the multiethnic Social Democratic Party (SDP). Thus, the mediation of the ethno-cultural cleavage is apparent in the way Đukanović's camp was established. At the time Đukanović's DPS made hardly any reference to national identity in Montenegro, while the remaining parties that coalesced around the DPS had very diversified agendas. The SNP, which became the major opposition player, retained some of the DPS's nationalist rhetoric from the early 1990s, which is attributable to its continued association with Milošević. Still, according to its founder, Momir Bulatović (2005, 238–242), the party was also significantly driven by a functional cleavage, i.e., it emphasized the corrupt nature of Đukanović's DPS, and the illegal enrichment of the elites at the time of the international embargo in the early 1990s.

The rift in Montenegrin politics created at this critical juncture was revealed on two occasions – the 1997 Presidential Elections and the 1998 Parliamentary Elections. Both elections produced extremely close results for the two factions of the former DPS. This reinforces the argument that two poles of critical mass were formed either in opposition to or in favour of Milošević's politics. This is illustrated in Table 2, which presents an overview of the parties and their affiliation in the 1998 Parliamentary Elections.

The dominance of functional cleavages at these elections is supported by the fact that the question of Montenegrin independence was not the main point on the agenda of either political bloc. Rather, it was the issue of support for or opposition to Milošević, and the future of political and economic reforms in Montenegro and in Yugoslavia. The degree of polarization is reflected in the election results, which reveal that a very small percentage of the political spectrum in Montenegro (0.4% of the electorate) was neutral on this issue. Kubo and Strmiska claim that this division was not based on the national sentiments of the population. They support this argument by looking at the 1991 census data, and by noticing the minimal support for the parties with "ethnic prefixes" (Kubo 2007, 163–180; Strmiska 2005 "The Making of Party Pluralism in Montenegro"). Hence, ethno-cultural cleavages were not captured and transplanted into party politics at the critical juncture in 1997.

Following the split in the DPS, the Montenegrin political scene remained polarized. Notwithstanding this, the shaping of the republic's political milieu was not finalized in 1997. Instead, the profiles of the political parties changed shape in the following years. This process took place in an environment created by the rupture in the DPS, Đukanović's detachment from Milošević, and the subsequent creation of the two opposed political blocs. By countering Milošević's policies from 1997 to 2000, the Montenegrin leadership embarked on a course of "creeping independence". The by-product of such a policy – which entailed detachment from the federal institutions – was that the DPS gradually transformed its opposition to the regime in Belgrade into a quest for statehood (van Meurs 2003, 63–82). This affected the nature of the 2000 critical juncture,[4] after which

Table 2. Polarization of Montenegrin political life in May 1998[i]

Party/Coalition	Affiliation	%
Liberal Alliance of Montenegro	AM	6.3
Serbian Radical Party "Dr Vojislav Šešelj"	PM	1.2
For Serbdom	PM	0.4
Serbian People's Radical Party in Montenegro	PM	0.2
Yugoslav United Left in Montenegro	PM	0.1
Democratic Alliance in Montenegro	AM	1.6
Bosniak-Muslim List in Montenegro	AM	0.1
Party of the Law of Nature	N/A	0.2
Socialist People's Party – Momir Bulatović	PM	36.1
Serbian People's Party	PM	1.9
Party protecting the savings in foreign currency	N/A	0.1
League of Communists of Yugoslavia – Communists of Montenegro	PM	0.5
"For a Better Life" – Milo Đukanović	AM	49.5
Party of Citizens having savings in foreign currency	N/A	0.1
Party of Democratic Action in Montenegro	AM	0.6
Democratic Union of Albanians	AM	1.0
Party of Human Ways	N/A	0.1
	Summary	
	Pro-Milošević	40.45
	Anti-Milošević	59.14
	Neutral	0.41

[i]Table constructed by this author with data from: Centar za Demokratsku Tranziciju, *Official results: Parliamentary Elections, 31 May 1998*. http://www.cdtmn.org/dokumenti/zvanicni-rezultati-parlamentarni-izbori-1998.pdf [accessed: 25 June 2011]

the structural cleavages prevailed over the functional ones until the resolution of the status question in the 2006 referendum on independence.

The referendum was the most recent critical juncture for Montenegrin party politics and it sparked the recalibration of the political scene. The DPS remained the major political player, having claimed victory at the referendum. However, prior to the elections in September 2006, the former unionists split into three factions of approximately equal size. The SNP – the pillar of the former unionist bloc – was the first party to show a willingness to change its political program and abandon its nationalist rhetoric. This change was generated immediately after the publication of the referendum results, and was manifested through attempts to balance the loss at the plebiscite with the preservation of the SNP's electorate. The continuing discord was mostly displayed by the SNS, which became the party representative of the Serbs in Montenegro. The SNS called for the formation of the "Serbian List" coalition. However, this call did not resonate well with the rest of the opposition bloc, since the SNP rejected the proposal as it considered itself a "civic" party. Moreover, new political forces entered the scene, the most notable example being the Movement for Change (PzP). The PzP grew out of an NGO focused on reforms and the development of economic policies different from the ones proposed by the government. Therefore, after the critical juncture of 2006, new functional cleavages emerged and changed the dynamics of political struggle in Montenegro.

Political agents and the rise of cleavages through ethno-cultural narratives

Since cleavages are representations of conflict in a society, looking at the way they are related to one another helps us to understand the political dynamics in that society.

Cleavages that emerge as a result of divisions in a polity can be independent, overlapping, or cross-cutting in relation to each other. If cleavages are independent, they are unrelated to other cleavages that have been created. For instance, in Albania the population is either Christian (Orthodox or Catholic) or Muslim. Although there are other cleavages in the country (e.g. class), the religious cleavage is largely unrelated to it and thus independent. If cleavages are overlapping, they reinforce one another and thus create deeper societal divisions and sharper distinctions among the population. Such is the case with Northern Ireland, whereby the religious cleavage overlaps with the political one, thus emphasising the distinction between nationalists and unionists. If a cleavage is cross-cutting, it is divisive but not in a neat fashion, as it can be associated with multiple groups. Such cleavages are often reinforced by other overlapping cleavages in societies with manifest ethno-cultural plurality. Switzerland is an example of a society in which the linguistic cleavage is supplemented by the religious one, and thus perpetuates the specificities of the different ethnic groups. In such cases, more often than not, the overlapping cleavage will have a manifest dominance in shaping the group, because it will make a clear distinction between communities.

In the case of Montenegro, some of these cleavages already existed, and were simply reinforced. Only after the political actors triggered the overlapping structural (ethno-cultural) cleavages did the inherent divisions among the people become apparent. The revival of ethno-cultural narratives that made a clear distinction between Serb and Montenegrin identities helped the two camps to shape their political identities. In the early 1990s, neither the religious, cultural, nor symbolic cleavages were markers that would distinguish "Montenegrin" and "Serb" aspects of identity in Montenegro. For this reason, and in contrast to the other successor states of the former Yugoslavia, identity in Montenegro was dual.[5] That is, a number of people felt "Montenegrin" and "Serb" at the same time. The divide over statehood in Montenegro eventually led to the reconstruction of "Montenegrin" and "Serb" identities and their association with pro-independence and unionist camps, respectively.

Religion: an ethno-cultural cleavage or a political epiphenomenon?

After the fall of the socialist regime, there was a reawakening of religious belief among the people of Eastern Europe. Some academics explain that phenomenon by focusing on the revival of religion (suppressed during the communist era) as a pillar of new identities across the region (Krastev and Mungiu-Pippidi 2004, 10–25). Although decades of socialist rule had created a strong attachment to the concept of "group" or "class", once socialism no longer exercised influence, people needed a substitute to recreate the nature of their group attachment, which could no longer be represented by "class". Thus, reverting to religion served as one of the tools that assisted the "re-imagination" of the identities of the newly formed states. Such was the case with the other republics in the former Yugoslavia. Nevertheless, in Montenegro the religious cleavage was not initially a source of differentiation among the Christian Orthodox population. Until 2000, Orthodox Christianity was a means of differentiating the majority of the population in Montenegro from Albanian, Bosniak, Croat and Muslim minorities. After the bifurcation of the Montenegrin political scene into pro-independence/pro-Montenegrin and unionist/pro-Serb camps, the association with predominantly the Serbian (SPC) or, to a lesser degree, the Montenegrin (CPC) Orthodox Church became a politicized ethno-cultural cleavage. However, the DPS elite also sought to attract non-Christian Orthodox minorities to their cause and thus were very careful over the question of religion (Morrison 2009a, 47). Due to this ambiguity over the position of the CPC among the DPS, the religious cleavage only reinforced the existing narratives when overlapping with other cleavages. In other words, the religious cleavage was never as dominant in Montenegro as it has been, for instance, in Bosnia and Herzegovina. Thus, the association with the Church as an epi-political institution became a layer of identity.

The CPC as it is today appeared in the early 1990s and claimed its historical existence in Montenegro until the unification of Yugoslavia in 1918, when it was subsumed by the SPC (Morison 2009a, 45–60; Ramet 2005, 255–285). Initially, the CPC was not recognized by the authorities of the state, who, throughout most of the 1990s, supported the SPC (*Pobjeda*, January 6, 1995, 2). Only when the identity of his camp was established as pro-independence did Đukanović acknowledge – yet not openly support – the existence of the CPC. The likely reasons for this were that 1) most of the DPS supporters identified with the SPC throughout the 1990s; and that 2) most of the historical religious buildings were owned by the SPC, which facilitated the identification of people with that church.

The complex relationship between the two churches – and their affiliation with the Montenegrin authorities – has roots in different interpretations of Montenegrin identity. The Metropolitan of the Serbian Orthodox Church claimed that "Montenegrin identity is a historical fiction. Serbs and Montenegrins are the same people, the same nation" (Santoro 1999, 8). The attitude of the SPC resonated strongly with the members of the opposition block who, according to the public opinion polls, identified primarily with this church, implying that the Metropolitan Amfilohije was the person they had greatest confidence in (CEDEM 2005). Public opinion polls further point to the importance of religion among the supporters of the pro-union bloc, who perceived the divide in Montenegro primarily as a rift in the Orthodox population (*pravoslavni živalj*). Consequently, for the unionist/pro-Serbian opposition, the emphasis on Orthodox Christianity was an important marker of identity. It helped create the image of ethnic identity firmly rooted in the religious cleavage.

The opposite was only partly true for the members of the pro-independence/pro-Montenegrin camp as the position of the CPC is controversial in the DPS and among its supporters. As a consequence, the religious cleavage in this political camp was not emphasized to the same extent as among the opposition members. The supporters of the DPS, which advocated independent statehood in the 2006 Montenegrin referendum, often identified themselves with the SPC rather than the CPC. The CPC was endorsed by minor parties promoting the independence of Montenegro, such as the SDP and LSCG. Thus, religion had a largely political connotation for the pro-independence camp. As a political epiphenomenon, the CPC challenged the religious dominion of the SPC. The CPC provided a point of reference for those people in the pro-independence camp who cherished religion as a part of their identity, but did not wish to be identified with a church that had the prefix "Serb" in its name. Moreover – given the fact that orthodox Christianity does not have a centralized, but a national church system – for some members of the pro-independence camp, the existence of the CPC legitimized the separateness of Montenegrin identity and the quest for statehood. As a consequence, "the struggle for the church [became] essentially the struggle for statehood" (Santoro 1999, 8). Religion thus proved to be a political, rather than an ethno-cultural cleavage in the struggle over statehood and identity in Montenegro.

Revival of tribalism as an ethno-cultural cleavage

In Montenegrin society, the concept of the tribe is historically grounded in the collective memory, as a "military, political and moral collective" that controlled its members (Jovanović 1995, 65; Boehm 1983). However, the revival of a new form of tribal structure also became an ethno-cultural cleavage in the battle over statehood and identity. Through the ascription of individuals to a particular tribe, and tribes to a particular political movement, the history and tradition of Montenegro became tools through which a political idea reached the population. Throughout history tribes never went to war against each other for ideological or political reasons, and although "tribes changed with history, they always bore the responsibility for government in a unified Montenegro" (Calhoun 2000, 38).

In the context of the divide over statehood and identity, tribes became reinvented as an emblem of folk culture, so as to generate a feeling of national belonging. However, within a different socio-political context, this historical symbol gained a completely different meaning. According to Popović, the revival of tribal structures in Montenegrin society was a means for Milošević's followers to "build some new, alternative, however false, source of legitimacy" after their political defeats in the previous years (Popović 2002, 23). Against such a view, the unionist camp maintained that during 1999 and 2000, the gatherings – sports competitions, political discussions, poetry evenings – were assemblies aimed at revitalising this camp's political strength (*Pobjeda*, October–November, 1999). They were most attended in the northern part of Montenegro, where the support for the pro-union bloc was dominant.

These gatherings resulted in the formation of the Council of People's Assemblies, the central association of these tribes. Its name was reminiscent of historical gatherings of tribal chieftains during the dynastic rule. Such a reproduction of history was criticized by the government for its distortion of history and its appropriation for the achievement of political aims (*Pobjeda*, September 19, 1999, 1). In addition, these gatherings also provoked the reinvention of pro-Montenegrin neo-tribes as a challenge to the supporters of the Yugoslav idea. These new tribes – associated with the idea of independent Montenegrin statehood – were located southwest of the Zeta River. Unlike their northern counterparts, united under a central association with a clear political purpose, the congregations of the southern tribes usually took the shape of more informal folklore or sports gatherings.

According to Calhoun (2000, 35), these differences marked a rift between the Old Montenegrin tribes and the Brda tribes, giving the struggle over statehood and identity a geographical dimension. This division was important, since the Brda tribes were incorporated into Montenegro only in the nineteenth and twentieth centuries, by the acquisition of territory following the weakening of the Ottoman Empire. Subsequently, in light of the new political struggles, the Brda tribes associated themselves with unionist ideas and professed the idea of the Serbian origins of Montenegrins. This process was facilitated by a) these tribes' geographical proximity to Serbia; and b) the emphasis – in the political discourse – on these tribes' traditional ties with Serbia (Simić 1997, 124–131). Thus tribalism, as a politically driven ethno-cultural cleavage, helped to create new imagined lines of division such as regional differences between the North and South in Montenegro.

The divisive function of symbols

The "implicit meanings" of the symbols of the state, such as the flag, the coat of arms, or the national anthem, have often been connected to people's histories (Douglas 1975, 14). According to Andrijašević (1998, 28), "history, as an important element of the identity of a community, offsets the action, gives an example, strengthens hopes and reminds of a grand goal that needs to be achieved". Accordingly, symbols proved to be an important, politically generated, ethno-cultural cleavage in the polemic surrounding statehood and identity in Montenegro. Both camps reinterpreted history in order to give legitimacy to their claims in the eyes of the public. After 2000, the pro-independence interpretation of tradition distanced Montenegro from Serbia and the common state with it. The opposition camp challenged this view and tried to preserve the old symbols and their meaning, seeking to remain in the common state with Serbia. Since both claims were to a certain extent historically justified, the state symbols of Montenegro all became a central part of the debate on statehood and identity. In particular, the ruling DPS "utilised emotive rhetoric intended to appeal to the romantic inclinations of the Montenegrin people, [...] as a brave, honourable, and independent people. Contemporary Montenegrins, they argued, were presented with a unique historical mission – to correct the grievances felt by their forefathers who had to bear the loss of Montenegrin independence in 1918" (Morrison 2009b, 46).

The present symbols of the Montenegrin state still prove controversial, and a source of on-going political divisions (Milošević 2012). Having been adopted at the time of the divide over statehood and identity by the ruling DPS-led camp, they bear references to the independent Principality and later Kingdom of Montenegro, and thus to the Montenegrin state tradition. This "rather romanticized reworking of history blended with contemporary arguments" (Morrison 2009b, 46) reinforced the ruling elite's rhetoric for the need of an independent Montenegro as the continuation of the long tradition of statehood prior to 1918.

Hence, the politicization of symbols as an ethno-cultural cleavage was very much rooted in the debates over their historical meaning and connotations. In fact, at the peak of the divide, the pro-independence/pro-Montenegrin government adopted a new Law on State Symbols in 2004, which redefined the coat of arms and the flag of Montenegro. The Law described the coat of arms of Montenegro as "a golden crowned double-headed eagle with its wings in flight, with a sceptre in its right and an orb in its left claw on a red base. On the eagle's chest is a shield with a golden lion passant" (art. 4). Following Article 5 of the Law, the flag of Montenegro was red, bordered in gold, and with the coat of arms in the middle. The unionists claimed that a departure from history had been made, since the traditional Montenegrin flag used to be red, blue and white (like the Serbian one), with a white eagle (also similar to the Serbian coat of arms) (Đurković 2007, 6). However, an examination of the Montenegrin flags and coats of arms indicates that the new Montenegrin flag is a combination of the background of the dynastic army flag (red background with a golden border), the coat of arms of the Principality of Montenegro prior to the arrival of King Nikola (white eagle) and the colour of the eagle from King Nikola's flag. Actually, the army flag of King Nicholas did not have a golden border, and although the eagle was – unlike in the previous Montenegrin flags – golden, it did not have a lion on its chest, but the symbols of the ruler (Andrijašević, 2004, 51). This implies that state symbols became an important element of the DPS-camp's attempts to romanticize the image of the nation, and that the continuing conflict over their meaning perpetuates an ethno-cultural cleavage in Montenegrin society.

There was a similar controversy over the national anthem, whereby the government attempted to eliminate all reference to what may have been interpreted as a Serbian aspect of Montenegrin identity. In 2004, the text of the national anthem *Oj svijetla majska zoro* ("Oh, the bright dawn of May") was altered by the ruling elite. The controversial text of the anthem has, similarly to the state symbols, been created out of several historical texts. A portion of the anthem's text existed in the folk tradition of Montenegro, and was reworked in 1932 by Sekula Drljević, the interwar leader of the Montenegrin federalists who later collaborated with the Italians closely allied with the Croatian *ustaša* movement (Marković and Pajović 1996). While the meaning of the anthem has never been contested in the political discourse, the fact that two of its verses were written by Drljević is still controversial. By using Drljević's version of the text, the DPS leaders sought to reinforce the idea of Montenegro's tradition of statehood and the struggle for it, as the interwar federalist movement largely carried nationalist elements. However, the association of the federalists with fascism proved controversial not only between the two blocs, but also within the DPS itself. This has been emphasized in the recent statement by the Montenegrin President, Filip Vujanović, who noted

> I have no objection regarding the content of the two verses. On the contrary, I respect the content of those verses, and I am absolutely convinced that the final message is an excellent one: 'So may Montenegro live forever!', and I think that our anthem should end with that message. What is impossible to relate to the anti-fascist Montenegro is the authorship of those two verses. It is beyond any doubt that the authorship of those verses belongs to a man who does not belong to the anti-fascist movement in Montenegro, but who rather represents the negation of anti-fascism in Montenegro. (Vujanović 2011)

In this context, the discord over symbols in Montenegro points to the importance of history for the imagination of the nation. It also indicates how political elites can use those symbols and make them widely available to the public, yet wrapped up in their own agendas. Once such divisive symbols become a part of the polity's living reality, they bear in themselves a part of the political conflict and transform into another politically malleable ethno-cultural cleavage.

Language as an ethno-cultural cleavage

The question of language is inextricably related to education, the press, and the general transmission of ideas, as noted by most academic work on nationalism and identity (e.g. Hobsbawm and Ranger 1983; Gellner 1994; Anderson 1991). In the Balkans, ever since the romantic ideas of the unification of the South Slavs in the mid-nineteenth century, language has been an important aspect of how people viewed themselves (White 2000, 170–188). As a consequence of the events in the region in the 1990s, language developed a political aspect and became related to territory, i.e. to the "political organization of space" (White 2000, 181).

According to Article 9 of the 1992 Constitution, the "language in official use" in Montenegro was the *ijekavski* dialect of Serbian. Prior to the disintegration of Yugoslavia, the language was termed Serbo-Croatian/Croato-Serbian. After the break-up of the former Yugoslavia, the successor states enshrined separate languages in their constitutional frameworks, named after the state or having reference to it (Radojević 1989, 7). In the FRY, and in Montenegro, the official language remained Serbian, which changed after Montenegro became an independent state. The constitutional provisions related to language are a further indication of the politicization of a cleavage, which reinforced the ethno-cultural narrative of the ruling elite.

In Article 13, the Constitution of Montenegro of 2007 stipulates that the "official language in Montenegro is Montenegrin", while "Serbian, Bosnian, Albanian and Croatian" are "officially used languages". During the constitutional debate, the denomination of the language as Montenegrin faced fierce opposition from the former unionist bloc, which deemed it a political move (*Pobjeda*, June 20, 2006). The unionist bloc supported the preservation of the name of the official language as Serbian, arguing that, in line with the 2003 population census (Zavod za Statistiku Crne Gore 2003), 59.7 % of the people spoke the Serbian language, while 21.5% spoke Montenegrin.

At the same time, for the former pro-independence camp terming the language as Montenegrin gave legal guarantees to the political prevalence of their concept of identity based on historical grievances. The revival of the discourse over the Montenegrin language has been reinforced by the activities of the pro-independence cultural organizations, such as the Montenegrin PEN centre, and in the writings of the linguists Vojislav Nikčević and Borislav Jovanović. In the context of historical grievances, Jovanović claimed that "the Montenegrin language is still seen as linguistically deviant – as a variant, sub-variant [...]in line with the unitary and assimilationist philological conceptions. However, despite this suppression, the Montenegrin language is not a dead language" (Jovanović 2005, 10).

In addition to denominating the language as "Montenegrin", in July 2009, the Ministry of Education of Montenegro adopted new orthographic norms, according to which the Montenegrin alphabet no longer has 30 graphemes, but 32 (ś and ź have been added). Montenegro is the only former Yugoslav successor state that has changed the alphabet, which is another indicator of the politicization of language which has thus became a structural cleavage. The divisiveness of language has also been manifest in the 2011 population census (Zavod za Statistiku Crne Gore 2011), whereby 39.8% of the population declared Montenegrin to be their native tongue, against 42.9 % speakers of Serbian. Keeping in mind that 45% of Montenegro's population declared themselves Montenegrin and 28.7% as Serb in 2011, and the above-presented 2003 census results on language, there is an indication that the overlap between language and ethnic/national identity remains fluid. However, the process is largely unfinished, which points to the fact that the linguistic cleavage displays its ethno-cultural nature once politicized and adjoined to other structural cleavages.

Structuration and the typology of cleavages

In unconsolidated political contexts cleavages are particularly susceptible to manipulation by political actors. At the time of the divide over statehood and identity, Montenegrin political elites revived ethno-cultural narratives[6] and triggered the dominance of structural cleavages over the functional ones. In fact, in the late 1990s Montenegro was a society that was recovering from the effects of a negative transition, triggered by the instability that followed the disintegration of Yugoslavia (Popović 2002, 11–37). As a consequence of a series of political processes, Montenegro's political scene became highly polarized in 1997, and elite competition for power became significant. Given the dynamics of elite competition, and the change in the structure of opportunities and constraints generated by Milošević's departure from power, the politicization of cleavages became a major factor in attracting the electorate to the two camps. This politicization was possible due to the fluid cultural divides and the dual character of national identity throughout Montenegro's history (Roberts 2007). Consequently, old divides (e.g. religious, tribal, class, ethnic) became politicized and transformed into ethno-cultural cleavages. As such, they became quintessential for the establishment of the identity of both the leadership and the supporters of the pro-independence/pro-Montenegrin and unionist/pro-Serb camps.

Hence, the divide over Montenegrin statehood is therefore associated with a still on-going process in which cross-cutting ethno-cultural cleavages (the duality of national identity in Montenegro) are reorganized into overlapping ethno-cultural cleavages (Montenegrin vs. Serbian national identity).The overlapping cleavages that marked Montenegro's divide over statehood and identity helped in cementing ideas of the ethno-cultural particularity of Serbs and Montenegrins to the unionist and pro-independence camps respectively. That is, the more overlapping cleavages that were revived, the more it was possible to gather them round one political representation of identity. The fact that the two competing camps associated religion with ethnic and tribal belonging meant that the political competition occurred between two players and that these cleavages did not allow for the emergence of further competitors for power. In the case of Montenegro, this is illustrated by *those* people who felt Montenegrin, associated with the idea of independence, neo-Montenegrin tribes, and the CPC; and by *those* people who felt Serb, associated with the idea of the preservation of the common state, pro-Serbian tribes, and the SPC. The divide between the two camps in Montenegro cut deep into society, because overlapping cleavages tend to reinforce perceptions of identity.

Yet, the overlapping cleavages were necessary to crystallize the difference between the two camps, largely because many of the pre-existing cleavages were cross-cutting. That is, a very similar language, or the same religion could be associated with more than one camp. The actual difference between the Serb and the Montenegrin language, particularly prior to the standardization of the latter in 2009, was merely denominative. Equally, whether an individual would affiliate with the SPC or the CPC was a matter of political rather than religious choice. In cases of cross-cutting cleavages, people's perception of their own identity is usually malleable in that it is likely that it will be associated with their political or economic interests. In such cases, the activities of political elites have a pivotal role in determining individuals' ascription to identity camps by reinforcing the cross-cutting cleavage with an overlapping one. In the case of Montenegro, this explains the cases of *those* people who felt Montenegrin and voted for independence, but associated with SPC and spoke Serbian; or *those* people, for example, who felt Serbian, associated with SPC and spoke Serbian, but voted for Montenegrin independence. Therefore, in Montenegro, the overlapping cleavages overcame the cross-cutting ones as the determinant of the individuals' political choice.

Conclusion

Studying political parties and political systems of different countries in the world assumes an awareness of those moments in history in which social conflicts were frozen and transferred onto the political plane. The role of political elites in freezing conflicts and thus in establishing, changing, or perpetuating cleavages has only recently become a prominent research topic among political scientists (Enyedi 2006, 228–238), and this is largely due to the rise of new democracies in Europe. Looking at how political parties emerged in the post-communist world, Zielinski (2002, 185) noted that the degree of the politicization of cleavages is largely dependent on the activities of political elites, who may opt for instituting a particular type of cleavage as the core of political competition.

Against this background, this paper has contextualized and analyzed the multifaceted and complex factors that have given rise to cleavages in the recent contests over statehood and identity in Montenegro. It has argued that in polities in transition, in which the processes of state and nation building are unfinished or unconsolidated, cleavages related to ethnic identity become salient in political competition. As such, cleavages become axes around which the political parties, which usually represent different ethno-cultural groups, compete for power. Moreover, looking in more detail at the case of Montenegro, this paper also showed that memories of historical divisions, particularly those related to structural cleavages (over religion, language, and culture), are recreated as catalysts of modern political struggles.

This study has identified the critical junctures in the divide over statehood and identity in Montenegro, by looking at those moments in recent history in which conflict was frozen and transformed into cleavages. The paper examined four crucial moments, and maintained that the 1989 "anti-bureaucratic" revolutions and the 2000 fall of Milošević gave rise to structural (ethno-cultural) cleavages, while the 1997 split of the DPS and 2006 Montenegro's independence generated predominantly functional (class and operational) cleavages. The paper also outlined differences in the nature and intensity of the cleavages that emerged at different points in Montenegro's transition, and in the context of the division over statehood and identity particular attention was paid to the cleavages that took place after 1997. In fact, the split within the DPS in 1997 initiated a series of political struggles that had resulted in the establishment of two political blocs by 2006: pro-independence and pro-union. However, as no society functions as an isolated system, the shaping of people's identity and the divide into pro-independence Montenegrins and unionist Serbs that followed was a product of a larger process. This process entailed the interaction among elites, society and exogenous influences, such as the fall of Milošević in 2000, which triggered the reinvention of the agendas of political elites and prompted the rise of further ethno-cultural cleavages. The cumulative effect of the various cleavages helped the transition of Đukanović's camp from anti-Milošević to pro-independence and of the opposition camp from pro-Milošević to unionist. Montenegrin and Serbian identities, respectively, became hardened into these two camps.

The paper also looked at the different ethno-cultural narratives that were used to underpin the emergence of structural cleavages and their prevalence over functional ones. This susceptibility of cleavages to political agency gained prominence after the demise of the Milošević regime in Belgrade, when the focus of elite competition shifted towards the debate over statehood and identity. In that respect, past events provided enough reference for the Montenegrin leadership to find examples of historical justification for their claims related to either a) independent Montenegrin statehood and separate Montenegrin identity; or b) the unification with Serbia and the indistinguishability of Serbs and Montenegrins. The fact that the two competing camps selectively endorsed these narratives reinforced their arguments and made their claims "difficult to challenge, even to disbelieve" (Sinfield 1992, 33).

This transfer of historical memory has particular significance for societies undergoing a process of transformation after the fall of socialist rule. Old stories needed to be revived to justify social change. The memories of previous, living generations dated back largely to the period of socialist rule. Thus, historical narratives of the dynastic rule, heroism and glory gained salience in shaping people's identity because they transcended the period remembered by the living generations. The competing elites in Montenegro placed emphasis on these stories through their discourse, use of symbols, and erection of monuments. In this polarized environment, two competing streams of collective memory were revived in order to increase the appeal of the claims of the competing camps. The difference between these streams was not merely the selection of facts surrounding historical events. Rather, it was the interpretation of the facts that was used to justify the contemporary political claims.

The study concludes by arguing that different types of cleavage had different types of impact on political competition in Montenegro. Using Montenegro as a case-study, this paper argues that the number of identity camps depends on the type of cleavages (independent, overlapping, cross-cutting) in the polity. The more independent (unrelated to other cleavages) cleavages there are, the more identity camps will gain significance in the struggle for power; the more overlapping cleavages there are, the more likely they will coalesce around one political representation of identity. Yet, if the cleavages are cross-cutting (that is – cutting across several groups), then people's perception of their own identity is more likely to change. In such cases, the activities of political elites have a pivotal role in determining individuals' ascription to identity camps, as shown by the case of Montenegro.

Acknowledgements

This paper was originally presented at the 41st Annual UACES conference in Cambridge, in September 2011. It was written during my research fellowship at the University of Edinburgh (CITSEE project) and revised during my stay at the European University Institute in Florence. I am grateful to Prof. Bernhard Stahl and to Dr. Soeren Keil for their useful comments on an earlier draft. I am also thankful to Prof. Jo Shaw and Dr. Igor Štiks from the University of Edinburgh (CITSEE project) for their academic and professional guidance.

Notes

1. All factions are rounded to the first decimal.
2. Negative transition: stability to instability.
3. See section 2.2.
4. The 1999 Kosovo war did not feature as a critical juncture in Montenegro, because it did not cause any major political shifts. Rather, the handling of the Kosovo war by Đukanović's camp was a part of the policy of "creeping independence". For the pro-Milošević camp, the conflict reaffirmed the existing political beliefs based on close links with Serbia.
5. Identity in Slovenia articulated itself through both linguistic and religious particularities; in the case of Croatia, religion was a clear marker of identity from the identities with which it shared the same language; in Macedonia language was a marker of difference from identities with which it shared the same religion; and the case of the three conflicting identities in Bosnia and Herzegovina proved the importance of religious cleavages in the process of identity reconstruction after the break-up of Yugoslavia.
6. The party political cleavages that existed in Montenegro's history did not reproduce themselves during the divide (see Morrison). Rather, the narrative of the divide between Greens and Whites, opposing and supporting the unconditional unification of Montenegro with Serbia in 1918, became entrenched in the narratives that helped to establish the identities of the pro-independence and unionist camps.

References

Anderson, Benedict. 1991. *Imagined Communities*. London: Verso.
Andrijašević, Živko. 1998. *Crnogorske Teme*. Podgorica: Istorijski institut.
Andrijašević, Živko. 2004. *Nacija s greškom*. Cetinje: Đurđe Crnojević.
Bartolini, Stefano. 2005. *Restructuring Europe. Centre formation, system building and political structuring between the nation-state and the European Union*. Oxford: Oxford University Press.
Bieber, Florian. 2003. "Montenegrin politics since the disintegration of Yugoslavia." in *Montenegro in Transition: Problems of Identity and Statehood,* edited by Florian Biebar, 11–42. Baden-Baden: Nomos.
Boehm, Christopher. 1983. *Montenegrin Social Organization and Values: Political Ethnography of a Refugee Area Tribal Adaptation*. New York: AMS Press.
Bulatović, Momir. 2005. *Pravila ćutanja*. Niš: Zograf.
Calhoun, Steven. 2000. "Montenegro's Tribal Legacy." *Military Review* 80 (4): 32–40.
Centre for Democracy and Human Rights (CEDEM). 2005. *Public Opinion in Montenegro: December 2005*. Podgorica: CEDEM.
Centar za Demokratsku Tranziciju (CDT). 2001. *Official results: Parliamentary Elections, 22 April 2001*. http://www.cdtmn.org/dokumenti/zvanicni-rezultati-parlamentarni-izbori-2001.pdf
Centar za Demokratsku Tranziciju (CDT). 2002. *Official results: Parliamentary Elections, 20 October 2002*. http://www.cdtmn.org/dokumenti/zvanicni-rezultati-parlamentarni-izbori-2002.pdf
Centar za Demokratsku Tranziciju (CDT). 2006. *Referendum 21/05/2006* (23 May 2006). http://www.cdtmn.org/izbori/referendum06.php
Darmanović, Srđan. 1992. "Montenegro: Destiny of a Satellite State." *Eastern European Reporter* 27 (March–April): 27–29.
Douglas, Mary. 1975. *Implicit Meanings*. London: Penguin.

Đilas, Milovan. 1947. "O crnogorskom nacionalnom pitanju." *Članci 1941-1946*. Beograd: Kultura.
Đurković, Miša. 2007. "Montenegro: Headed for New Divisions." *Conflict Studies Research Centre* 07/09 (Swindon: Defence Academy of the United Kingdom, March): 1–14.
Enyedi, Zsolt. 2006. "Party politics in post-communist transition." In *Handbook of Party Politics*, edited by R. S. Katz and W. Crotty, 228–238. London: Sage.
Federal Statistical Office. *Population Census 1981, 1991*. 1992. Belgrade: FZS.
Gellner, Ernest. 1994. *Encounters with Nationalism*. Oxford, UK and Cambridge, MA: Blackwell.
Hobsbawm, Eric, and Terence Ranger. 1983. *The Invention of Tradition*. Cambridge: Cambridge University Press.
Hodson, Randy, Duško Sekulić, and Garth Massey. 1994. "National Tolerance in Yugoslavia." *American Journal of Sociology* 99 (6): 1534–1558.
International Crisis Group. 2000. *Montenegro: In the Shadow of the Volcano*. Balkans report 89 (21 March).
Jovanović, Borislav. 2005. *Crnogorski književni urbanitet*. Cetinje: Đurđe Crnojević.
Jovanović, Jagoš. 1995. *Istorija Crne Gore* Cetinje: Izdavacki Centar.
Krastev, Ivan, and Alina Mungiu-Pippidi, eds. 2004. *Nationalism after Communism*. Budapest: CEU Press.
Kubo, Keiichi. 2007. "The issue of Independence and Ethnic Identity in Montenegro." *Southeastern Europe* 32 (1): 163–180.
Lipset, Seymour, and Stein Rokkan. 1967. *Party Systems and Voter Alignments*. New York and London: The Free Press-Collier-Macmillan.
Mair, Peter. 2001. "The freezing hypothesis. An evaluation." In *Party Systems and Voter Alignments Revisited*, edited by L. Karvonen and S. Kuhnle, 27–44. London and New York: Routledge.
Marković, Vlado, and Radoje Pajović. 1996. *Saradnja Četnika sa okupatorom u Crnoj Gori: dokumenti 1941–1945*. Podgorica & Cetinje: Republički Odbor SUBNOR-a Crne Gore.
Martin, Pierre. 2000. *Comprendre les évolutions électorales. La théorie des réalignements revisitée*. Paris: Presses de Sciences Po.
van Meurs, Wim. 2003. "The Belgrade Agreement: Robust Mediation between Serbia and Montenegro". In *Montenegro in Transition: Problems of Identity and Statehood*, edited by Florian Bieber, 63–82. Baden-Baden: Nomos.
Milošević, Milena. 2012. "Fate Of Montenegro's State Symbols in Balance." *Balkan Insight* (26 April). http://www.balkaninsight.com/en/article/fate-of-montenegro-s-symbols-still-uncertain.
Morrison, Kenneth. 2009a. *Montenegro: A Modern History*. London: IB Taurus & Co.
Morrison, Kenneth. 2009b. "The Political Life of Milo Djukanović." *Journal of Southeast European Studies* 1: 25–54.
Pavlović, Srđa. 2003. "Who are Montenegrins? Statehood, identity and civic society." In *Montenegro in Transition: Problems of Identity and Statehood*, edited by Florian Bieber, 83–106. Baden-Baden: Nomos.
Popović, Milan. 2002. *Montenegrin Mirror: Polity in Turmoil 1991–2001*. Podgorica: Nansen Dijalog Centar.
Radojević, Danilo. 1989. "Etničke odrednice jezika- Naziv nije neutralan." *Vjesnik*, 14999 (Zagreb: Vjesnik).
Radonjić, Radovan. 1998. *Tranzicije*. Podgorica: CID.
Ramet, Sabrina. 2005. "The Politics of the Serbian Orthodox Church." In *Serbia since 1989*, edited by Sabrina P. Ramet and Vjeran Pavlaković, 255–285. Seattle and London: U of Washington P.
Rastoder, Šerbo. 2003. "A Short Review of the History of Montenegro." In *Montenegro in Transition: Problems of Identity and Statehood*, edited by Florian Bieber, 107–138. Baden-Baden: Nomos.
Roberts, Elizabeth. 2007. *Realm of the Black Mountain: A History of Montenegro*. Oxford: Blackwell.
Rokkan, Stein. 1970. *Citizens, Elections, Parties. Approaches to the Comparative Study of the Processes of Development*. Oslo: Universitetsforlaget.
Rokkan, Stein. 1999. *State Formation, Nation-Building, and Mass Politics in Europe: The Theory of Stein Rokkan*. Based on His Collected Works, edited by Peter Flora with Stein Kuhnle and Derek Urwin Oxford: Oxford University Press.
Santoro, Lara. 1999. "From Baptism to Politics, Montenegrins Fight for Identity." *Christian Science Monitor* 91/103 (23 April): 7–9.

Shoup, Paul. 1968. *Communism and the National Question in Yugoslavia*. New York and London: Columbia University Press.
Simić, Andrei. 1997. "Montenegro: Beyond the Myth." In *Crises in the Balkans: Views from the Participants*, edited by Constantine P. Danopoulos and Kostas Messas, 113–134. London & Colorado: Westview Press.
Sinfield, Alan. 1992. *Faultlines: Cultural Materialism and the Politics of Dissident Reading*. Oxford: Oxford University Press.
Strmiska, Maximilian. 2005. "The Making of Party Pluralism in Montenegro." *Conflict Prevention*, 2005. http://www.conflict-prevention.net/search
"Ustav Republike Crne Gore". 1992. *Službeni List Republike Crne Gore* 48/92. Podgorica: Službeni List. ["Constitution of the Republic of Montenegro". Official Gazette of the Republic of Montenegro 48/92].
"Ustav Crne Gore". 2007. *Službeni List Crne Gore* 1/07. Podgorica: Službeni List. ["Constitution of Montenegro". Official Gazette of Montenegro 1/07].
Vujanović, Filip. 2011. "Vujanović: Državna himna ne zbližava već odvaja ljude." *Vijesti Online*, (30 September). http://www.vijesti.me/vijesti/vujanovic-drzavna-himna-ne-zblizava-vec-odvaja-ljude-clanak-40300
White, George. 2000. *Nationalism and Territory*. Oxford: Rowman & Littlefied Press.
Zavod za Statistiku Crne Gore. 2003. *2003 Population Census of Montenegro*. http://www.monstat.cg.yu/Popis.htm
Zavod za Statistiku Crne Gore. 2011. *2011 Population Census of Montenegro*. http://www.monstat.cg.yu/Popis.htm
Zielinski, Jakub. 2002. "Translating Social Cleavages Into Party Systems: The Significance of New Democracies." *World Politics* 54 (2): 184–211.

The role of the EU in promoting good governance in Macedonia: towards efficiency and effectiveness or deliberative democracy?

Marija Risteska

CRPM, Skopje, Macedonia

Good governance has been used as a development tool by international organizations and the European Union (hereinafter: EU) which has included it in cooperation agreements and promotes it within its Enlargement Policy. This paper analyzes the good governance approach in the EU's relations with Macedonia and its effects on the country's democratic policy making. The analysis shows that the Europeanization of Macedonia has an impact on the democratic processes in the country with suboptimal results as its technocratic approach in assessing the country's readiness for EU membership has proved to be detrimental for the deliberative democratic processes. The intensive pressure for effectiveness and efficiency results in finding short cuts in rule transfer through copying and pasting legislation from member states and limiting the democratic policy making to political deliberation rather than to wide policy consultations between state and non-state actors.

Introduction

There is a bulk of literature that focuses on EU enlargement towards Central and Eastern Europe, but little of it provides answers on Western Balkans countries' EU accession. What these sources also fail to address is what the role of the EU is in promoting good governance. This paper intends to change that predicament. Its main objective is to study the role of the EU in the promotion of good governance in Macedonia, and identify the channels through which diffusion of good governance principles, values and practices occur. By using an analytical framework developed by Börzel (2009) and in particular, by using legitimacy as an analytical tool, the paper offers answers to the primary research question: what is the impact of Europeanization in Macedonia; does it foster effectiveness and efficiency of policy implementation or enhance the deliberative process of decision making? It examines the historical processes of cooperation development between Macedonia and the EU. It presents the EU approach to good governance in Macedonia by scrutinizing legislation, EC reports and official statistics. To demonstrate the effect of the EU good governance policy on democracy building in Macedonia, the paper presents evidence on the deliberative policy processes from qualitative research (face-to-face interviews) that the author conducted in the period of 2008 to 2011 with civil servants working in policy analysis units in line-ministries in the Macedonian Government, politicians as well as officials of the European Union.

The EU role in promotion of good governance – analytical framework

Schimmelfennig and Sedelmeier proposed that the best model to explain the EU accession process is one of "external incentives" for "rule transfer" from the EU based on conditionality applied to the democratic consolidation and the harmonization with the acquis, with outcomes subject also to domestic adoption costs (2004). EU has great leverage to ensure that the desired policies are adopted as it regularly monitors progress through its diplomatic presence in the EU Delegation offices in each country, and this is enhanced through its control over the financial assistance programs. Through these instruments the EU is able to punish governments which resist reforms through the instrument of conditionality, and by preventing governments who fail to meet the required conditions from passing through the next stage of the accession process. The effectiveness of this system of what Dimitrova (2002) has called "enlargement governance" as a system of transferring policy to the Western Balkans is apparent from the cases of Croatia and Macedonia which have travelled furthest along the path of European integration. National programs for the adoption of the *acquis communautaire* have involved a whole-scale policy transfer of EU compatible legislation to the applicant states.

The "external incentives" model presupposes that the applicant country is making a rational choice in accepting the conditions of accession in exchange for the award – membership status in the EU. However, as Grabbe (1999, 6) points out, EU membership is a moving target due to the ever-changing rules of accession which affects the consensual understanding on the side of both the candidate country and the EU. What is more, empirical studies showed that "the EU puts different emphasis on the way it justifies its policy of conditionality to domestic actors in the various Western Balkan countries – a differentiation closely linked to the specificity of each case" (Noutcheva 2007). Hence, Grabbe (2006) points out that the EU's "transformative power" is limited by the complexity of the actor constellations involved. This paper accepts that conditionality is flexible in nature and that it includes both formal technical requirements on candidates, but also the informal pressures on domestic actors of which behavior the success of EU conditionality depends.

This understanding of EU accession conditionality as a process, rather than set of rules, is especially endorsed when analyzing the EU role in promotion of good governance. Governance as a discipline on the rise, from being debated in international development organizations to systematically being mainstreamed in their development strategies, has been also included in the European Union's cooperation agreements with the eastern neighborhood countries and promoted in its enlargement policy. The European model of good governance is therefore spread and promoted through accession conditionality. What is good governance for the EU is defined in the White Paper on European governance which also identifies five principles of good governance: openness, participation, accountability, effectiveness and coherence. The White Paper fundamentally underscores the concomitant presence of each of the above-noted principles in terms of their effective and successful implementation, and ultimately the achievement of good governance (Chowdhury and Skarstedt 2005).

In order to analyze the EU's approach to the promotion of good governance Tanja Börzel proposes distinguishing two dimensions (2009):

(1) Good governance as an administrative concept;

This understanding builds on the work of König and Adam (2001, 29–30) and Fuster (1998) associating good governance with the setting of a sound administrative and regulatory framework, mainly provided by the state, to facilitate efficiency and effectiveness of government (Börzel 2009). This notion concentrates in essence on state-building. In this respect state-building is understood as a process of developing governance capabilities that enhance the capacity of the state to enforce political stability and enhance economic viability. This process is dependent on both internal and external actors.

(2) Good governance as a political concept;

This understanding is based on the work of scholars such as Mcfaul (2004–2005), Carothers (2002), and Burnell (2000) who focus on respect for human rights and democracy (Börzel 2009). This notion concentrates in essence on building democratic institutions that will ensure deliberative decision making processes and wide citizens' consultations. It especially sets emphasis on situation analysis and defining various options for resolution of policy problem(s), and checking which option creates value for citizens. In this dimension of good governance importance is given to participation of various actors in the process of decision making, state and non-state.

Scharpf (1999) on the other hand has defined that there are input and output dimensions of legitimacy as well. In this respect input legitimacy requires political decisions to be made in a participative or consultative process that will allow the solution of the problems to correspond with the preferences of the affected people. The output legitimacy on the other hand is about solving societal problems in an effective and efficient manner. So, the input perspective focuses on whether the citizen's interest is taken into consideration when decisions are made, whereas the output perspective focuses on whether the decisions are perceived to be in the interest of citizens.

Hence, the two divisions in the understanding of good governance Börzel (2009) is making – i.e. the administrative and the political concept – interact with the two dimensions of legitimacy Scharpf (1999) deducted in an important way. Namely, good governance as an administrative concept is dependent on the EU's pursued objectives to increase output legitimacy in accession countries, as it focuses on efficiency and effectiveness of government to implement EU policies. Whereas good governance as a political concept is dependent on the EU pursued objectives to increase input legitimacy in accession countries; it is focused on democratic processes in decision making and respect for human rights.

The investigation of the existence of legitimacy requires evidence that government is effective and that it is just and fair and that these features of government help legitimate it (Levi and Sacks 2005). The widespread belief that government is good and legitimate is demonstrated through support and loyalty the government gets from its people. In this respect Levi and Sacks (2005) noted that "the legitimacy of a government we might consider a good government requires the belief that government deserves support because according to evidence and rational it is serving the collective good and doing so in a relatively equitable manner". While Börzel's model for analyzing the role of the EU in promotion of good governance (2009) allows for the depiction of the two dimensions of good governance, it does not provide mechanisms for generating evidence whether the policies adopted and implemented in the Europeanization process are serving the collective good in an equitable manner and, therefore, whether they increase legitimacy of government.

This paper will use legitimacy as an analytical tool for studying the role of the EU in the promotion of good governance in Macedonia. It will not generate evidence of legitimacy of government in the Europeanization process of Macedonia. When analyzing the impact Europeanization has on Macedonia the paper establishes a dichotomy between input and output legitimacy. The aim of this approach is to scrutinize the effects of the EU's promotion of good governance and its contribution to an efficient, effective, and even inclusive formulation and implementation of collectively binding norms (Héritier 2003).

The Europeanization of Macedonia: a two stage journey

In the Western Balkans the EU is perceived as a "referenced model for modernization of the political, economic and social systems of the aspiring countries in transition" (Ioakimides cited in Demetropoulou 2002, 89). For Macedonia, becoming a member of the European Union has been a strategic goal since independence was declared in 1991, but formal relations between Macedonia as an independent country and the EU are still very recent. Although the Arbitration Commission of the Peace Conference on the former Yugoslavia[1] declared that Macedonia met the conditions set by the EC for international recognition, due to Greek opposition the first contractual relation between the EU and Macedonia was initiated in 1996 when the PHARE program was signed, followed by a cooperation agreement (in 1997) and opening of the Office of the EU Resident Envoy in Skopje (in 1998). The EU proposed a new Stabilization and Association Process (SAP) for five countries of Southeastern Europe and on 16 June 1999 adopted a positive conclusion of a feasibility study to open negotiations with Macedonia on a Stabilization and Association Agreement (hereinafter: SAA), that was signed in 2001 with which in essence the Europeanization process of Macedonia commenced. The Europeanization process, for analytical purposes, can perhaps be divided into two periods.

In the first period 2001–2004, the EU had a role of "*an active player*" in mediation and conflict resolution (Noutcheva et al. 2004), but also acted as a soft arbiter facilitating the gradual move towards association with the EU of the countries of the region.[2] After the break up of Yugoslavia in Macedonia a new concept of the state did not have to be developed; as David Chandler noted, "the failed Yugoslav state once had strong state institutions and a developed economic-planning administration" (2006, 221). However, the EU had an important role in the development of political and institutional mechanisms for conflict management and with that provided a significant contribution to state-building.

In contrast to the wars in Croatia and Bosnia and Herzegovina, where its action was sordidly belated, during the 2001 Macedonian conflict the EU proved capable in close cooperation with the United States and the Organization for Security and Cooperation in Europe (OSCE) to use effectively soft foreign policy instruments to prevent another Balkan bloodshed. The EU, through the Policy Unit of the High Representative for Common Foreign and Security Policy, offered a package of state-building measures including: border control assistance, refugee support, local government, and judicial reform, including enhancement of minority rights in order to promote interethnic relations. At critical moments during the crisis, the European Commission offered incentives to the Macedonian political elite to stop the conflict, the most visible example being the signing of the Stabilization and Association Agreement (hereinafter SAA) in early April 2001, and an aid package of 40 million Euros for 2001, through its CARDS program for Western Balkans. Giving European future perspective to the country and financial support to facilitate the accession path was expected to stop the ethnic conflict in Macedonia, and eventually moved the Macedonian politicians closer to a negotiated conflict settlement that occurred in August at Ohrid. The Ohrid Framework Agreement envisioned a series of political and constitutional reforms designed to address ethnic Albanian demands for equal standing, featuring power sharing.

Macedonia applied for EU membership in 2004, with which the second period of the country's Europeanization process commences. In this period the EU acquires a new role, providing models of governance and policy options – *continuously acting as a framework* – as the country converges its legislation to the EU's *acquis* (Noutcheva et al. 2004). Developments were highly dependent on the political debates and events in the EU[3] and internal political dynamics in Macedonia.[4] Despite the fact that the overall enlargement was at a stalemate, in five years' period the country progressed from applicant to candidate country status, acquiring visa liberalization (granted in December 2009) and a recommendation to start negotiations from the European Commission renewed each year since 2009, and endorsed by a Declaration of the European Parliament in 2010. Although the country continuously managed to fulfill the EC set of rules endorsed by conditionality, the European Council has not yet decided on the start of negotiations with Macedonia delaying the decision until a "mutually acceptable solution"[EC (2009) 533 final, p. 24] of the name issue with Greece[5] is reached. The resolution of the name issue extends the list of conditions for EU accession and is seen to deviate from the original conditionality based on the Copenhagen criteria and overshadows the pre-accession reform process in Macedonia. Though the EU perceives its role in the Europeanization process of Macedonia as consistent (Radio Free Europe interview with Commissioner Füle from November, 2011), from Macedonia's perspective, "the accession process seems more about responding to the concerns raised in EU members' capitals than about fulfilling the membership criteria" (FRIDE).

The EU's approach in promoting good governance in Macedonia: between state-building and democracy building

Since the European Council in Strasbourg 1989 the EU defined the respect for democratic principles and human rights as essential elements for assessing the membership capacity of the Central and Eastern European countries. However, the democracy building was soon substituted with promotion of good governance. With the democratization processes consolidating, the EU started promoting the effectiveness and efficiency of institutions and especially after the latest enlargement of Romania and Bulgaria, which received much criticism of insufficient progress in administrative capacity-building and the fight against corruption (Gabanyi 2005, 31, 28; 2006). Hence, such an approach was reaffirmed with the opening of Chapters 23 (Judiciary and Fundamental Rights) and 24 (Justice, Freedom and Security) in the start of negotiations with Montenegro to allow for track record to be generated by the time of accession (Interview in Berlin with the Head of the Desk for the Balkans of the Federal Chancellary). Therefore, ability to implement EU policies in an effective and efficient manner becomes the number one priority of the EC when assessing the membership capacity of an acceding state. Considering that the high level dialogue between Macedonia and the European Commission follows the same pattern of the negotiation process it is expected that the priorities of the EC will resemble those enforced in Montenegro.

Promotion of good governance in EU documents

While the enlargement policy certainly, as a whole, entails democracy building in Macedonia the EU exported democratic governance, it is especially focused on the statebuilding and promotion of effective government. This has become visible in the EU's attempt to stabilize the whole of the Western Balkans (Börzel 2009). In this respect Krastev noted that the Europeanization of the Balkans has technocratic features, where "any democracy is evaluated on the basis of its level of institutionalization" and where governance is tackled by "minor technocratic efforts, such as training ministerial staff or aiding cabinet offices, rather than major efforts at bolstering state capacity" (2002, 44; cited in Carothers 2002, 17).

In the Macedonian case, the SAA in its preamble calls for a commitment in political, economic and institutional stabilization through the development of civic society and democratization, institution building and public administration reform, enhanced trade and economic cooperation, the strengthening of national and regional security, as well as increased cooperation in justice and home affairs (SAA FYR Macedonia OJ L 49/1). However, the agreement does not provision any vehicles of democratization, while it endorses the EU focus on state-building, as it provisions that the parties will attach particular importance to the reinforcement of institutions at all levels in the areas of administration in general and law enforcement and the machinery of justice in particular. This includes "the consolidation of the rule of law ... and the independence of the judiciary, the improvement of its effectiveness and training of the legal professions" (Art. 74).

The Commission periodically assessed the implementation of the SAA and in the progress reports it looked at whether Macedonia complied with democracy, human rights, and the rule of law criteria. These assessments also show how vague the EU approach is in assessing the level of democratization, i.e. "the public administration has some way to go before it can adequately fulfill all the tasks required of it in a functioning democracy based on the rule of law" (First Annual SAA assessment report [COM(2002)163] p.3). The opinion of the Commission and their advice to the Macedonian government is very clear and up to the point when assessing output legitimacy, such as the following: "weakness of the judiciary and the consequent difficulties for law enforcement remain; corruption is a serious cause for concern and it is crucial that the government tackles this energetically through an action plan of specific measures" (First Annual SAA assessment report [COM(2002)163] p.3). The same wording is repeated in the Second annual SAA assessment report [COM (2003)139, p.1], but changed in the Third annual SAA assessment report where the decentralization process and the implementation of the Ohrid Framework Agreement are seen as main mechanisms for "strengthening the rule of law, as well as for commitment and a sense of responsibility from all components of the population" [COM (2004)204, p.3]. Multiple sources in the Macedonian Government also confirm that in the first period of EU–Macedonia relations, governed by the SAA, the democratization efforts of the EU were more related with decentralization and minority rights protection rather than development of deliberative and democratic policy making.

Promotion of good governance through EU financial instruments

In 2000, the EU introduced CARDS (Community Assistance for Reconstruction, Development, and Stabilization) as an instrument of financial assistance for the Western Balkans. CARDS financed actions that were identified in the annual program for the country and/or multi-annual program as was the case in 2005–2006. The overview of the country programs shows that the democratic processes in the country were not supported with this financial instrument in 2001, contrary to all preceding years. Hence, the actions that were supported since 2002 were related to the mitigation of further in-country divisions (mainly inter-ethnic), and the improvement and promotion of inter-ethnic relations after the conflict of 2001. The only other democracy building area CARDS supported was the development of civil society capacity (where CSO cooperation was on the agenda in 2002, networking in 2003 and advocacy and lobbying in 2004). The strengthening of civil society capacity for participation in the country's policy making process has not been subject to CARDS 2001–2006 program. On the other hand the same program in the same period provided support for the state to enforce political stability and enhance economic viability such as: building institutional capacities for the enforcement of certain policies (border management, immigration and asylum); enforcement of laws such as the enhancement of professionalism of the judiciary, as well as for the rule of law and the fight against crime and corruption such as the reform of the police. All these actions were state-building actions and aimed to increase the capacities to enforce policies and therefore enhance output legitimacy. CARDS also supported the decentralization process by building central government capacity for the devolution of competences.

The term good governance appears for the first time in the 2005–2006 Multi-Annual Program and targets two broad areas: Justice and Home Affairs (JHA) and public administration reform. The JHA interventions focus again on increasing state capacity that enhances output legitimacy. This is also the case with the projects proposed in the domain of public administration reform that include administrative capacity building in several areas (statistics, telecommunication, customs and taxation management of the Commission's programs post-2006).

The efforts of the EU in Macedonia, in increasing capacity of a border police, training customs officials and supplying technologically sophisticated surveillance and communications hardware, are however in function for the European Commission's Directorate General (DG) on Home Affairs, as this capacity to manage EU regulations on migration is directed towards suspension of criminal trafficking in drugs, people and other illicit goods through the Balkans to the EU (Woodward 2011). In addition, there is no evidence of whether the effective implementation of EU migration policies facilitated through the built capacity of the border police, customs officials and so on generates output legitimacy for the Macedonian citizens, in other words whether the results from the implemented policies are of interest of Macedonian citizens.

The transnational channel was used in the post 2006 period to pursue objectives on input legitimacy through the assistance provided with the European Instrument for Democracy and Human Rights (hereinafter EIDHR). With this instrument civil society organizations are supported to: (i) pursue common agendas for human rights and democratic reform based on mutual cooperation; (ii) build consensus on disputed or controversial areas of policy in deeply divided societies, by means of civil society dialogues; (iii) enhance political representation and participation by means of initiatives by the civil society in dialogue with the "political society"; (iv) enhance the inclusiveness and pluralism of civil society [DG RELEX/B/1 JVK 70618].

The Europeanization effects on Macedonia

The process of Europeanization has three distinct effects on Macedonia's politics: it emphasizes reforms that support enhancement of government effectiveness in implementation of policies that are approximated with EU law, and has limited effect on development of democratic practices of participatory policy making; hence, in the policy making process there is limited involvement of civil society (NGOs, academia, businesses, interest groups and media); finally the approximation process is characterized by the transfer of policies from the EU to Macedonia without much adaptation to local circumstances and reflection of the Macedonian citizens' needs.

The accession negotiations are not yet opened, and it is expected, based on the experience from the last enlargement, that the EU will naturally concentrate in the forthcoming negotiations phase on the capacity of the administration/government to effectively implement and apply the *acquis communautaire*. The above suggests that the external governance in managing the EU "integration" of Macedonia risks further weakening of the standing capacity of the Macedonian state institutions and marginalizing democratic processes.

Government effectiveness instead of democracy

The SAP remains the cornerstone of the EU policy towards the country. With the new partnership instrument the EU seeks to enhance its support for institution building, improve political co-operation and provide the possibility for the country to participate in Community programs (European Commission 2001). The European Accession Partnership Agreement also strengthens the EU conditionality on Macedonia, as it identifies the short-term and long-term objectives against which the country is evaluated on an annual basis using the European Commission's Progress Reports as a main tool. It also introduces the new financial instrument through which conditionality is endorsed, the Instrument for Pre-Accession (hereinafter IPA). With this shift, the reform of the public administration and civil service as well as the management of public finances finally got on the agenda in 2006.

However, the European Accession Partnership Agreement introduced in 2006 has reinforced the output legitimacy orientation of the EU in Macedonia. Among the short term priorities envisaged in the European Partnership Agreement, the ones focusing on output legitimacy – such as track record in judiciary reform, in anticorruption and police reform, and improvement of the rule of law – outnumber those focusing on democracy building and increasing input legitimacy, such as constructive and inclusive dialogue, and the introduction of the merit-based civil service system. Though the Agreement states very clearly that the country should "strengthen administrative capacity, notably by developing the capacity for strategic planning and policy development" and "implement effectively the measures adopted to ensure transparency in the administration, in particular in the decision-making process, and further promote active participation by civil society", all IPA MIPD actions for the period of 2007–2010 do not envisage support to the policy development/making system. The focus in the area of democracy and rule of law is on public administration reform strategy and public internal financial reform (MIPD in 2007). The implementation of the strategies in these two areas is supported with the subsequent accession partnership strategy for the period 2008–2010. In fact, the promotion of good governance is effectuated through particular assistance to judicial reform, police reform and fighting corruption. This again emphasizes government effectiveness instead of democracy.

The democratic decision making does not appear as a priority to any of the Macedonian counterparts, nor it it found in the statements of the EU officials. Instead of calling for invigorating policy dialogue between the state and non-state actors, as was the case in other countries in the accession period (i.e. CEE), the European Commission in Macedonia focuses more on the "political dialogue". Namely, as in no other case before, the European Commission in Macedonia uses the term "political dialogue" not just to qualify the relations between the EU and its Macedonian counterparts (usually used in international relations to describe the dialogue between the parties that are in a relationship governed by a certain agreement, i.e. the Accession Partnership Agreement), but to describe the dialogue between political parties in the country. Dialogue between political parties is part of deliberative decision making and is important when parties are ethnically based. Until 2008 the EC Delegation in Macedonia insisted on political dialogue to be fostered outside of the institutions (i.e. during meetings of the party leadership that usually took place in the MPs' club). Experts criticized this approach (i.e. Siljanovska 2001) as it weakened the Parliament as the main venue for deliberative decision making. Hence, an abundance of documents, primarily communications between the Commission, the Parliament and the Council, such as the conclusions on Macedonia in relation to the Enlargement Strategy, call for a "strengthened political dialogue" in 2010 [COM(2010)660 final]; or assess that "political dialogue has improved: the governing coalition is stable, the political climate is more cooperative and the parliament is more effective" in 2009 [COM(2009)533 final]. Even the Accession Partnership in 2008 under short-term priorities enlists the "promotion of a constructive and inclusive dialogue, in particular in areas which require consensus between all political parties, in the framework of the democratic institutions" [(2008/212/EC)]. Finally, none of these EU documents, which are playing a vital role in guiding the reforms and influencing the good governance practices in the country, mention the involvement of non state actors in inclusive and participatory policy making (i.e. businesses, civil society organizations and various interest groups). This EU approach is, however, on one hand reflection of the fierce competition between the position and opposition parties in Macedonia, where the opposition is more vocal in calling for their involvement in decision making, and the Government is not presenting a persuasive case of wide political consensus building on for Macedonia important matters (i.e. UN facilitated name issue talks, NATO membership reforms, EU accession reforms, Ohrid framework agreement related reforms and etc.). On the other hand, the EU rhetoric mitigates the risk that decisions are made unilaterally in the coalition government which might have repercussions on the peace and stability of the country and on the effectiveness of policy implementation. This again demonstrates that "the EU applies differentiated pressure across applicants, dependent on whether certain issue was regarded as problematic and security relevant in the particular case" (Schwellnus 2008, 187).

Hence, the noted limited EU approach in diffusion of democratic values and practices in Macedonia should be considered just as an addition to the efforts of the Government to govern democratically. The domestic political actors must show awareness for participatory and consultative policy making, and not rely only on the external incentives provided by the EU for reform of the public sector.

Non involvement of civil society in policy making

As noted in Chapter 2 the input (legitimacy) perspective of good governance focuses on whether the citizen's interest is taken into consideration when decisions are made. This is fostered through policy dialogue and deliberative decision making in which both state and non state actors are involved. The inclusion of other non state actors, apart from political parties, such as academia, expert groups, interest groups, businesses and civil society organizations is fundamental for the decisions to reflect citizens' interests.

Considering that policy dialogue is not an objective for the Macedonian political elite, and is neither a priority for the EU officials as noted above, a review of the institutional infrastructure available for participatory policy making is useful in order to depict what the impact the EU's approach on good governance in Macedonia is.

The transnational channel, facilitated through the EIDHR (continuing where CARDS stopped as civil society organizations were explicitly eligible for Community assistance within CARDS (CARDS 2000: Art. 2b, OJ L 306/3)), pursues reform objectives for democracy building and strengthening input legitimacy from 2006 onwards. Yet, defining the functions and competences of non-state actors within the cooperation framework of the Stabilization and Association Process does not necessarily institutionalize the demand for the involvement of civil society and interest groups in inclusive policy making.

The Macedonian government, however, reformed the policy development system since 2006. The country adopted a new legal framework that provisions an orderly process with one single actor to coordinate policy making in respective areas (a Ministry, or the General Secretariat of the Government for horizontal issues) and limited information gaps (Risteska, Page, and Spasovska 2010). The policy development process is predominantly focused on legislation as the main instrument for policy-making, although other instruments (information, taxes, subventions and so on) are also employed. The aim of the new policy development system is to ensure policies are based on evidence, consultative, transparent and responsive to the needs of citizens, and to some extent to increase input legitimacy of decisions. For these purposes the Macedonian government, with the adoption of the Law on Free Access to Information [OG RM 13/2006; 86/2008 and 6/2010] and changes to the Rules of Procedure of the Government, requires each Ministry to publish its draft legislation on its own website as well as on the Single National Registry of Regulations. Consequently, consultations with the stakeholders have become more accessible to the public at large.

The new system envisages a general framework for decision making that includes a procedure for two types of consultations involving different bodies that have a stake in the implementation. The first type of consultations are concerned with the collection of opinions on the decision from the relevant ministries and agencies (i.e. inter-ministerial consultations); the second type of consultations are public consultations and aim at gathering views from civil society, businesses and interest groups (wider public) to be fed into the design of the regulation as well as the assessment of its possible impact on the concerned parties. The interviews in Parliament depict that civil society is not interested in taking part in public debates; "we have problems persuading trade unions and employer association to provide feedback on the changes of the Labor law" (Interview with Cvetanka Ivanova, 2011). Similar dissatisfaction is noted by representatives of the policy development units of the line Ministries in the Macedonian government who doubt the capacity of the civil society to produce policy relevant contributions (comments) to the drafted legislation that is subject to consultation ("Usually civil society lobbies for specific interest of individuals whereas the role of the Government is to defend the public interest" Interview with Aleksandar Popovski, 2011).

Both types of consultations are carried out on a routine basis, in a late and rather short stage of the policy-making process (Risteska et al. 2010), so they do not have significant impact on the decision to be made. As a result the consultations are most often used to collect opinions on a draft decision, and the opinions collected from the institutions are mostly about issues of nomo-technical nature (how the Law is written with a focus on linguistic issues) or of compliance of the draft Law with the remaining legal framework in jurisdiction of the public bodies invited to take part in the consultations. In public consultations the question of how to enhance participation of non state actors (such as civil society organizations, interest groups, the academia, research centers and the media) in policy-making still remains (Risteska et al. 2010). In a situation like this the EU role will be vital to push for more consultative and inclusive policy making open to the whole civil society. Since the Macedonian domestic political actors show limited awareness of the need to enhance the democratization efforts in policy making and willingness for such change, an "external incentive" by the EU for democratic development of policies (the principles of participation, transparency, responsiveness and fairness) is highly needed to strengthen the democracy building objectives and balance the influence the EU has on good governance practices in the country.

Policy taking rather than policy making

Since civil society is not yet involved in policy making, one should not expect the policy making process in Macedonia to be initiated with identification of a policy problem. The need to approximate the Macedonian legislation with that of the EU is the key policy making driver in Macedonia nowadays. The pressing EU agenda is outlined in the National Program for the Approximation of Legislation (hereinafter NPAA). The NPAA envisages the adoption of around 100 laws every year. The adoption of the legislation that allows for conformity with EU law has a "fast track" in the Parliament that is facilitated through several instruments: (i) the government decree to mark all EU accession related legislation with an EU flag, which will than be given priority in government and Parliament procedure; and (ii) a government decree for a table to accompany every EU related draft legislation when it is sent to Parliament (the table provides an overview of transposition of EU law with the proposed draft law and is supposed to inform Parliament on the level of the approximation made with the specific draft law). This system also ensures that only EU related laws are prioritized in Parliament procedure and not other laws that are not related to the EU agenda.

The Schimmelfennig and Sedelmeier proposed model of "external incentives" (2004, 661, 663–664) seems to be able to especially explain the accession process of Macedonia in 2008 when the pressure of meeting EU benchmarks was especially high and the "fast track" adoption of EU legislation took speed in the summer period resulting in a record adoption of 172 pieces of legislation (of which 50 were newly drafted legal documents and 122 were changes to existing legislation) in an emergency procedure, which is usually used to prevent or eliminate major disturbances in the economy, in the interests of the security and defense of the country, or in case of major natural disasters, epidemics or other extraordinary and urgent needs. It is estimated that in July and August 2008 the Macedonian Parliament was discussing each of these 172 laws for not more than 40 seconds at times when the opposition did not participate in the work of the Parliament. This mere rule transfer was heavily criticized as undemocratic, and assessed "as detrimental to the quality of the laws" [COM(2008) 674. This way of prioritizing the EU agenda and the commitment to meet the EU benchmarks was eventually rewarded in October 2009 when the Commission recommended to the European Council the start of accession negotiations with Macedonia, despite the democratic deficit in policy making.

Unfortunately, the intensive pressure to conform to EU legislation as soon as possible is also identified as the main reason why in-depth situation analysis, detailed impact assessments and consultations with stakeholders are not practiced by the Macedonian civil service in the process of policy development (various discussions at the conference "Better Regulation Policy as a Tool for Enhancing the Rule of Law", Skopje 2011). Though recognizing that these procedures will increase input legitimacy, "long consultation procedures and deliberative democratic policy making procedures will just be a slow down for the process of the approximation of Macedonian legislation with EU law" (Interview with Jana Stojkova, 2011). Therefore the main approach used in policy making is policy transfer directly from EU regulations or lessons learnt from countries that are considered as suitable comparative examples to Macedonia (a number of interviewees from both the Macedonian Government and the EU Delegation in Skopje in the period 2008–2011 identified Slovenia, Croatia, Ireland and Estonia as countries used as reference points when developing new policy related to the EU agenda). In both cases Macedonian policy makers are not developing policies, but are rather taking ready-made policy solutions. The main problem of such transfers is the non-adaptability to Macedonian circumstances. Though some EU legislations, such as the directives, are of compulsory and coercive nature, the transfers of others, such as the recommendations, are of purely voluntary nature. In both cases transition periods might be negotiated when transposing both directives and recommendations, especially if they cause either social or economic constraints to the country. These constraints are detected in the process of situation analysis and impact assessment of the new laws, the two policy development tools that are hardly practiced. Therefore, the level of adaptation of EU legislation (directives and even recommendations) to Macedonian conditions is minimal.

This suggests that the accession process is of a one-sided nature. The enormous implementation load, the time pressure, and the strong emphasis on effectiveness rather than evidence based policy making renders the accession into a predominantly technical and administrative process of rule-transfer. However, it also evidences that without input legitimacy achieving output legitimacy or effective and efficient implementation of these policies is impossible. Citizens cannot find the results of the implemented policies to be in their interest if the policies that are being implemented are not in their interest. And to be in the interest of citizens, policies need to be consulted with citizens and reflect their needs.

Conclusions

The EU has developed and applied an effective approach to transform the political and economic structures of the countries that aspire for EU membership. Through its conditionality principle, the EU affects governance in accession countries. The role of the EU is perceived as a "referenced model for modernization of the political, economic and social systems" (Vachudova 2003) in the Western Balkans. However, the case of Macedonia shows that the Union is compelling short term changes that might undermine what is best in mid-to-long term for Macedonia in building authoritative institutions. In particular, the case of Macedonia shows that the EU's main concern is the output legitimacy dimension of governance, where effective and efficient enforcement of laws are an absolute priority. This derives from the orientation of the EU to state-building in post-conflict societies such as Macedonia. This model is argued to bring poor results as it misunderstands the reality of Macedonia and is in conflict with the goals of peace and development that state-building aims to achieve.

The Europeanization of Macedonia demonstrates the one-sided nature of the accession process, where the good governance expectations are more on the side to effectively implement rather than democratically deliberate policies – the implementation load is enormous, and so is the time pressure, which renders the accession into a predominantly technical and administrative process of rule-transfer. It also shows that the development of a transnational channel to pursue reform objectives on input legitimacy (focused mainly on the openness and democratization of the decision making process) is limited. This in turn reduces the EU's impact on the democratization of Macedonia. With the accession negotiations firmly set on an intergovernmental track, neither the Commission nor the Macedonian government have made any effort to systematically involve non-state actors in the adoption of the *acquis* as in other accession countries. In Macedonia, defining the functions and competences of non-state actors within the cooperation framework of the Stabilization and Association Process does not necessarily institutionalize the demand for the involvement of civil society and interest groups in inclusive policy making. The political dialogue among political parties in Macedonia and between the EU and Macedonia does not strengthen such demands either.

The policy dialogue between state and non-state actors is not targeted with any of the major EU documents on Macedonia that otherwise are playing a vital role in guiding the reforms in the country. In them, involvement of non state actors in inclusive and participatory policy making (i.e. businesses, the civil society organizations and various interest groups) is not mentioned. The new policy development system in the country sets the structure for a policy dialogue to be invigorated through public consultations that are short (conducted within two weeks as compared to the EU average of 40 days) but have become compulsory in the policy making process. Hence the participation of civil society in policy dialogue still remains an issue, and therefore the policies are not reflecting the interests of citizens and the input legitimacy is limited. Since the Macedonian domestic political actors show limited awareness of the need to enhance the democratization efforts in policy making, an "external incentive" by the EU for democratic development of policies (the principles of participation, transparency, responsiveness and fairness) is especially important to be strengthened in Macedonia, to allow for more balanced influence on good governance practices in the country.

Notes

1. Also commonly known as the Badinter Arbitration Commission. The commission was set up by the Council of Ministers of the European Community on 27 August 1991 to provide the Conference on Yugoslavia with legal advice.
2. Fostered through the Thessaloniki process promoted in 2003.
3. Notably the enlargement fatigue after the accession of Bulgaria and Romania and the failure of the Constitutional treaty.
4. Where the 2005 EU candidate country status and the recognition of the constitutional name of the country by the United States of America did not help the Social Democrats to stay in power after the 2006 Parliamentary elections; the critics on the new government to provide policy dialogue; the intensified negotiations for resolution of the name issue with Greece; the blockage of the NATO accession which was followed by the early parliamentary elections in 2008.
5. Since the independence of Macedonia in 1991, Skopje and Athens have been locked in a dispute over the use of the name Macedonia. The constitutional name Republic of Macedonia was opposed by Greece to provoke ambiguity between the country and the adjacent Greek region of Macedonia. The dispute is under international mediation within the United Nations where the Republic of Macedonia entered into membership under the provisional reference the Former Yugoslav Republic of Macedonia (FYROM) after the two countries signed Interim Accord in 1995. Republic of Macedonia applied for membership in NATO and the EU under the provisional reference and is experiencing blockade from Greece, contrary to what the Interim Accord regulated. For this reason Republic of Macedonia instituted proceedings before the International Court of Justice (ICJ) against Greece in 2008. The ICJ ruling that "the Hellenic Republic, by objecting to the admission of the former Yugoslav Republic of Macedonia to NATO, has breached its obligation under Article 11, paragraph 1, of the Interim Accord of 13 September 1995" (Summary No.2011/6) was made on 5 December 2011.

References

Börzel, Tanja. 2009. "Transformative Power Europe? The EU Promotion of Good Governance in Areas of Limited Statehood", *ERD Workshop* "Transforming Political Structures: Security, Institutions, and Regional Integration Mechanisms", Florence, April 16–17.

Burnell, P. 2000. *Democracy Assistance: International Cooperation for Democratization*. London: Frank Cass.
Carothers, Thomas. 2002. "The End of the Transition Paradigm." *Journal of Democracy* 13 (1).
Chandler, David. 2006. *Empire in Denial: The Politics of State-building*. London: Pluto Press.
Chowdhury, N., and C. E. Skarstedt. 2005. "The principle of good governance." *A Legal Working Paper in the CISDL "Recent Developments in International Law Related to Sustainable Development" Series*.
Dimitrova, A. 2002. "Enlargement, Institution Building and EU's Administrative Capacity Requirement." *West European Politics* 25 (4): 171–190.
FRIDE Activity brief, 5 June 2009. "The Road from Skopje to Brussels: Macedonian Euro-Atlantic Integration Challenges".
Fuster, Thomas. 1998. *Die "Good Governance" Diskussion der Jahre 1989 bis 1994: Ein Beitrag zur jüngeren Geschichte der Entwicklungspolitik unter spezieller Berücksichtigung der Weltbank und des DAC*. Bern/Stuttgart: Haupt.
Gabanyi, Anneli Ute. 2005. "Rumänien vor dem EU-Beitritt." *SWP-Studie* 31: 28.
Gabanyi, Anneli Ute. 2006. "Rumänien und Bulgarien – EU-Beitritt 2007 mit Auflagen." *SWP-Aktuell 2006(A 27)*.
Grabbe, Heather. 1999. "A Partnership for Accession? The Implications of EU Conditionality for the Central and East European Applicants." Robert Schuman Centre Working paper 12(99). San Domenico di Fiesole: European Institute.
Grabbe, Heather. 2006. *The EU's Transformative Power: Europeanization Through Conditionality in Central and Eastern Europe*. Basingstoke: Palgrave Macmillan.
Héritier, A. 2003. "New Modes of Governance in Europe: Increasing Political Capacity and Policy Effectiveness?" In *The State of the European Union, 6 – Law, Politics, and Society*, edited by T. A. Börzel and R. Cichowski, 105–126. Oxford: Oxford University Press.
Interview with Jana Stojkova, Republic of Macedonia's Government Sector for Economic Policies and Regulatory Reform, 19 October 2011.
Interview with Cvetanka Ivanova, Member of Parliament and Head of the Commission for labor and social policy, December 2011.
Interview with Aleksandar Popovski, Head of legal department, Ministry of economy, December 2011.
Ioakimides, P. 2002. "European Union and the Greek state". cited in "Europe and the Balkans: Membership Aspiration, EU involvement and Europeanization Capacity in South Eastern Europe." L. Demetropoulou." *Southeast European Politics* 3 (2–3): 89.
König, K., and Markus Adam, eds. 2001. *Governance als entwicklungspolitischer Ansatz, Forschungssymposium. September 2000*. Speyer: Hochschule für Verwaltungswissenschaften Speyer.
Krastev, Ivan. 2002. "The Balkans: Democracy Without Choices." *Journal of Democracy* 13 (3).
"Law on Free Access to Information of Public Character." *Official Gazette of the Republic of Macedonia* 13/2006; 86/2008 and 6/2010.
Levi, Margaret, and Sacks, Audrey. 2005. "Achieving Good Government—And, Maybe, Legitimacy." Paper presented at the Arusha conference "New frontiers of social policy.".
Mcfaul, M. 2004–2005. "Democracy Promotion as a World Value." *The Washington Quarterly* 28 (1): 147–163.
Noutcheva, Gergana, Nathalie Tocci, Bruno Coppieters, Tamara Kovziridze, Michael Emerson, and Michel Huysseune. 2004. "Europeanization and Secessionist Conflicts: Concepts and Theories." *Journal of Ethno-politics and Minority Issues in Europe* 5 (1): 1–35.
Noutcheva, Gergana. 2007. Fake, Partial and Imposed Compliance: The Limits of the EU's Normative Power in the Western Balkans.
OSCE Conference. 2011. "Better Regulation Policy as a Tool for Enhancing the Rule of Law." Skopje.
Risteska, M., A. Page, and N. Spasovska. 2010. "Monitoring of the Implementation and Ex-post Evaluation of the Legislation – Comparative Experiences, Options and Capacities." *OSCE*.
Scharpf, F. W. 1999. *Governing Europe. Effective and Legitimate?* Oxford: Oxford University Press.
Schimmelfennig, Frank, and Ulrich Sedelmeier. 2004. "Governance by Conditionality: EU Rule Transfer to the Candidate Countries of Central and Eastern Europe." *Journal of European Public Policy* 11 (4): 661–679.
Schwellnus, G. 2008. "Minority Protection as a Condition for Membership." In *Questioning EU Enlargement*, edited by H. Sjursen, 186–200. London: Routledge.

Siljanovska Davkova, Gordana. 2001. "Macedonian Transition – From Unitary Toward Binational State." co-author. Magor: Skopje.

Vachudova Milada, Anna. 2003. "Strategies for Democratization and European Integration of the Balkans." In *The Enlargement of the European Union*, edited by Marise Cremona, 141–160. Oxford: Oxford University Press.

Woodward, Susan. 2011. "Varieties of State-Building in the Balkans: A Case for Shifting Focus." In *Advancing Conflict Transformation. The Berghof Handbook II*, edited by B. Austin, M. Fischer and H. J. Giessmann. Opladen/Framington Hills: Barbara Budrich Press.

Internet sources

Boege, V., Brown, A., Clements K., and Nolan, A. "On Hybrid Political Orders and Emerging States: State Formation in the Context of 'Fragility' Berghof Research Center for Constructive Conflict Management. Web 04 September 2012. <http://edoc.vifapol.de/opus/volltexte/2011/2595/pdf/boege_etal_handbook.pdf>

COMMUNICATION FROM THE COMMISSION TO THE COUNCIL AND THE EUROPEAN PARLIAMENT Enlargement Strategy and Main Challenges 2008–2009 [COM(2008) 674 final] Web 04 September 2012. <http://ec.europa.eu/enlargement/pdf/press_corner/key-documents/reports_nov_2008/strategy_paper_incl_country_conclu_en.pdf>

COMMUNICATION FROM THE COMMISSION TO THE EUROPEAN PARLIAMENT AND THE COUNCIL Enlargement Strategy and Main Challenges 2009–2010 [COM(2009) 533 final] Web. 04 September 2012. <http://eur-lex.europa.eu/LexUriServ/LexUriServ.do?uri=COM:2009:0533:FIN:EN:PDF>

COMMUNICATION FROM THE COMMISSION TO THE EUROPEAN PARLIAMENT AND THE COUNCIL Enlargement Strategy and Main Challenges 2010–2011, [COM(2010) 660] Web. 04 September 2012. http://ec.europa.eu/enlargement/pdf/key_documents/2010/package/strategy_paper_2010_en.pdf>

COUNCIL DECISION of 18 February 2008 on the principles, priorities and conditions contained in the Accession Partnership with the former Yugoslav Republic of Macedonia and repealing Decision 2006/57/EC [EC(2008) 212] Web. 04 September 2012. <http://eur-lex.europa.eu/LexUriServ/LexUriServ.do?uri=OJ:L:2008:080:0032:0045:EN:PDF>

Enlargement of the European Union : An historic opportunity , European Commission 2001. Web. 04 September 2012. http://ec.europa.eu/enlargement/archives/pdf/press_corner/publications/corpus_en.pdf

Radio Free Europe interview with Commissioner Füle from November, 2011 Web. 04 September 2012. <http://www.makdenes.org/content/article/24377868.html>

REPORT FROM THE COMMISSION. The Stabilisation and Association process for South East Europe. First Annual Report. [COM(2002) 163 final, p.3] Web. 04 September 2012. <http://eur-lex.europa.eu/LexUriServ/LexUriServ.do?uri=COM:2002:0163:FIN:EN:PDF>

Report from the Commission – The Stabilisation and Association process for South East Europe – Second Annual Report {SEC (2003) 339; SEC (2003) 340; SEC (2003) 341; SEC (2003) 342; SEC (2003) 343}. [COM(2003)139, p.1] Web. 04 September 2012. <http://eur-lex.europa.eu/smartapi/cgi/sga_doc?smartapi!celexplus!prod!CELEXnumdoc&lg=en&numdoc=503DC0139>

Report from the Commission – The Stabilisation and Association process for South East Europe – Third Annual Report}. [COM(2004)202] Web. 04 September 2012. http://eur-lex.europa.eu/smartapi/cgi/sga_doc?smartapi!celexplus!prod!DocNumber&lg=en&type_doc=COMfinal&an_doc=2004&nu_doc=202

Stabilization and Association Agreement between the European community and member states and former Yugoslav Republic of Macedonia, Council of the European Union 6726/01 Web 08 February 2013 http://ec.europa.eu/enlargement/pdf/the_former_yugoslav_republic_of_macedonia/saa03_01_en.pdf

Another "strategic accession"? The EU and Serbia (2000–2010)

Bernhard Stahl

International Politics, University of Passau, Passau, Germany

The South-eastern enlargement currently suffers from defections, compliance problems and blockades; the results of the European Union's policy since 1999 can be called mixed at best. The "Serbian question" – for instance – remains unsolved since Serbia still means a "problem child" of the international community. The thesis generated in this paper is that all of these problems are indicators of a basic identity conflict. This conflict stems from entirely different identities, i.e. world views, perception of the state, political cultures and the meaning of international politics. The EU's enlargement policy – in its ideal type – is precisely meant to overcome this conflict by "Europeanizing" the acceding states. Yet the argument here is that the EU also pursues goals beyond Europeanization – for instance "stabilization" – hence the EU might be interested in accessions despite the fact that the Copenhagen criteria have not been fulfilled. Such "strategic accessions", as experienced with Romania, Greece and Cyprus, tend to hinder the EU's external governance and foster enlargement fatigue in the long run. The case of Serbia serves as an example for demonstrating that Serbia is not complying with the basic standards of EU integration and that the EU is not really enforcing compliance. As a result, we are heading towards a "strategic accession" in the Serbian case.

Introduction

Since the demise of the Ottoman Empire in the Balkan Wars of 1912–13, issues of territoriality, belonging, *irredenta* and violent ethno-political conflict have not been resolved in a sustainable manner. With the Kingdom of the Slovenes, Croats and Serbs and the Yugoslav Federation the Serbian question could be frozen for some time, only to re-emerge in the Yugoslav Wars (1991–95). Yet the international community's efforts to stabilize the region by forced diplomacy in 1995 and intervening militarily in the Kosovo War of 1999 triggered a sea-change: From that time on, the EU has committed itself to the fate of the region. It is common knowledge that its Western Balkans' policy serves as a crucial test for becoming a credible and serious foreign policy actor. Yet, as the EU Commission's most current status report admits, the south-eastern enlargement currently suffers from defections, compliance problems and blockades; the results of this "tough love" (Blockmans 2007) can be called mixed at best:

- Ethnic tension in Macedonia could be calmed down by the EU's intensive shuttle diplomacy in 2001. Yet the country's further rapprochement is blocked by Greece. Macedonia sued Greece at the International Court of Justice (ICJ).
- Turkey's accession is staggering along since Cyprus' accession to the EU, due to the un-solved issue of Northern Cyprus and Germany's, France's and Austria's objections in principle.

- The state of Bosnia and Herzegovina is unstable since the ethnical cleavages cannot be overcome. The mandate of the HR in Sarajevo has been prolonged indefinitely(!).
- The EU's endeavour to hold the state union of Serbia and Montenegro together failed. Montenegro declared independence in 2006.
- Ten years after the Kosovo war, the results of the EU's state-building policy are devastating: the status talks failed; Kosovo's unilateral declaration of independence in February 2008 was only recognized by 22 out of 27 EU member states; the state-building and democratization results are doubtful; Russia has estranged itself from the EU using Kosovan independence as a pretext for its Georgian policy; the EULEX mission in Kosovo is becoming increasingly contested locally and the future accession is over-shadowed by the Kosovo issue.

The thesis generated in this paper is that all of these problems are indicators of a basic identity conflict. This conflict stems from entirely different identities, i.e. world views, perception of the state, political cultures and the meaning of international politics. The EU's enlargement policy – in its ideal type – is precisely meant to overcome this conflict by changing the identities of acceding states. The key analytical term to denote this is "Europeanization" which in a merely technical sense means to adopt the *acquis communautaire* of the Union but from an identity perspective means to become "like us".

Now, what happens if a country does not comply with the EU's *acquis*? In a strict interpretation of the EU's objectives, the country would be rejected. My argument here is that this is not always the case. The EU's enlargement policy also pursues goals beyond Europeanization – for instance "stabilization" – hence the EU might be interested in accessions despite the fact that the criteria have not been fulfilled. Such accessions I will call "strategic accessions". I will take Serbia as an example for demonstrating that, on the one hand, Serbia is not complying with the basic standards of EU integration and, on the other hand, that the EU is not really enforcing compliance. As a result, we are heading towards a "strategic accession" in the Serbian case.

The thesis generated here is that the EU in her relationship to Serbia is pursuing another strategic accession which tends to weaken her actorness and undermines her capacity to shape the union's neighbourhood in the long run. Analytically speaking, this is because Serbia's cooperation with the International Criminal Tribunal for the former Yugoslavia (ICTY) and the Kosovo status issue interfere with the ideal-type Europeanization principle.

In order to highlight the two-sided problems, the EU-Serbia relations will be examined in detail. It will be demonstrated how the Kosovo question and the war criminals affair emanate on Serbia's accession. The chronological and analytical account of the relations between the EU and Serbia mainly relies on primary sources and focuses on the interactive dynamics of the negotiations. The EU here is treated as a plural actor comprising community institutions as well as member states. The analytical time frame starts with Milošević's demise from power (2000) and ends with Serbia's application for membership (2010). While the Commission and the High Representative are most important regarding the EU's relations to Serbia, member states remain crucial for (de-)blocking the negotiations.

A post-modern power meets a modern power

In his IR-study from 2001, Georg Soerensen assumes that the foreign policy behaviour is primarily determined by its state constitution. By so doing, he differentiates between three categories of states: modern, post-modern and post-colonial states. In the following, I will start from the taxonomy provided by Soerensen and complement them with some insights from historical institutionalism and identity theory. Serbia can be characterized as "modern state" composed of a centralized state, a strong feeling of community (a "nation-state") and a rather introverted economic system[1] (Soerensen 2001, 74–83). Such modern states are susceptible to security dilemmas and threat perceptions which have been accentuated by Serbian history. The European Union, by contrast, can be denoted as a *"post-modern state"*, characterized by *multi-level governance*, de-centralized decision-making structures, post-national citizenship, multiple identities and a globalized economy (Soerensen 2001, 87–91). Post-modern states remain rather unimpressed with international security dilemmas and strive instead for creating security communities.[2] Of course, this does not mean that the EU cannot be irritated by external security risks, but they leave her identity largely untouched.[3] The rapidly growing literature on EU foreign policy reveals some more identity features of the Union. To be sure, the EU assumes very different roles when dealing with her environment (Ferreira Nunes 2011). In most policies and vis-à-vis most global actors there is a tension between the application of her normative principles on the one hand and a certain "pragmatism" on the other (Lucarelli and Manners 2006, 207). Regarding the Western Balkans, Anastasakis (2008) has observed an increasing blend of realist, functional and normative intentions on behalf of the EU. The pragmatic actor EU tends to be "risk averse" which basically means avoiding making definite choices (Laïdi 2010). Her conflict management can be described as being "reactive" (Gross and Juncos 2011, 148), largely driven by internal constraints – this is why Bickerton (2011, 118) calls the EU an "introspective power". Studies on the discursive legitimation of foreign policy show a "Westphalian discourse" which justifies foreign policy intervention in order to stabilize a region to keep the peace (Gariup 2009, 83). The big member states' realist foreign policy identity, therefore, can be externally challenged by formative events such as destabilization moves of conflict parties. In Fierke's and Wiener's (1999, 725) words: Candidates may turn promises into threats.

This basic EU role as a "stability exporter" is complemented by her normative ambition. Alas, a normatively based foreign policy has largely failed when confronted with autocratic regimes (Panebianco 2006; Smith 2006). But in its backyard, the promise of enlargement serves as an additional and promising foreign policy tool. It evidently represents a special foreign policy which "(...) is the capacity to make and implement policies abroad that promote the domestic values, interests and policies of the European Union." (Smith 2002, 8). Thus, by the accession process, the post-modern EU tends to project her identity onto the SEE region. Hence, enlargement can be conceived of as being an identity problem: Who shall be allowed to belong to "us", under which conditions? The incorporation of the *acquis* serves as a central pre-requisite to ascertain the "identity match". By concluding the negotiations the applicant has become most similar to "us".

The focus on the EU's identity only represents a starting point for the analysis. Since we know from social-constructivist theorizing that interaction tends to change the actors involved and – at the end of the day – also modifies the common political structure (Wendt 1987), some arguments on the actors' interaction patterns are in order.

As argued above, the EU's identity on the one hand delimits the legitimate room for common action of the European Union. On the other hand, a candidate country which fails to approach this common identity is most likely to be rejected. If identities enable or curtail common action they send strong signals as to what the likely behaviour of member states will be in the future, thus affecting whether and to what extent external actors' policies converge with those of the Union. Yet, the Union's identity does not remain undisturbed by accessions since by acceding "[i]ncumbents and outsiders continuously seek to define and redefine the boundaries of the community, between 'us' and 'them', and to interpret and reinterpret the organizational norms." (Schimmelfennig and Sedlmeier 2005, 16). Hence, interaction in the enlargement process tends to change the

EU identity itself. Consequently, the EU as post-modern power largely follows its common identity features:

- Belief in bargaining strategies for resolving conflicts,
- Status quo orientation (e.g. on territorial issues),
- Belief in symbols for transition to democracy (such as constitution, governmental change),
- Truthfulness of other governments' statements.

At the end of the day, Serbia should be "Europeanized" which would then be expressed by full membership to the EU. Analytically, this means a "process of constriction, diffusion and institutionalization of formal and informal rules, procedures, policy paradigms, styles, 'ways of doing things' and shared beliefs and norms" (Radaelli 2003, 10). Fulfilling the Copenhagen criteria seems to guarantee a "Europeanized" Serbia. Formally speaking, the EU's enlargement policy orientates itself according to the well-known Copenhagen criteria which encompass a stable political system, a functioning market economy and the entire adoption of the *acquis communautaire*. A fourth criterion which has been gaining importance in the last decade is now termed "integration capacity". This criterion cannot be met by the acceding countries but refers to the European Union itself. This evidently points to the Union's enlargement fatigue. After the failure of the Constitutional Treaty it has been used to postpone any possible accession until EU treaty revisions were finally worked out, i.e. the Lisbon Treaty was put into force. Yet for the South-Eastern Enlargement (SEE), one more criteria emerged. Substantial cooperation with the ICTY has become an additional requirement. This criterion has been used as a precedent by the EU to suspend Croatia's accession talks until the Croatian government effectively cooperates. Yet the criteria were never straightforward goals which could have been measured easily (Grabbe 2006, 31). Terms like "democracy" or "functioning market economy" were never properly defined by the Union (Grabbe 2006, 32). In the case of the eastern enlargement, the Commission has been compensating for this by interpreting the "adoption of the *acquis*" broadly. For instance, the *acquis politique* – all CFSP member state actions – were incorporated in the negotiations.

But to what extent are all of these EU principles, norms and laws not only officially accepted but also accepted domestically? We know from the process of norm diffusion that this requires not only the purported prevailing of norms. Rather, the complex learning process should be complete in a way that norms are "lived" – ideally, they are so deeply engrained in one's own value system that they have become part of oneself (Finnemore and Sikking 1998). Evidently, this is not always the case and takes time. As Vachudova (2001, 15–16) has argued, for the Eastern enlargement the CEEs have taken two different paths of transformation after 1991. In some societies former regime dissidents took over so that nationalists and regime members were sidelined in the political process. For the dissidents, reforms and transformation were political goals *per se* which were only supported by the European perspective. Examples for this kind of pathway were Estonia, Poland, and the Czech Republic. By contrast, in some other CEEs members of the former *nomenklatura* succeeded in remaining in power and spurred nationalist discourses in society which were intended to distract from the role they have played in the past and their non-interest in profound reforms. As Dyker (2004, 29) has argued, such nomenklatura nationalism went well with economic rent-seeking in the former Yugoslavia. Those rent-seeking élites may discredit European integration *in toto* for minimizing interference with their personal ambitions. Yet in that case they run the risk of being out-voted due to the general pro-integration attitudes of the people. That is why a declaratory pro-integration rhetoric seem to more attractive. Following Lampedusa's famous motto "if we want everything to remain as it is, it will be necessary for everything to change" this requires a rhetorical double-game: In the European realm, those élites and governments pretend to have properly fulfilled the *acquis* requirements despite evident non-compliance while blaming the EU for "un-due and unfair" accession delays at home. In terms of the "norm-cascade model" these societies stick to the first step. Norms are simply used as a means to please the EU without attaching real meaning to it, a case of "fake compliance" (Noutcheva 2007). Bulgaria, Romania, and Cyprus represent evident examples for this pathway.

Admittedly, methodologically speaking, the question to what extent norms are incorporated in the society remains a tricky one. Since I cannot examine this in detail here, I will resort to a methodological "bridge". If those norms are really incorporated, Serbia should "mean what it says". So her changed identity would become visible on the behavioural foreign policy level. Consequently, the question is to what extent Serbia's foreign policy propels norms and values which are consonant with those of the EU. From a positive point of view, one might observe a type of policy convergence which represents a certain "identity match".[4] In a normative sense, the question is raised in how far Serbia is striving to become "a force for the good" for the region. In light of the Europeanization theory imperfect norm internalization can be called a failed Europeanization down-load (cf. Börzel 2005, 46). Conversely, Serbian foreign policy does not produce cooperative and EU-consonant foreign policy results – failed Europeanization up-load.

The enlargement process is an interactive one in which the actors mutually impact each other. By condensing the theoretical insights from above, I will differentiate between two ideal-types of accession. The first type is that which takes place in accordance with the (ideational) rules of European integration. Acceding countries undertake great efforts in order to become members and finally "belong" to the Union. The process is driven by intrinsically motivated élites (former dissidents) which perceive accession as the result of a far-reaching domestic transformation. Consequently, the candidates have adopted both the *acquis communautaire* and the *acquis politique* in its entirety and qualify themselves for membership based upon their own endeavours. The efforts of alignment therefore take place prior to accession and - according to the theory of sociological institutionalism – correspond to an *"exclusive strategy of community-building"* (Schimmelfennig 2003, 74). In addition to technically adopting the goods of integration, the joining society also shares the fundamental idealistic idea of European integration which has been exemplified by the Franco-German partnership: conciliation and solidarity. In a complex societal learning process, EU norms have not only been accepted but even internalized. As one basic requisite, the society has acquiesced to its territory and (usually) multi-ethnic composition. As a result, such a country has internally started to come to terms with the dark spots of its past. So the emerging "historical truth" tends to converge with the historical truths of its neighbours which enables regional conciliation and stability. Such an ideal-type of accession can be termed as "idealistic accession." Their constitutive traits are the idealization of the European project and the significance of each country's respective contributions (membership achieved by efforts).

Yet, as enlargement history tells us, accessions can also be enabled despite a lack of own efforts by candidates to qualify themselves. This has several facets: a first motive is based upon the observation that states join simply because others have done so. The accession therefore takes place out of economic necessity merely in order for the state not to become marginalized.[5] The underlying assigned role of the EU is that of a "paymaster" (Bretherton and Vogler 2006, 20). Secondly, old member states have at times linked the accession of a state to the hope for stability either for the political system of the joining state or for the region as a whole.[6] Thirdly, there is the identity factor within the acceding country as a motive. The own cultural sense of belonging to Europe dominates the orientation of the ambitions. The majority of the elite as well as of the population believes that this sense of cultural belonging suffices to qualify a country for accession to the EU. The efforts of alignment prior to accession are therefore kept to a minimum and are merely of a declaratory character (*fake compliance*). In this case the Union can only hope for socialization after accession (*"inclusive community-building"*). These three overlapping motives for accession are summed up here under the term "strategic accession." Countries which have joined with such strategic motives in mind, have largely not adopted the core values of European integration – conciliation and solidarity (*"partial idealization"*).

Strategic accessions put a strain on the consolidation of European integration in two regards. First of all, it is assumed that a partial idealization of the European project leads to an undetermined socialization: the majority of the respective society does not share the permissive consensus of European integration, which ranks Union solidarity above respective national interests. Obstructive foreign political behaviour of individual states is the result of this whenever national gains face the risk of being sacrificed for the interests of the Union. Secondly, strategic accessions have a negative impact on the attitude of the population and elites of the existing members. The populations of member states view the accession as "premature" and "incomprehensible." The consequence is a decline of the permissive consensus in the old member states.

Looking back: experiences of strategic accessions

The most striking example of a strategic accession is Cyprus' in 2004. The basic question had been whether Cyprus would be able to join as a united Cyprus or not. The Union could have made unification a pre-condition but finally shied away from doing so. Via the majoritarian Turkish population in North-Cyprus, Ankara would have gained a lever for accession. By not conditioning the accession, the Turkish government came under pressure to compromise (Verheugen 2005, 83–84). The two options were heavily disputed in the Council particularly between France and Greece (Sajdik and Schwarzinger 2008, 68). Eventually, Greece threatened to veto the entire Eastern enlargement should Cyprus be pre-conditioned (Nugent 2004, 38). When the Union gave in to the Greek blackmail the plan worked for the North: The Turkish Cypriots were condoned by Ankara to support unification in the decisive referendum. But the Greek Cypriot's president Papadopoulos broke the promise his pre-decessor had given to Brussels recommending unification and promoted a "No" in the referendum (Verheugen 2005, 84, 93). The Greek population followed his advice and thus only the South of Cyprus joined the EU in 2004. The strategic accession triggered immediate consequences for the EU's relationship to Turkey. In June 2006, Nikosia attempted to block the start of the accession talks with Ankara (*NZZ*, June 13, 2006). Then Ankara objected to accepting ships from Cyprus which meant a break of the EU–Turkey trade agreement. As a consequence, the Union blocked 8 out of 35 negotiation chapters (Lavenex and Schimmelfennig 2007, 147–148). Cyprus has successfully taken the EU as a hostage.

Apart from the integration of Cyprus, the two stragglers', Romania and Bulgaria's, accession proved increasingly problematic. Initially, the European Commission had not wanted to start accession negotiations, but the Council – mainly due to Great Britain's pressure – overruled this (Noutcheva and Bechev 2008, 121–122). In 2002, at the summit in Copenhagen, the heads of state decided that both states would be permitted to join in 2007, regardless of their efforts towards alignment. France was able to have its way in this case by wanting to name a specific date and thereby deviating from previous procedure. This was surprising insofar as the countries had only implemented reforms under great pressure and the threat of strict conditionality (Noutcheva and Bechev 2008, 119–120). Considering the constructive role of both states during the Kosovo conflict, the Council opted for a strategic accession and gave both states definite dates of accession (Phinnemore 2005). Despite the fact that the Commission diagnosed severe deficits – for example in their judicial systems – Romania and Bulgaria were allowed to join in 2007. The Commission attempted to compensate for these deficiencies by implementing "cooperation and control procedures", in order to enforce efforts of alignment after the accession. Accordingly, in the summer of 2008, the Commission could limit the validity of Romanian and Bulgarian court decisions throughout Europe. Following Brussels repeated criticism of the employment of subsidy aids,[7] the Commission froze aids worth €500m and withdrew the authorization of two Bulgarian public authorities. In November 2008, the Commission extended its sanctions to include previously promised PHARE funds (*FAZ*, November 26, 2008). Not only the flourishing corruption, but the unsolved contract killings in Sofia's underworld continue to baffle Brussels.[8] The worried voices concerning Romania also became increasingly louder. Observers diagnosed a regression in comparison to the status quo at the time of accession. Following initial success in combating corruption and nepotism, the political elite of the country teamed up against the investigators – both the dedicated Minister of Justice Macovei and the head of the anti-corruption authority were dismissed (*FAZ*, July 15, 2008). The strategic accessions of Cyprus, Romania, and Bulgaria had negative consequences for the reception of enlargement policies in the old countries and promoted an "enlargement fatigue" in the old member states. The dramatic backlashes on the attitude towards European integration of the populations in the old member states also contributed to the rejection of the Constitutional Treaty and the Ireland Referendum or its successor, the Lisbon Treaty.

In this regard, the Union's youngest accession – Croatia's – also evokes mixed feelings. On the idealistic side stands the rather strict EU behaviour during the negotiations which even led to a temporary suspension of the accession talks due to Croatian non-compliance with ICTY claims. More important, the formerly nationalist conservative party HDZ changed course and the nationalist discourse in Croatia was tamed and made compatible with "Europe" (Jović 2011). Yet on the strategic side stands the non-completion of the *acquis communautaire*. In March 2011, the Commission has still stated serious concerns regarding Croatia's judicial system.[9] Some weeks later, the ICTY's verdict against some Croatian war criminals had triggered anxiety in Croatia and pro-integration attitudes fell dramatically. Due to those "political reasons" the Commission decided to conclude the negotiations and gave the green light for accession only four months after the rather negative report (*SZ*, June 11–13, 2011). While the Commission promised to further assess Zagreb's rule of law record it relinquished further delays to the accession date. Only some months after the EU had approved Croatia's political maturity Prime Minister Kosor praised the Croatian war criminal Gotovina as "national hero" in his election campaign which caused tensions with Serbia (*FAZ*, August 10, 2011). Moreover, the parliament passed a law which granted Croatian citizens immunity from Serbian prosecution of war crimes (*FAZ*, November 4, 2011). Norms of conciliation have been taken over but not been incorporated – an indicator of a "strategic accession".

The EU and Serbia

The EU's main goal in the Western Balkans is to achieve permanent peace in the region following the horrors of the wars in 1991–95 and 1998–99. This in itself poses a great difference to the eastern enlargement: while the political-moral motive of and bid for historical justice was omnipresent in the reasoning behind the eastern enlargement, this aspect has lost significance in favour of the challenge of attaining stability (Lang and Schwarzer 2007, 121; Avery and Batt 2007, 2). Altmann (2005, 208) sums this up as follows:

> In contrast to the acceding countries of eastern central Europe, the countries of the West Balkans were not promised the prospect of full EU membership based upon notable reform efforts and outstanding, speedy transformation progress. Rather, these states 'earned' this prospect due to the fact that after the mutual destruction of their partly well-developed socio-economic structures, they now present a region which threatens the stability of Europe. [author's own translation from German]

A clear indicator of European efforts towards stability was the establishment of the "Stability Pact for South-Eastern Europe" after the end of the Kosovo War 1999, which was re-dedicated in 2008 and then known as the "Regional Cooperation Council."

The southeast European enlargement shall serve as an example to demonstrate to what extent the tensions between idealist and strategic accessions have emerged. Based upon the example of the EU's policy towards Serbia, I shall outline how the main tool of conditionality was overridden and thereby discredited by strategic motives on both sides.

Serbia – a non-saturated nation-state

In international politics terms, the former Yugoslavia had been a true success story since it provided peace and prosperity to the Balkans and even served as a leading power of the reputable non-aligned movement from the 1960s to the 1980s. Therefore, it used to be commonplace that Yugoslavia would be among the first to be able to join Western institutions after the wall came down in 1989. This perception entirely vanished with the dissolution of Yugoslavia which brought about war, ethnic cleansing and genocide. In the course of events, Serbia was increasingly seen as the main culprit of the horror. To be more precise, in the public discourses in the EU countries, the autocratic regime of Slobodan Milošević was held responsible – not the Serbian people.[10] This was the main justification for militarily attacking the state institutions and symbols of power in the Kosovo bombing campaign of 1999. Historically speaking, the Eastern question was now being transformed into a "Serbian question": Without a peaceful, democratic, territorially saturated Serbia, so the common wisdom goes, the Balkans remain unstable.

But Serbia has been carrying heavy historical baggage. Since Serbia's gaining independence from the Ottoman Empire in the beginning of the nineteenth century, every generation had to endure war and territorial adjustments as a common experience. The state of permanent warfare and crises in the nineteenth and twentieth centuries precipitated a society haunted by tension and threats (Janković 2006, 42–43). Despite all these wars, Serbia has remained a non-saturated nation-state until today whose territory is under permanent re-construction. During and after the dissolution of Yugoslavia the Serbian territory changed five times:

- 1989: Milošević suspended the autonomy of Kosovo and Vojvodina (granted by the 1974 constitution) in Serbia (at the time still a "republic" in Yugoslavia)

- 1991–92: After Slovenia, Croatia, Macedonia and Bosnia-Herzegovina have left Yugoslavia, the Serbian and Montenegrin republics became "Rump-Yugoslavia".
- 2003: The EU compels Yugoslavia to create the state-union of "Serbia and Montenegro".
- 2006: The EU recognizes Montenegro as a sovereign state.
- 2008: 22 out of 27 EU member states recognize Kosovo's independence.

We know from transition theory that the lack of territorial saturation leads to defects in democratization and political culture.[11] In the Serbian case, *"xenophobic nationalism"* has prevailed being *"a vital part of Serbian culture today"* (Ramet 2007, 42). Politics equals a form of warfare; political competitors are perceived as enemies (Ramet 2007, 42).

When Milošević was ousted from power by mass demonstrations in 2000, the EU reacted enthusiastically, promising to commit itself to the democratization and stabilization of the new Serbia. The incoming Djindjić government enjoyed a very positive reception in the West and was massively supported, for instance by German economic aid. Djindjić's assassination in early 2003 even made the EU intensify its efforts. Yet the real turning point in the EU-Serbian relations was the Thessaloniki EU Council in June 2003, where the EU perspective of the entire region was confirmed. Under the procedure of "Stabilization and Association Process" the EU established an Enhanced Permanent Dialogue with Serbia a month after the Thessaloniki Summit, which actually upgraded the already existing EU-FRY Consultative Task Forces (Djordjevic 2008, 89). Following this, the EU tried to speed up the process of Serbia's rapprochement to the Union, considering that the accession process turned out to be the EU's most successful foreign policy tool in transforming acceding states (Ralchev 2004).

As demonstrated elsewhere (Stahl and Harnisch 2009b, 42–45), it would be over-simplified to grasp a society's identity as homogenous and uniform. Rather, we shall comprehend Serbia's foreign policy identity as divided into two large discursive camps. These camps are split according to their basic understanding of society, of the role of modernity and tradition, and also of the foreign policy objectives. On the one hand, the national-conservative/traditional side is characterized by an introverted, pre-modernist and rural political agenda. In the political arena, this strand is represented by the Serbian Radical Party (SRS), the Serbian Progressive Party (which split from the SRS in 2008), the Democratic Party of Serbia (DSS) and various smaller parties and allied groups such as New Serbia (NS). In society, the Orthodox Church – the most reputable institution in Serbia today – shares the traditional and nationalist worldview. On the other hand, the Liberal Party (LDP), the expertocrat G17+ and president Tadić's Democratic Party (DS) all represent a modernist, European and more internationalist strand of society. Milošević's Socialist Party (SPS) is somewhat torn between the camps due to its anti-US agenda and nationalist but modernist programme. In most cases – the Kosovo question being no exception – the nationalist discourse has dominated over the modernist one. As a consequence, the modernist camp was never strong enough (with the exception of the Djindjić years during 2001–03) to govern without the support of at least one nationalist party.

The following case study will demonstrate how the EU and Serbia interact and how this has been paving the way to another strategic accession.

Promoting fake compliance – the EU, Serbia and the ICTY[12]

After Djindjić's murder, Serbia's transition to democracy stumbled. The young and dynamic Prime Minister had gained a reputation by delivering Milošević to The Hague where he was facing accusations on war crimes, crimes against humanity and genocide. Yet, at the same time, Mladić had been living in Belgrade protected and financed by the defence forces. In the 2003 elections, the Serbian Radicals won 27.6% of the vote becoming the strongest party, Milošević's Socialists achieved 7.6% while the more modernist parties, G17+ and the Democratic Party (DS), scored 11.5% and 12.6% respectively. Positioned between them, the national-conservative Serbian Democratic Party (DSS) together with New Serbia (NS) received 17.6% and the monarchist Serbian Renewal Party (SPO) were able to achieve 7,6% of the vote. In terms of power politics, Serbia's domestic scene after Milošević was characterized by a "cohabitation" situation: After his victory in the presidential elections in summer 2004, President Tadić represented a more modernist direction while Prime Minister Koštunica stood for the national-conservative clientele. The latter formed a minority government which consisted of the DSS-NS, the G17+ and the SPO which was partly supported by the Socialists (SPS).

In June 2004, the Serbian Parliament, with the votes of the Radicals, the Socialists and the government parties (without G17+) decided to grant financial aid to Milošević's and Sešelj's relatives.[13] The EU reacted with irritation claiming that only if full cooperation with the ICTY was provided, the Stabilization and Association Agreement talks (SAA) could be opened. In April 2005, the Serbian government extradited four army generals to the ICTY. Since the new Prime Minister Koštunica (DSS) had shown his explicit disdain for the tribunal, he had promised not to detain ICTY indictees by force and so the generals pretended to have come "voluntarily". Yet as one of the generals appeared in his pyjama and slippers in The Hague this remains debatable (ICG 2005, 2). The extradition was accompanied by a media chorus which did not lay stress on the terrible crimes the indictees were accused of. Rather, their heroic attitude was praised since they sacrificed themselves to secure Serbia's way to Europe. President Tadić justified the extradition with functional needs. He claimed that non-extradition would diminish Serbia's chances to keep Kosovo (*BETA*, cf. *DW*, October 11, 2004). The EU then decided to tie Serbia to a European track. In October 2005, the Commission and the Council agreed on opening the Stabilization and Association Agreement talks (SAA) which serve as a pre-requisite for the membership application. This start meant a *"leap of faith"* (Commissioner Patten) since the usual conditions were not yet met (cf. Reuter 2005, 380). In March 2006, enlargement commissioner Olli Rehn made it entirely clear that the detention of Ratko Mladić, the former leader of the Bosnian Serbs military forces and the no. 1 on the ICTY's wish list, served as a non-negotiable pre-condition for further EU integration. Consequently, Prime Minister Koštunica promised to the international community that Mladić would be delivered in the following month (Raith 2006, 40). Since the Serbian government did not deliver, the EU suspended the SAA in May 2006 for an indefinite period of time. When the ICTY chief prosecutor, Carla Del Ponte, confirmed that cooperation on behalf of Serbia was insufficient the EU stayed on track and prolonged the suspension. Meanwhile in Belgrade, the centre-conservative minority government broke apart since the modernist G17+ party no longer tolerated Koštunica's non-cooperative policy vis-à-vis Brussels and The Hague.[14] Prime Minister Koštunica lamented that "[t]he policy of a permanent setting of conditions, that has been conducted for a while towards Serbia, is deeply wrong and so far produced exclusively negative effects." (*EUobserver*, June 19, 2006).

The January election of 2007 saw slight losses for the ruling national-conservatives under Koštunica while the Radicals went up to a new high of 28.6%. Since the DS under Tadić gained 10% (up to 22.7%, partly at the expense of G17+) and the Liberal Democrats entered the Parliament (5.3%), Koštunica formed a new government including the DS. This more "European" Koštunica government (2007) found a positive reception in the West. Romania, Italy and Greece claimed to replace the restrictive conditionality concerning Mladić with a more flexible definition of cooperative behaviour (*EUobserver*, January 23, 2007). In May, another fugitive, Mladić's assistant Zdravko Tolimir, was found in Bosnia and transferred to The Hague. This success was officially attributed to the cooperation between Bosnian and Serbian secret services. In fact, the severely ill suspect used to live in his house in Belgrade before he was secretly brought to Bosnia by night. There, he was placed in an empty house where a NATO command could find him (*Economist*, June 9, 2007). The EU followed the plea made by some of the member states and subsequently unblocked the SAA. In November, the Commission announced the finalization of the SAA just before the Serbian presidential elections, although the initial requirement of *"full cooperation with the ICTY"* had not been achieved. This was clearly meant to help the DS candidate Boris Tadić against his challenger Tomislav Nikolić from the Radicals. Among member states, only the Dutch government – for identity reasons related to the massacre in Srebrenica – did not follow suit and refused to sign the SAA before the Serbian government delivered the main suspect for the Srebrenica genocide, Ratko Mladić. To offer something, the EU thus created an "Interim agreement on trade issues" (ITA) and raised the prospect of visa-free access to the Schengen space for Serbian citizens. Yet, as critics such as former RELEX Commissioner Patten argued at the time, all these incentives would undermine the conditionality principle (*Frankfurter Rundschau*, October 11, 2007). In January 2008, the Commission once more offered Serbia talks on lifting the visa obligations. In June 2008, another war criminal suspect at large, Stepan Župljanin, was delivered to The Hague. Since the EU did not move – due to Dutch objections – the Serbian government detained Radovan Karadžić, the former political leader of the Bosnian Serbs, in Belgrade. Evidently, he had been living unnoticed in the Serbian capital for years. The HR Solana reacted in an enthusiastic manner:

> This is a turning point in fulfilment of well-known conditions set to Serbia on its path to integration with Europe. The EU shall immediately consider what conclusions are to be made from this positive development of events and I am sure we shall move ahead together with Serbia. I very much hope that this shall make possible for the chief prosecutor of the Hague Tribunal to say that the cooperation is developing in good direction. We also expect from the authorities in Serbia to continue with their efforts on locating and arrest of the remaining two fugitives still at large.[15]

Subsequently, Solana lobbied to lift the Dutch veto on the SAA but to no avail. By so doing, he demonstrated that he recommended easing the conditionality principle (Solana 2009). Yet the Netherlands still refused to put the SAA into force without Mladić. In Serbia, the pre-eminent split on Europe triggered further effects in the party system: When the ITA was put to the Serbian parliament the Radical party split over the issue and Nikolić left the party to launch the "Serbian Progress Party". In many ways, this was a remarkable event in the post-Milošević era. Since Nikolic also supports European integration as such Serbia now enjoys a domestic quasi-consensus on this vital issue (Teokarevic 2011, 62).

In July 2009, the Commission announced to suggest visa-free EU travel for Montenegro, Macedonia and Serbia (*BBC*, July 15, 2009). Enlargement Commissioner Füle raised some hopes on the EU's goodwill but insisted on Serbia's will of cooperation. As long as the main supposed war criminals remain at large, ICTY prosecutor Brammertz lamented, cooperation remained incomplete. On 2 June 2010, Mladić was detained by Serbian security forces in a house in Lazarevo (Vojvodina). On 20 July, the last suspected war criminal on the ICTY list, Goran Hadžić, was also detected in Northern Serbia. After having handed over

Mladić and Hadžić, the EU representatives reacted enthusiastically and praised Serbia's cooperation.[16] When Tadić subsequently visited Berlin he emphasized that since Serbia fulfilled its promise, now it is the EU's turn to deliver: Serbia expects candidacy status by the end of 2011 which should be followed by immediate start of negotiation talks (*DW*, June 29, 2011). The leader of the Socialist party and Minister of the Interior, Ivica Dačić, warned the EU not to set "new conditions" for Serbia: "If anyone in the EU does not want Serbia to join, they should speak up. If the EU does not want us, we will have to live without it." (cf. *B92*, July 21, 2011). Mladić's detention, however, should not be interpreted as the nation's recognition of international law. A majority of Serbs still disapproves of the deliverances to The Hague. This is hardly surprising, as the ICTY is not perceived as a frontrunner of international justice at all. On the contrary, for instance, when the ICTY issued its verdict against some former protagonists of the Milošević regime for crimes against humanity and war crimes committed in Kosovo, this was met with complete disapproval by all political parties in Belgrade (*FAZ*, February 28, 2009). President Tadić revealed a different motive: For every day without Mladić, Serbia had to pay a high price suffering from a credibility problem.[17] Hence, it is not international justice and reconciliation which was at stake for Serbia but rather – considering the bad economic situation in Serbia – that Tadić's DS urgently needed the candidate status to succeed in the upcoming elections in spring 2012 (*SZ*, July 21, 2011). President Tadić revealed in a speech in Kragujevac why candidate status is so important for his country. It would make it easier to attract FDI and additional funds for improving the Serbian infrastructure (*B92*, December 6, 2011).

Offering accession to the EU – demanding stabilization for Kosovo

While building up state institutions in Kosovo since 1999, the EU denied responsibility to assess the status question and stuck to a "silencing strategy". The situation reached a nadir when Milošević was purged in October 2000 and Serbia's peaceful transition to democracy gave additional credence to the argument not to raise the I-Word (ICG *Roadmap* 15). When the Serbian government proposed to divide Kosovo in May 2001, the international community harshly rejected the initiative (Cohen 2002, 32). Several European Councils and the EP explicitly stressed the non-violation of borders, territorial integrity and sovereignty in SEE at the time.[18] In November 2001, the Belgian Presidency declared: "We have not changed our minds. We are not in favour of independence" (cited in ICG *Roadmap* 2 [4]). In April 2002, the Commission stated that her association strategy was not meant to further split-up the region.[19] The EU's state-building policy was based on an identity consensus that undergirded the Rambouillet accords. These accords had foreseen a substantial autonomy for Kosovo but no independence. The Kosovo War did accentuate but did not principally alter this position. EU member states and their partners had left their soldiers in harm's way to end human rights violations and a broader destabilization of the Western Balkans but not to bring about independence. Moreover, Kosovo independence held the risk of setting in motion another Balkan domino effect – triggering secessional violence in Bosnia too (Weller 2008, 185). The pogroms against Serbs and other minorities in Kosovo in March 2004 activated the Serbian government which re-iterated its plans for a "cantonization" of the province (Judah 2004, 20–22). But UN Special representative Eide, the contact group and the EU rejected the idea by excluding further territorial changes, be they the unification with Albania or the division of the province.[20] In effect, the violent pogroms had transformed the Western position in favour of Kosovo-Albanian aims.[21] Serbia's position hardened immediately. The Serbs in Kosovo, supported by Belgrade, turned their back on UNMIK and the EU, boycotting common institutions in Kosovo (Koeth 2010, 232).

Following these events, Premier Koštunica made the Kosovo question his core theme in the election campaigns of 2006, 2007 and 2008, forcing President Tadić to respond. Since the EU had rejected the cantonization plan twice in 2001 and 2004, he called for a "national consensus on Kosovo". Consequently, Tadić closed ranks with Koštunica's DSS, the Socialists and the Serbian Radicals. The President agreed to a new Serbian constitution which hailed Kosovo as an integral part of Serbia. Since the fall of Milošević in 2000, the work on the constitution had been pending. In a sudden coup, it was rushed through Parliament when amended by the Kosovo stipulation. Remarkably, for securing a majority in the referendum on the constitution, the government erased the Kosovo-Albanians from the election register (*DW-world*, October 26, 2006). By so doing, the Kosovo-Albanians were deprived of a core right of citizenship. This clearly indicates that the government's later slogan "Kosovo is Serbia" only alludes to the territory but not to 90% of its inhabitants.[22] The uniting on the domestic front was complemented by a foreign policy reorientation: Tadić and Koštunica sought support for the Serbian position in Moscow.

In early 2006, the Serbian government issued a resolution on Kosovo in which Serbia agreed to start talks on the autonomy of the region. At the same time, Koštunica's chief adviser Simić made clear that these talks would not touch upon independence since this had been excluded by Resolution 1244 (*B92*, January 18, 2006). During the on-going negotiations, Brussels and the member states encouraged Belgrade to demonstrate more flexibility. The EU-Parliament, for instance, affirmed the argument of "new realities" in Kosovo which had established state-like structures.[23] The Commission, too, seemed convinced by chief negotiator Ahtisaari's arguments but refrained from public pleas concerning independence. As early as March 2006, enlargement commissioner Rehn had sent a clear signal to Belgrade: "[...] there can be no return for Kosovo to Belgrade's rule [...]".[24] After the Ahtisaari plan failed, the President of the Commission, Barroso, warned Belgrade that "(f)or Serbia [...] can be no role in the EU if it does not cooperate for a Kosovo solution" (ICG *Stalemate* 10 [68]).

The idea of a "grand bargain" – granting fast-track integration into Euro-Atlantic structures in exchange for the Serbian recognition of Kosovo – was popular in Brussels and Washington for some time. The EU and the US felt increasingly tempted to bargain on the SAA and Kosovo. So NATO decided in November to invite Serbia to the alliance's Partnership of Peace programme. In December, Greece, Italy and Denmark urged the EU to lift the SAA suspension but the UK, France and the Netherlands objected to the initiative (*EUobserver*, December 11, 2006). Yet Brussels offered Belgrade negotiations on visa procedures. Surprisingly, Rehn declared in March that candidate status could still be in reach for 2008 (*EUobserver*, March 7, 2007) which was met with disbelief in some member states. Moreover, Italy had proposed to grant Serbia candidate status in exchange for Kosovo's independence (*NZZ*, September 24, 2007).

Meanwhile in 2007, the ongoing Kosovo negotiations resonated badly with the Serbian public. When UN chief negotiator Ahtisaari launched his plan for the province, Premier Koštunica called his plan "an act of legal aggression" (*EUobserver*, March 27, 2007) and refused to meet him when he came to Belgrade to present his plan. A Serbian daily newspaper, the *Kurier*, even compared the UN chief negotiator to Hitler (cf. Ramet 2007, 52). In December, the parliament agreed on a resolution proclaiming Serbia a "neutral country". This move is without precedent in Eastern Europe, since all countries have been pursuing a "NATO first, EU second" strategy in order to complete their "going West". In a positive grasp of this stance one might recall Yugoslavia's leading role in the non-aligned movement. A rather negative interpretation would suppose the "Russian card" behind this (Teokarevic 2011, 73). Furthermore, one might concede that the Serbian élite has not been distancing itself from Milošević's Kosovo endeavour in a way which would have allowed to understand the NATO bombing of 1999 as something belonging to "his past". This exactly had been Blair's, Chirac's and Schröder's justification for the "bombing campaign": NATO was attacking Milošević's authoritarian regime, not the Serbian people (see footnote 10). The Serbian élite did not follow this interpretation and still feels closer to Milošević than to NATO.

At the G8 meeting in Heiligendamm (GER), France's president Sarkozy proposed another round of Kosovo negotiations limited to 120 days in order to offer a final chance for compromise (Weller 2008, 58). Such a round would be a worth-wile enterprise if only to ensure EU unity (Ker-Lindsey 2009, 75–76). A "Troika" – made up of representatives from the EU, the US, and Russia – was meant to resume the negotiations. Interestingly, the troika even dared to break away from the guideline the CG + , UNMIK and the EU had agreed upon earlier. The EU's representative, German diplomat Ischinger, floated the idea of whether territorial changes could be an option. But both conflict parties rejected his proposal (Weller 2008, 60). None too soon, Serbia's president launched a substantial proposal offering far-reaching autonomy for Kosovo including access to international financial institutions, a flag and a national anthem. But Tadić's efforts were undermined by Prime Minister Koštunica's un-inspired pleas and came too late to make the Kosovars move (Weller 2008, 65). Indeed, the international community had already given up all hopes that a final compromise was still in reach. Rather, the prolonging of talks served the double purpose to turn Russia around and – more importantly – to gain some time for finding a compromise within the EU on how to deal with looming independence.[25] At least, Germany was now also willing to recognize Kosovo's independence without the UN's consent (Ker-Lindsey 2009, 89). When the troika's endeavours finally failed on 14 December 2007, even the European Council came to the conclusion that further negotiations were pointless.[26] Furthermore, Solana was mandated to concretely prepare the EULEX-mission. This mission was meant to replace UNMIK and support the build-up of proper self-governing institutions. Solana succeeded in convincing the non-recognizing member states – in particular Cyprus to agree to EULEX.[27]

The Slovene presidency vainly attempted to convince the Dutch government to sign the SAA (*B92*, January 16, 2008). But Koštunica rejected any deal with the EU linking the SAA to Serbia's goodwill on the Kosovo question. Prime Minister Koštunica refused to sign the ITA, arguing that Kosovo cannot be part of a deal even if this would mean blocking accession: "Belgrade will not bargain on Kosovo" (*EUobserver*, September 20, 2007). He also insisted that the EULEX mission would prejudice statehood. The EULEX mission would help to establish a "puppet state" on Serbian soil, "the most dangerous precedent after WW II" (*BBC*, December 14, 2007). By contrast, President Tadić argued that EULEX would be "status-neutral" so that Serbia's position on Kosovo would by no means jeopardize its EU integration. In order to support Tadić, the EU's special envoy to Kosovo, Pieter Feith, announced that EULEX deployment in Northern Kosovo would be postponed to after the Serbian elections (*B92*, March 13, 2008).

The unilateral Kosovar declaration of independence on 17 February 2008 triggered protests in Belgrade and Northern Kosovo. In the Serbian capital demonstrators looted western bank subsidiaries and supermarkets, and attacked the Turkish, British, Croatian, German and US embassies and a border check-point in Kosovo. A furious Prime Minister commented on the declaration of independence: "It has to be legally annulled the moment it was legally proclaimed by leadership of convicted terrorists" (cf. *BBC*, February 12, 2008). Accordingly, Serbia's government did not protect the Western Embassies. Prime Minister Koštunica even praised the Serbian youth for their commitment and wisdom

(*B92*, February 27, 2008). Some sources also suggest that the government in Belgrade orchestrated attacks on a UN border check-point in Northern Kosovo (*BBC*, March 18, 2008). The EU's High Representative, Javier Solana, condemned the violence and suspended the SAA (*NYT*, February 23, 2008). Yet, only six weeks later, he ignored his earlier words, pushing for an early signing of the SAA just before the approaching Serbian elections in May (*DW*, April 17, 2008). In addition, the EU publicly recommended to vote for the "Pro-European" parties and again invited the government to sign the ITA.

In April, only a few weeks before the elections, the Serbian president and the Finance Minister Djelić travelled to Luxemburg and signed the SAA with EU officials. Meanwhile at home in Belgrade, the Serbian Prime Minister declared the President's signature as void and denounced the signing of the SAA as "Solana's agreement" (*B92*, April 10, 2008). The politics of farce peaked when the Netherlands and Belgium stated that the SAA would not be put into force before Mladić was sent to the ICTY. At least, the EU marketing campaign for Tadić paid off: In the Serbian elections of May 2008, Tadić's coalition "Serbia for Europe" (including DS, G17+, SPO) achieved 39% and declared itself the winner of the elections. The Pro-European parties gained 6% vis-à-vis the centre parties around Koštunica. This result was praised in the Western press as a huge victory for Europe. But still, the pro-European parties did not hold the majority in parliament. President Tadić therefore formed a government with the Socialists – the party of the former dictator Milošević – as a junior partner, assuring the EU that Serbia would remain on an integration track.

This change in government did not, however, mean any change concerning a Kosovo consensus. Even after Kosovo's declaration of independence in February 2008, all Serbian parties further agreed on a "united state policy" on Kosovo (*B92*, February 12, 2008). Instead of accepting EU incentives, Serbia launched a diplomatic lobbying campaign against Kosovo's independence. In October 2008, Serbia won the UN Assembly's approval for bringing the Kosovo issue to the International Court of Justice. Hence, the EU countries were pressed to legally justify their position on Kosovo's independence. The EU's position vis-à-vis Serbia had further weakened because of the five member states unwilling to recognize Kosovo's independence (Slovakia, Romania, Greece, Cyprus and Spain). As a consequence, the EU herself became a schizophrenic actor whose appeals to come to terms with Kosovo became hollow.

In February 2009, the Serbian office for EU integration stated that the Serbian Parliament failed to put ca. 25 SAA laws into force: Only 17 out of the planned 64 laws were passed in Parliament (cf. *B92*, February 6, 2009). In the same month, Olli Rehn stated that "applying for EU candidacy is not advisable in 2009" (*B92*, February 12, 2009). The Serbian government followed his advice: It applied for membership in January 2010. By so doing, it ignored the usual sequence in the accession process and delivered an application before the SAA was in force.

In a revealing statement, the Western powers seemed increasingly doubtful whether their strategy on Serbia still worked. In early 2010, Western powers complained openly in a letter to Serbia's Foreign Minister, Vuk Jeremić, that their incentive-based approach had been exploited by the DS:

> We have tolerated until now the Serbian aggressive rhetoric regarding Kosovo, because we believed that with time passing it could be taken off the agenda. Our partners in Belgrade have told us that the statements of minister Jeremic about Kosovo aimed to protect President Tadić from attack by Serbian nationalists, and the initiative to ask the ICJ for an advisory opinion on the Declaration of Independence was just a manoeuvre to remove Kosovo from the political agenda in Serbia. None of this seems to be the case (...).[28]

The ICJ opinion,[29] released in July 2010, gave a boost to the EU majority fraction's view that Kosovo's independence should be treated as a *fait accompli*.[30] Yet the five non-recognizing member states did not make use of the opportunity to change their mind. Serbia, by contrast, intended to launch a proposal to the UN General Assembly criticizing the ICJ's opinion. The British and German Foreign Ministers warned Belgrade not to continue this policy (*EUbusiness.com*, August 27, 2010) and the EU put great pressure on Belgrade to change the proposal. After the Serbian government had diluted the text, HR Ashton and most member states re-iterated their will to grant Serbia a "fast-track" to membership (*EUobserver*, June 10, 2010). Yet the ICTY's prosecutor, Serge Brammertz, openly clashed with Enlargement Commissioner Füle and HR Ashton over the issue while the Netherlands and Germany remained sceptical on whether to grant further rewards to Serbia (*EUobserver*, October 7, 2010). It was these two countries, supported by Britain, which inhibited granting the candidate status to Serbia by the end of 2011. The reasons given pointed to the violent clashes around border posts in Northern Kosovo which left some KFOR soldiers injured. When the Serbian government promised to stop the violence and agreed to informal talks with the Kosovo-Albanians on technical border issues the three sceptics gave in: In March 2012, Serbia received candidate status.

Conclusions

The EU–Serbian relations have been troublesome throughout the last decade. Brussels proved to be a torn actor. On the one hand, the deficient accessions of Cyprus, Bulgaria and Romania have increased the awareness that strategic accessions should be avoided beforehand since EU pressure tends to evaporate after a country has joined. On the other hand, the "Serbian question" has been haunting the region for so long that stability seems to be an end in itself. In the course of events, as this study has been trying to demonstrate, the EU has increasingly leaned towards stability aims sacrificing its idealist ambitions.

By and large, this is the common pattern in the three main areas of EU-Serbia relations: the cooperation with the ICTY, the accession process itself (namely the SAA), and the Kosovo issue. In all of these realms, policy results are mixed at best, including complete foreign policy failures.

First, regarding the cooperation with the ICTY, EU tactics to insist on the fugitives have proved successful at first glance. Beyond doubt, the fact that all of the indictees on the The Hague wish-list could be delivered to the tribunal means an enormous reputation gain for international law, the fight against genocide and for universal values. Yet the price the EU paid was that Serbia's compliance obviously remained superficial and did not help Europeanization. The successful deliverances to The Hague by no means represent a "normative shift" in Serbia. The financial assistance to their families, the "hero rhetoric" and the continuous insults of international institutions such as the ICTY and the UN chief negotiator Ahtisaari – even by government members – have demonstrated quite the contrary. Serbia only "sacrificed" its heroes for national survival and the Koštunica and Tadić governments used the fugitives simply to overcome SAA negotiation deadlocks. Indeed, the transitional justice issue has been "hijacked" by the Serbian political élite serving their purpose (Subotic 2009). Serbia reacted to the financial incentives not because of norm internalization. Neither idealization of the European project, nor any societal conciliation effort has been linked to the war criminals issue.

The lack of any conciliation motive has also been extremely pertinent in the Kosovo negotiations which ended in a complete policy disaster. The EU proved herself a status orientated, defensive post-modern power which was neither willing nor able to address the status question in time. As a consequence, the EU has been a driven actor, driven by the US push for unilateral independence, driven by Russian intransigence and driven by Albanian and Serbian militarist radicals in Kosovo. Not only was the EU split on the issue, its plan to inherit Kosovo's state-building from UNMIK was successfully undermined by the Serbian (legally correct) insistence on status neutrality for EULEX. This stance is hardly tenable vis-à-vis Priština and already caused violence against EULEX. Serbia lost the Kosovo case at the ICJ but nevertheless re-iterated its Kosovo policy. By so doing, Serbia demonstrated its instrumental understanding of international institutions. When intending another un-compromising resolution to the UN General Assembly, the EU immediately reacted by granting further incentives for softening it. So even the loss of the ICJ case was utilized by Serbia to get the EU speeding up SAA ratification. However, it seems hard to imagine Kosovo and Serbia joining the EU without even recognizing each other. The case of Cyprus – when the EU's incentive strategy had also terribly failed – is well remembered in Brussels. Yet the member states are already split as to whether recognition should be made a pre-condition for Serbia's accession or not.[31]

Thirdly, the Europeanization effects have been meagre. Regarding Serbia's "up-load" record its cooperation within the international community remained problematic: It did refuse to negotiate pro-actively on Kosovo, the government did not hinder violence against Western embassies and Kosovo border posts, it does not support EULEX and it did not change course after the ICJ opinion. Rather, it made things more difficult for the international community by asking for an ICJ opinion, by choosing Russia as preferred partner, by hiding the war criminals, by hardly showing any interest in regional cooperation. The same applies to the Europeanization "downloads". As the Commission's latest progress report and scientific evidence[32] reveal, Serbian governments do not seem interested in passing "European" laws at adequate speed and forcing their implementation. This insight regrettably fits in with the non-interest of the Serbian parties and large parts of its élite to promoting societal modernization. By acquiescing to this for the (superficial) sake of stability the EU evidently demonstrated its non-interest in profoundly reforming Serbia. Rather, the EU trusts in its soft power means to stabilize Serbia and hopes that time will heal the Serbian identity problem. Considering the insight that the EU's leverage fades away as soon as a country joins the union (Slobodchikoff 2010) this looks like a recipe for failure.

The EU's policy to prefer short-term stability gains to long-term norm internalization also reflects its split actorness – and identity. Overall, the more stability-minded actors – the Council, the High Representative and the member states favouring "fast track accession" (e.g. Greece, Italy, Slovenia, Austria) – have been dominating the actors insisting on effective compliance (Commission, European Parliament, the Netherlands, Belgium). The inconsistent positioning of the "Big-3" (France, United Kingdom, Germany) has led to the EU oscillating between stability short-term and idealist long-term considerations.

In a social-constructive light, the staggering accession process triggers another unintended consequence: The EU feels tempted to grant Serbia new labels and incentives even if the government does not deliver. This window-dressing rhetoric meets Serbian fake compliance well. Given the Serbian identity based on external attribution, the EU's oscillating rhetoric resonates well in this identity construction: It strengthens the public opinion that Serbia deserves EU membership *per se* and the EU is conspiratorially hindering Serbia's overdue accession.[33] By so doing, the EU undergoes rhetorical self-entrapment[34] which will further enhance enlargement fatigue and possibly lead to referendum failures in future ratifications on another strategic accession.

Notes

1. In 2010, Serbia imported twice as many goods as it exported. Its trade with the neighbour countries is weak, Croatia and Bosnia only account for 3% (each) of the imports. European Commission (EUROSTAT): Fact sheet "Serbia. EU bilateral trade and trade with the world." *DG Trade*, March 21, 2012.
2. A "Security Community" is defined as a "transnational region comprised of sovereign states whose people maintain dependable expectations of peaceful change" (Adler and Barnett 30).
3. In another paper, I have extended the argument to the "post-colonial power" Kosovo and attributed the west's failure to settle the Kosovo problem to the inherent identity problems in the triangle 'post-modern EU – modern Serbia – post-colonial Kosovo'. cf. Stahl (2013) 100jähriges Scheitern.
4. Kubicek (2003) speaks of a "cultural match".
5. The historic examples are Denmark and Ireland which simply joined the EC following the UK.
6. The historic example here is Greece which was allowed to join the EC in 1981 although the Commission stated non-maturity at this early stage. But the member-states overruled the Commission's recommendation by wishing to gratify the overcoming of dictatorship (Nugent 2004, 27–28). As the current financial crisis reveals, Greece has never implemented the *acquis*.
7. Elitsa Vucheva: "Commission softens tone on Bulgaria, Romania corruption", *EUobserver* July 23, 2008.
8. See Carola Kaps: "Wirtschaft blüht, Korruption auch", *FAZ* July 21, 2008, p.10.
9. European Commission: "Interim Report from the Commission to the Council and the European Parliament on Reforms in Croatia in the Field of Judiciary and Fundamental Rights." Negotiation Chapter 23, COM 110, Brussels: 2 March 2011.
10. This discursive pattern proved very successful in convincing the British, German and French public to start the "bombing campaign" against Serbia (Stahl and Harnisch 2009a 108, 150, 193).
11. Transition theory claims that borders have to be fixed and identity questions to be settled before democracy can thrive. See Schmitter 1995, 49; Linz and Stepan 1996, 5–86.
12. The following descriptive part is a modified version from Stahl (2011) (*Perverted conditionality*).
13. Šešelj, until today the leader of the Serbian Radical Party, was the leading politician of Serbia's "nationalist turn" in the late 1980s and 1990s. He deliberately went to the ICTY in The Hague to face numerous accusations. The verdict on his case is expected soon.
14. See the interview with the resigned vice-chancellor Miroljub Labus: "*The Prime Minister broke his promise*" (*B92*, May 3, 2006).
15. Cf. "*What Serbia can expect from EU after extradition of Radovan Karadzic*", *Blic*, July 23, 2008.
16. Commissioner Füle spoke of "splendid news" (Radio Free Europe) while EU President van Rompoy called it "a milestone for Serbia, the region and international justice", statement, 26 May 2011. Accessed July 18, 2011. http://www.consilium.europa.eu/uedocs/cms_data/docs/pressdata/en/ec/122242.pdf
17. Interview with President Tadić, *FAZ*, June 3, 2011.
18. European Council. *Conclusions of the presidency*. Paragr. 65. Stockholm: 23-24 March 2001. Accessed June 29, 2010. http://www.consilium.europa.eu/ueDocs/cms_Data/docs/pressData/de/ec/ACF191B.html; European Council. *Conclusions of the presidency*. Paragr. 60. Nizza: 7-9 Dec. 2000. Accessed June 29, 2010. http://www.consilium.europa.eu/ueDocs/cms_Data/docs/pressData/de/ec/00400.%20ann.d0.htm; European Parliament. *Resolution on the situation in Kosovo*. Paragr. 8. Strasbourg: 15 Feb. 2001. Accessed June 29, 2010. http://www.europarl.europa.eu/sides/getDoc.do?pubRef=-//EP//TEXT+TA+P5-TA-2001-0097+0+DOC+XML+V0//DE
19. European Commission. *Report of the Commission. The Stabilization and Association process for SEE. First Annual Report*. Brussels: 3 April 2002, 10. Accessed January 18, 2008. http://eurex.europa.eu/LexUriServ/LexUriServ.do?uri=COM:2002:0163:FIN:DE:PDF
20. United Nations Security Council. *Report on the Situation in Kosovo*. New York: 6 Aug. 2004, 3–7. Accessed June 29, 2010. http://www.securitycouncilreport.org/atf/cf/%7B65BFCF9B-6D27-4E9C-8CD3-CF6E4FF96FF9%7D/kos%20S2004%20932.pdf; United Nations Security Council. *A comprehensive Review of the Situation in Kosovo*. New York: 7 Oct. 2005, i-iv. Accessed June 29, 2010. http://www.securitycouncilreport.org/atf/cf/%7B65BFCF9B-6D27-4E9C-8CD3-CF6E4FF96FF9%7D/Kos%20S2005%20635.pdf

21. One parliamentarian of the Kosovo Assembly went so far as to publicly call the riots a *"legitimate revolt by the Albanian population"* and a *"lesson for the international community"*, cited in Narten 2009, 273.
22. As Schmitt (2008, 187, 210) has noted, this attitude of the Belgrade élite can easily be traced back to the first and second Yugoslavia.
23. European Parliament: *Entschließung zur Zukunft des Kosovo und der Rolle der Europäischen Union*. Buchstabe H, 29 March 2007. Accessed November 11, 2007. http://www.europarl.europa.eu/sides/getDoc.do?pubRef=-//EP//TEXT+TA+P6-TA-2007-0097+0+DOC+XML+V0//DE
24. Cf. Krasniqui, Ekrem: "EU says Serbia can't rule Kosovo again." *EU-Observer* 9 March 2006. Accessed March, 15 2006. http://euobserver.com/24/21096
25. Judah, Tim: *Kosovo Talks Unlikely to Come to Anything*. Balkan Investigative Reporting Network, 10 Aug. 2007. Accessed August 29, 2008. http://kosovo.birn.eu.com/en/1/70/3845
26. Brussels European Council. *Extract from the Presidency Conclusions*. Brussels: 14 Dec. 2007. Accessed August 20, 2008 http://www.consilium.europa.eu/uedocs/cmsUpload/071214-Extract_from_EUROPEAN_COUNCIL.pdf
27. Council Joint Action 2008/124/CFSP of 4 February 2008 on the EU Rule of Law Mission in Kosovo.
28. Diplomatic note by the foreign ministries of Germany, France, Italy, the United Kingdom and the United States to the Serbian Foreign Minister, Vuk Jeremić, cited in: *waz.euobserver* 9 Feb. 2010.
29. The ICJ ruled, in essence, that the Security Council Resolution 1244 had not ruled out Kosovo's declaration of independence. In this regard, the unilateral declaration of independence was not in breach with international law as Serbia is claiming.
30. For instance, the German foreign minister Westerwelle, when visiting Belgrade, claimed that "Kosovo's borders are fixed" (*Die Welt*, August 27, 2010).
31. The Belgian Minister for European Affairs seems to be in favour (*EUobserver* 9 March 2010) whereas the British Ambassador to Serbia claimed the opposite (*B92*, June 24, 2008).
32. See http://europa.eu/rapid/pressReleasesAction.do?reference=MEMO/11/693&format=HTML&aged=-0&language=EN&guiLanguage=en 30 Nov. [2011] and Ratiu 423.
33. In an article in a German newspaper, the Serbian president Boris Tadic explicitly made this point when he tried to lobby for the candidate status just one day before the EU summit; cf. Boris Tadic: "Serbien am europäischen Wendepunkt." *FAZ*, December 8, 2011, 10.
34. This term was introduced by Frank Schimmelfennig in his work on Eastern enlargement. EU governments had promised the uniting of Europe using grand rhetoric. When they uttered concerns regarding the domestic policy preferences they were reminded of their promise. So they felt obliged to adhere to their initial rhetoric and did not dare to further object to enlargement – a case of "self-entrapment".

Primary Sources:

Serbian and Montenegrin sources:

BETA (http://www.beta.co.rs/default.asp?lan=en)
B92 (http://www.b92.net/eng/)
Blic (http://www.blic.rs/)
DAN (http://www.dan.co.me/)

International sources:

BBC
Deutsche Welle (DW) (http://www.dw-world.de/dw/0,,265,00.html)
Die Welt
Economist
EUbusiness.com (http://www.eubusiness.com/)
EUobserver (http://euobserver.com/)

Frankfurter Allgemeine Zeitung (FAZ)
Frankfurter Rundschau
IWPR – Institute for War and Peace Reporting (http://iwpr.net/)
NYT – New York Times
NZZ – Neue Züricher Zeitung
SZ – Süddeutsche Zeitung

Acknowledgements

I would like to thank the two anonymous reviewers for helping me clarify some of the theoretical and empirical aspects of the article. Also, many thanks to Katharina McLarren and the respective panel participants of the ecpr conference in Reykjavik for their useful comments on an earlier version of the article.

Bibliography

Adler, Emmanuel, and Michael Barnett. 2002. *Security Communities*. Cambridge: Cambridge University Press.
Altmann, Franz-Lothar. 2005. "EU und Westlicher Balkan: Eine schwierige Verlobung." *Südosteuropa* 53 (2): 185–212.
Anastasakis, Othon. 2008. "The EU's Political Conditionality in the Western Balkans: Towards a More Pragmatic Approach." *Southeast European and Black Sea Studies* 8 (4): 365–377.
Bickerton, Christopher J. 2011. *European Union Foreign Policy: From Effectiveness to Functionality*. London: Palgrave Macmillan.
Blockmans, Steven. 2007. *Tough Love. The European Union's Relations with the Western Balkans*. The Hague: T.M.C. Asser Press.
Börzel, Tanja A. 2005. "Europeanization: How the EU Interacts with its Member States." In *The Member States of the EU*, edited by Simon Bulmer and Christian Lequesne, 45–76. Oxford: Oxford University Press.
Bretherton, Charlotte, and John Vogler. 2006. *The European Union as a Global Actor*. 2nd ed. New York: Routledge.
Cohen, Leonard J. 2002. *Serpent in the Bosom: The Rise and Fall of Slobodan Milošević*. Boulder: Westview Press.
Djordjevic, Olivera. 2008. *The limits of Europeanization 'from without': Is there an EU-driven democratization process in Serbia?* UNISCI Discussion Papers, N° 18, Oct.
Dyker, David A. 2004. *Catching Up and Falling Behind: Post-Communist Transformation in Historical Perspective*. London: Imperial College Press.
Ferreira Nunes, Isabel. 2011. "Civilian, Normative, and Ethical Power Europe: Role Claims and EU Discourses." *EFAR* 16: 1–20.
Fierke, Karin M., and Antje Wiener. 1999. "Constructing Institutional Interests: EU and NATO Enlargement." *Journal of European Public Policy* 6 (5): 721–742.
Finnemore, Martha, and Kathryn Sikking. 1998. "International Norm Dynamics and Political Change." *International Organization* 524: 887–917.
Gariup, Monica. 2009. *European Security Culture: Language, Theory, Policy*. Farnham and Burlington: Ashgate.
Grabbe, Heather. 2006. *The EU's Transformative Power. Europeanization through Conditionality in Central and Eastern Europe*. Houndmills and New York: Palgrave/Macmillan.
Gross, Eva, and Ana E. Juncos. 2011. *EU Conflict Prevention and Crisis Management: Roles, Institutions and Policies*. London: Routledge.
International Crisis Group. 2005. "Kosovo: Toward Final Status." *Europe Report Nr. 161*, 24 Jan. http://www.crisisgroup.org/home/index.cfm?id=3226&1=1
International Crisis Group. 2002. "A Kosovo Roadmap (I): Addressing Final Status." *Europe Report Nr. 124*, 1 March. http://www.crisisgroup.org/home/index.cfm?id=1640&1=1

International Crisis Group. 2007. "Breaking the Kosovo Stalemate: Europe's Responsibility." *Europe Report 185*, 21 August http://www.crisisgroup.org/home/index.cfm?action=login&ref_id=5018
Janković, Nikola. 2006. *Die serbische Nation zwischen Ethnonationalismus und Internationalismus im 21. Jahrhundert: Analysis*. Michael-Zikić-Foundation, University of Bonn.
Jović, Dejan. 2011. "Turning Nationalists into EU Supporters: The Case of Croatia." In *The Western Balkans and the EU: 'The Hour of Europe'*, edited by Jacques Rupnik (33–45). Chaillot Papers No. 126. Paris: European Union Institute for Security Studies.
Judah, Tim. 2004. "Serbia's Kosovo policy." In *European and US Policies in the Balkans*, edited by Franz-Lothar Altmann and Eugene Whitlock (19–24). SWP Paper. Berlin: Stiftung Wissenschaft und Politik.
Ker-Lindsey, James. 2009. *Kosovo: The path to Contested State-hood in the Balkans*. London and New York: I.B. Tauris.
Koeth, Wolfgang. 2010. "State Building without a state: The EU's Dilemma in Defining Its Relations with Kosovo." *European Foreign Affairs Review* 15: 227–247.
Kubicek, Paul, ed. 2003. *"The European Union and Democratization"*. London: Routledge.
Laïdi, Zaki. 2010. "Is Europe a Risk-Averse Actor?" *EFAR* 15: 411–426.
Lang, Kai-Olaf, and Daniela Schwarzer. 2007. "Argumente für eine neue Erweiterungsstrategie – die Diskussion über die Aufnahmefähigkeit der EU." *Integration* 30 (April): 117–128.
Lavenex, Sandra, and Frank Schimmelfennig. 2007. "Relations with the Wider Europe." *JCMS* 45: 143–162.
Linz, Juan, and Stepan Alfred. 1996. *Problems of Democratic Transitions and Consolidation: Southern Europe, South America and Post-Communist Europe*. Baltimore: JHU Press.
Lucarelli, Sonia, and Ian Manners. 2006. "Conclusions." In *Values and Principles in European Union Foreign Policy*, edited by Sonia Lucarelli and Ian Manners, 201–215. London and New York: Routledge.
Narten, Jens. 2009. "Dilemma of Promoting 'Local Ownership': The Case of Postwar Kosovo." In *Dilemmas of State-Building. Confronting the Contradictions of Postwar Peace Operations*, edited by Roland Paris and Timothy Sisk, 252–283. New York: Taylor and Francis.
Noutcheva, Gergana. 2007. *Fake, Partial and Imposed Compliance. The limits of the EU's Normative Power in the Western Balkans*. CEPS working document No. 274, July.
Noutcheva, Gergana, and D. Bechev. 2008. "The Successful Laggards: Bulgaria and Romania's Accession to the EU." *East European Politics and Societies* 22 (1): 114–144.
Nugent, Neill, ed. 2004. *European Union Enlargement*. Houndsmills: Palgrave.
Panebianco, Stefania. 2006. "The Constraints on EU Action as a 'Norm Exporter' in the Mediterranean." In *The European Union's Roles in International Politics: Concepts and Analysis*, edited by Ole Elgström and Michael Smith, 136–154. London and New York: Routledge.
Phinnemore, David. 2005. *"And we'd Like to Thank...": Romania's Integration into the European Union*. Paper presented to UACES 34th Annual Conference and 10th Research Conference, Zagreb, September 5–7.
Radaelli, Claudio. 2003. "Europeanization of Public Policy." In *The Politics of Europeanization*, edited by Kevin Featherstone and Claudio Radaelli, 27–56. Oxford: Oxford University Press.
Ralchev, Plamen. 2004. *The EU Conditional Assistance as a Policy Tool Towards Southeastern Europe*. FORNET, Brussels. http://www.fornet.info/documents/Ralchev-Present ation20Feb2004.pdf
Raith, Michael. 2006. "Quo vadis Belgrad? Serbien zwischen europäischer Integration und nationalistischer Isolation." *Südosteuropa Mitteilungen* 5 (June): 36–49.
Ramet, Sabrina P. 2007. "The Denial Syndrome and its Consequences: Serbian Political Culture Since 2000." *Communist and Post-Communist Studies* 40: 40–58.
Reuter, Jens. 2005. "Serbien und die EU – Wie weit ist der Weg nach Bruessel?" *Südosteuropa* 53 (3): 376–403.
Sajdik, Martin, and Michael Schwarzinger. 2008. "European Union Enlargement. Background, Developments, Facts." In *Central and East European Policy Studies*. Vol. 2, New Brunswick and London: Transaction Press.
Schimmelfennig, Frank. 2003. *The EU, NATO and the Integration of Europe. Rules and Rhetoric*. Cambridge: Cambridge University Press.

Schimmelfennig, Frank, and Ulrich Sedlmeier. 2005. "The Politics of EU Enlargement: Theoretical and Comparative Perspectives." In *The Politics of EU Enlargement. Theoretical Approaches*, edited by Frank Schimmelfennig and Ulrich Sedlmeier, 3–30. London: Routledge.

Schmitt, Oliver Jens. 2008. *Kosovo. Kurze Geschichte einer zentralbalkanischen Landschaft*. Wien: UTB.

Schmitter, Philipp C. 1995. "Von der Autokratie zur Demokratie. Zwölf Überlegungen zur politischen Transformation" *Internationale Politik* 50 (6): 47–52.

Slobodchikoff, Michael O. 2010. "The New European Union: Integration as a Means of Norm Diffusion." *Journal on Ethnopolitics and Minority Issues in Europe* 9 (1): 1–25.

Smith, Hazel. 2002. *European Union Foreign Policy: What it is and What it Does*. London: Pluto Press.

Smith, Karen E. 2006. "The Limits of Pro-active Cosmopolitism: The EU and Burma, Cuba, and Zimbabwe." In *The European Union's Roles in International Politics: Concepts and Analysis*, edited by Ole Elgström and Michael Smith, 155–171. London and New York: Routledge.

Soerensen, Georg. 2001. *Changes in Statehood. The Transformation of International Relations*. Basingstoke and New York: Palgrave MacMillan.

Solana, Javier. 2009. *Wellicht gaat Nederland anders over Servië denken*. Interview in NRC Handelsblad 2 April: 7.

Stahl, Bernhard. 2011. "Perverted Conditionality – the Stabilisation and Association Agreement Between the European Union and Serbia." *European Foreign Affairs Review* 4 (16): 465–487.

Stahl, Bernhard. 2013. "100-jähriges Scheitern: Die internationale Gemeinschaft und der albanisch-serbische Identitätskonflikt." In *Das neue Kosovo: Eigenstaatlichkeit, Demokratie und Europa*, edited by Konrad Clewing and Vedran Dzihic. Südosteuropäische Arbeiten, Oldenburg-Verlag (forthcom.)

Stahl, Bernhard, and Sebastian Harnisch, eds. 2009a. *Vergleichende Außenpolitikforschung und nationale Identitäten Die Europäische Union im Kosovo-Konflikt (1996–2008)*. Series "Außenpolitik und Internationale Ordnung", Baden-Baden: Nomos-Verlag.

Stahl, Bernhard, and Sebastian Harnisch, eds. 2009b. "Nationale Identitäten und Außenpolitiken: Erkenntnisse, Desiderate und neue Wege in der Diskursforschung." In *Vergleichende Außenpolitikforschung und nationale Identitäten. Die Europäische Union im Kosovo-Konflikt (1996–2008)*, edited by Bernhard Stahl and Sebastian Harnisch (31–58). Series "Außenpolitik und Internationale Ordnung", Baden-Baden: Nomos-Verlag.

Subotic, Jelena. 2009. *Hijacked Justice: Dealing with the Past in the Balkans*. Ithaca: Cornell University Press.

Teokarevic, Jovan. 2011. "Ten Years of Post-Milosevic Transition in Serbia: Problems and Prospects." In *The Western Balkans and the EU: 'The Hour of Europe'*, edited by Jacques Rupnik (59–78). Chaillot Papers, No. 126. Paris: EU Institute for Security Studies.

Vachudova, Milada Anna. 2005. *Europe Undivided. Democracy, Leverage, and Integration After Communism*. Oxford: Oxford University Press.

Verheugen, Günther. 2005. *Europa in der Krise*. Köln: Kiepenheuer & Witsch.

Weller, Marc. 2008. *Negotiating the Final Status of Kosovo*. Chaillot Paper 114, ISS.

Wendt, Alexander E. 1987. "The Agent Structure Problem in International Relations Theory." *International Organization* 41: 335–370.

EU Member State-Building in the Western Balkans: (Prolonged) EU-protectorates or new model of sustainable enlargement? Conclusion

Jens Woelk

University of Trento and EURAC, Bolzano, Italy

More than 20 years after the violent break-up of Yugoslavia European efforts to create sustainable States in the Western Balkans, as discussed in the papers of this Special Issue, have brought about some progress, but a lot of work remains. This conclusion will draw on some of the themes developed in the previous papers and contrast to what extent EU Member State-Building provides a new framework for enlargement and what the key questions of sustainable expansion of the EU and functional state-building through conditionality will be. It concludes that the EU's current engagement with the Western Balkans faces many problems and obstacles and therefore some reconsideration might be necessary.

The Western Balkans: a testing ground for the future of Europe

100 years ago, in Sarajevo in June 1914, Europe entered a century of self-destruction; 20 years ago, in April 1992, the beginning of the siege of Sarajevo marked another dark chapter of European history with the rest of Europe standing apart. Today, Sarajevo, Bosnia and Herzegovina, and the whole region of the Western Balkans are again the litmus-test for the Continent and for the integration capacity of the European model of democracy and pluralism (Toniatti 2010).

The specific reciprocal relationship between the Balkans and Europe is the common denominator of this Special Issue on "*Europeanization, State-Building and Democratization in the Western Balkans*". According to all contributors there is no doubt that the Balkans are a part of Europe, and that there is a specific Europe responsibility in assisting the area in its difficult transformation which is rightly considered specific and thus different from the transformation in CEE in the 1990s. Although the final objective is the same, the starting point and conditions differ as well as the context suggesting changes in the path to accession for the Western Balkans.

Until a decade ago, full European responsibility had been invoked and the opening of a clear and credible European perspective for the whole area was at the center of the debate. After the EU's commitment, in particular after the summit in Thessaloniki, security issues moved to the background and the perspective of EU accession became the main focus. Despite general improvement of the situation and undeniable progress in a number of fields, more recently the focus of the debate has shifted to the difficulties on the "rocky road" towards European integration of the Western Balkans (Pippan 2004), due to the unexpected (or underestimated?) duration and intensity of international and EU intervention (on the constitutional implications see Marko 2007). A sober evaluation of the current situation in the region, based on the EU Commission's progress reports, does not leave too much room for optimism: in some cases, the Commission's reports might better be referred to as "no-progress reports" (in contrast with the general positive impression some years before, e.g. Batt 2004). It is evident that there is still much to do, but there is much less clarity on how actually to do it. In addition, while there is clearly an "enlargement fatigue" on the EU side raising doubts regarding the political will of the EU and the Member States (Pickering 2011, 1941), also the Western Balkans seem to suffer already from a (pre-)"accession fatigue" (Rupnik 2010, 2011a); in the end, the status quo is not unattractive for many.

A thorough assessment and new impulses as well as strategies are thus needed to create new momentum: can **"EU Member State-Building"** be the answer, i.e. a specific path to EU membership creating, in parallel, the preconditions for being a sustainable State as well as for a future Member State? How should this path look like, based upon a critical evaluation of the current experience with the Stabilization and Association Process (SAP) and conditionality? This, as well as the acknowledgement that the EU's transformative power is limited, is the central concern addressed by this Special Issue.

Sovereignty and integration: the historical example of post-WW II

For underlining both the importance and dimension of the task of integrating the Western Balkans as well as the potential of cooperation and integration, often reference to the historical achievement of overcoming the divisions between the "arch-enemies" France and Germany is made (also by Soeren Keil, initiator of this special issue, in his introduction to this special issue, p. 3). In fact, one should add, by contrast with the Treaty system of Versailles and Trianon after WW I, the post-WW II order in Western Europe was built on cooperation and inclusion (in particular of Germany) rather than on external control and domination. This important lesson from history – stability and prosperity through cooperation and inclusion – makes the insistence on regional cooperation in the Western Balkans plausible as well as the trajectory of their future inclusion in the European Union.

However, using this comparison with the post-conflict situation in Western Europe after WW II, the **voluntary character of integration** must not be underestimated (in fact, this element contrasts with the external control of the process in the Western Balkans). Integration has become possible only by renouncing on parts of national sovereignty, i.e. by opening up the sovereign legal (and constitutional) systems, thus transforming independent States into "interdependent" ones within a framework of economic and legal integration and multilevel governance. The gradual process leading to this situation has been characterized – from the perspective of the Member States – as "Europeanization" (or, more recently, as "EU-isation", Haughton 2007, 234). Today, membership in the EU has become such a characteristic feature, also from a legal point of view, that it is hardly possible to even imagine the same Member States (and their legal systems) without it.

However, since the failure of ratifying the Constitutional Treaty the EU finds itself in a constitutional crisis, as has become particularly evident during the current economic crisis. The main question now is whether there are absolute limits to EU integration (and which ones)? The debate raised by some Constitutional Courts on the "constitutional identity" of Member States, i.e. the essential and specific elements of statehood that have to be respected and guaranteed vis-à-vis the supremacy of EU Law, is fundamental as the answer would, turned around, also allow a precise definition of the European Union itself. And regarding future Member States as well as State-Building, the question translates into the problem of how much influence can and may the EU exercise on constitutional structures and principles, both in terms of legitimacy and of opportunity (i.e. sustainability).

Transition: one moment in time or lasting process?

The process of constitutional, legal and societal transition in the Western Balkans is still under way. Within only one decade (1990–2000), the dissolution of the socialist system, tragic civil wars, transformation of the economic systems into market economies and a fast constitutional transition had to be managed by the new States in order to be admitted into international organizations, such as the Organization of Security and Cooperation in Europe (OSCE) as well as the Council of Europe (CoE). Membership in both is required for moving closer to membership in the European Union (EU), which has become a main goal for all Western Balkan States. European integration is founded upon the idea of sharing sovereignty and upon the conscience of converging constitutional values and principles. Like in a federal system, European integration requires a minimum of homogeneity: "united in diversity", but as truly "integrated States" sharing certain fundamental values and principles. This is why the "rehabilitation" of the Western Balkan States is conditioned by the respect of certain standards (conditionality), with the consequent adoption and absorption of foreign legal models and the monitoring of their implementation and of compliance with "European standards".

In constitutional terms, transition refers to the change from one constitutional system to another one, both based on different values and fundamental principles. Thus, the question of the (democratic) legitimacy of such a profound change is raised regarding the very change as well as the new constitutional system. As, usually, the change from one constitutional system to another does not occur in the framework of pre-existing procedures, democratic consensus becomes a constituent pre-requisite in the transition towards the pluralistic and democratic constitutional system, e.g. through a referendum on the nature of the State or through free and multiparty elections of a constituent assembly.

The result of modern constitutionalism in Europe is a model of constitutional systems based on strong and detailed guarantees regulating the legitimate use of power, in particular through the separation of powers as well as through checks and balances, and providing for a system of Human Rights protection. Through the establishment of an international regime of Human Rights Treaties the latter has also become the basis, at international level, for the legitimate use of international powers of intervention and sanction (even substituting popular support, as it happened in Bosnia and Herzegovina and Kosovo).

The Western Balkans on their way towards European integration are therefore characterized by the internationalization of their constitutional law and by the visible circulation of constitutional models, which creates a paradox: although for most States in the Western Balkans the context is still strongly characterized by the mirage of State sovereignty, international pressure and monitoring regarding the adoption and implementation of "international and European standards" – i.e. criteria elaborated outside the sovereign sphere of the new States – actually limit their sovereignty even before their effective integration. Moreover, the application of these "European standards" is often much more severe than for the "old" and already "integrated" Member States leading to – perceived and real – "double standards".

But does the historical comparison with post-WW II Western Europe really fit?

An important difference, highlighted by Soeren Keil in the first part of his introduction and illustrated by the examples in the contributions, is the enormous complexity of the situation in the Western Balkans. Although the threefold transformation – political-legal, economic and social – and the consequent rapid and comprehensive changes are a common challenge to all countries in the region, the specific situation within the single countries differs considerably despite their common past, their relatively small dimension and their common goal of joining the EU. The complexity is highlighted in all contributions: while Gëzim Krasniqi's focus is on the complex relations between the different actors (minorities, kin- and host-States and international organizations), reminding us, however, that none of these actors should be considered a monolith (Krasniqi 19), Valery Perry and Soeren Keil address the differences in the approaches of international actors and the resulting difficulties in integrating their work. The consequence of this complexity is – necessarily – a differentiation in conditions and approach vis-à-vis the single states (setting certain limits to a regional approach).

However, a common feature is the weak character of all states in the region, some of which are even still contested from within or by their neighbors: "unfinished States" (Surroi 2011) are not secure in their very existence and unable to perform their basic functions. By consequence, the preconditions for Europeanization and membership are simply not given in Bosnia, Kosovo, and only – to some extent – in Serbia and Macedonia. The paradox of European integration is that in order to transfer and share parts of substantial sovereignty, it is necessary to first become a sovereign State (traditional style). This is why "EU Member State-Building" as a specific form of State-Building, with the objective of future integration in mind and preparing for it, is increasingly advocated as a necessary means for "building impossible States" (e.g. Bieber 2011, 1783–1802).

EU Member State-Building: from the outside?

The main difference compared to the origins of European integration is that the process in the Western Balkans is not an endogenous one, but "mainly externally driven, coercive and increasingly demanding" (Anastasakis 2005, 82). In fact, it makes a huge difference for accession that integration within the existing EU is already highly advanced. By consequence, accession is mainly transformed into a question of compliance with the *acquis comunautaire*, which explains the concentration on "technical" issues, the output-orientation of the process and "neutral" institution-building as the principal means for assisting the candidates (which have to be transformed from weak and "unfinished" to strong and fully functioning States).

From the EU perspective, "enlargement" does not only refer to the inclusion of new Members, but is also an important active tool of external policy (although limited to its immediate European neighborhood). The consequence is active and direct intervention in order to prepare future members, even before reaching the formal status as candidates. This often means, at least in practice, unilateral imposition, supervision and evaluation of "European standards", disguised as a merely "technical exercise" rather than negotiated accession.

However, any direct intervention necessarily means direct involvement within the internal affairs and politics (various examples have been given by the authors of this special issue).

In extreme cases, in particular in Kosovo or Bosnia and Herzegovina, **direct involvement risks to create a culture of dependency** instead of strengthening the State. In particular it risks to delay or to even compromise the "ownership" of the process as precondition for future accession. (for Bosnia, see Venneri 2007) While the "democratic deficit" has become a commonplace when referring to the EU, the dynamics of direct intervention and dependency create a "democratic deficit" within the (future) candidate States, too. Mere ratification of EU guidelines (as in the Macedonian case according to Risteska's analysis) and unclear domestic political responsibility risk to provoke lasting damage in the democratization process and political culture of future Member States. Even worse, formal compliance through the adoption of new legislation does not guarantee effective implementation and penetration of the new standards in the legal system. In addition, an "absorption capacity" exists: how many reforms in the judiciary or the public administration are sustainable in a short period of time?

Five paradoxes in the Western Balkans

On the basis of these observations, five major paradoxes in the relationship between the EU and the Western Balkans can be identified:

1) The **"sovereignty paradox"** has already been illustrated above and relates to the subjects of the relationship. The formally sovereign States are already treated as such, although most of them still have to fill formally established democratic and rule of law structures with substance: discrepancies are particularly visible when the implementation of legislative reforms is evaluated! By consequence, any dialogue with the State occurs necessarily through the political and societal elites which control the institutions. However, despite their official commitment to EU integration, these are not rarely opposed to any change by principle, as their interest is, above all, in maintaining the status quo (as the best guarantee for their continuous power and control): the costs of change for domestic elites have to be more thoroughly considered (see in particular Džihić and Wieser 2011).

2) The **"No-blueprint paradox"** is the usual answer to the question "which are the 'European standards' to be applied"? While the latter, if *acquis*-related and thus technical in nature, are usually quite clearly defined in EU secondary law, there is much less certainty in issues related to the constitutional sphere. In particular, there is no blueprint for the constitutional order of a (future) Member State, as also the single constitutional systems of the Member States are different and as this diversity is considered to be a value in itself. Although numerous issues related to accession have, at least, constitutional implications, e.g. the judicial system, the EU does not predispose models or solutions. The situation is complicated by the fact that diversity is a dominant feature throughout the region, slightly mitigated by common past and traditions (which are, however, often either seen as compromised after transition or not known by foreigners and consultants).

3) The **"good will" paradox** refers to the fact that the EU legal system is mainly based on the voluntary respect of the rules by its members. This creates difficulties with enforcement, at least vis-à-vis States. The European Court of Justice can issue a statement of violation of (technical) Treaty duties by the States. However, effective and adequate reaction to (presumed) non-compliance with political and constitutional duties is extremely difficult: this has become clear in the "Austrian crisis" in 2000, and is also evident in the recent cases of Hungary and Romania.[1] The adoption of sanctions for violations of fundamental principles, now foreseen in art. 7 Treaty of the European Union, requires a high degree of political consensus among the Member States; they are clearly *ultima ratio*-measures. The voluntary

nature of integration (for Member States) corresponds to the conviction that integration is an advantage and not an obligation, by contrast with the coercive character of conditionality for candidates often perceived by the latter as unilateral imposition of "European standards".

4) But the scarce effectiveness of sanctions, which might be framed as **"no damage-paradox"**, is not only due to this voluntary character. Sustainable States have to be both capable and willing to integrate. Sanctions vis-à-vis (potential) candidates might consist in the freeze or blockade of technical and financial assistance or even negotiations. It means that progress will be blocked or delayed (as it has been announced by the EU Commission in July 2012, in case of Bosnia not amending its Constitution in order to comply with the ECtHR judgment in the Sejdic-Finci case). However, experience shows that sanctions might worsen the situation rather than improving it, which suggests prudence and preference for carrots rather than sticks! In fact, frequently the Commission seems to react to non-compliance-behavior with "nothing more than verbal warnings urging domestic political elites to pursue the required criteria" (Mihaila 2012, 27).

5) The fifth paradox can be addressed as the **"mirror paradox"**: the EU's capacity of acting as a catalyst for reforms depends very much on its own attractiveness (Privitera 2007, 153). In the last years the EU itself is not in good shape due to the consequences of the failure of the Constitutional Treaty, of "enlargement fatigue" after the last two rounds of enlargement in 2004 and 2007, and of the economic and financial crisis. This does not only mean that the EU is more occupied with itself and much less concentrated on the Western Balkans, although success in the region will clearly be crucial also for the EU itself and its external action. Inevitably lesser engagement also has serious and negative consequences for the progress made by the (potential) candidates as reform efforts depend on incentives and realistic perspectives. The appeal of membership alone is simply not enough.

Assisted states and participated conditionality: a plan for EU Member State-Building

The main question concerns how to find solutions for sustainable change and create incentives for overcoming these paradoxes. The contributions in this special issue suggest some alternative elements to the current approach.

It is immediately clear that you cannot build any slightly difficult construction without having a plan. Thus, also State-Building and in particular the more sophisticated EU Member State-Building need a detailed construction plan. The more so, as many architects and builders are involved in an exercise requiring a high degree of coordination and cooperation. However, the Sovereignty paradox seems to justify and reinforce the No-blueprint paradox calling for abstention from interfering with fundamental decisions which have to remain with the State (sovereign even in the period of construction). But while this emphasis on independence already contrasts with the general situation of interdependent States in a globalized world, it is also unrealistic in an emerging European constitutional space built on common principles and traditions and even counterproductive, if the result shall be a "Member State of the EU".

In Europe, at a general level, some important fundamental principles and values are shared. The OSCE "Charter of Paris for a New Europe" of 1990, proclaims "democracy as our only form of government". Democracy, human rights, including the rights of persons belonging to minorities, and the rule of law (art. 2 TEU codifying the Copenhagen criteria for membership) have become core principles and values, thus excluding systems contrasting with them. But these values and principles are quite abstract and need to be shaped concretely through their implementation. At this level, concrete guidance is missing. In the Member States, historical experiences have led to different solutions which all fit under the common principles; this diversity in the constitutional structures is worth to be preserved and even a value in itself (art. 4 TEU). The independence of the judiciary, for instance, can be guaranteed by self-administration through a judicial council (like in Italy, Spain and France), but this is not the only way to do so (as Austria, Germany and the UK, all without such an institution, demonstrate); even in the case that such a judicial council is established (actually it has become the pre-dominant model in CEE and SEE), differences may regard its actual powers, its composition, etc. Only once a decision has been taken for a specific model is it possible to monitor and check its compliance with the general principles, its conformity with requirements resulting from the *acquis comunautaire* as well as its effective operation in practice.

Contributing to the inflationary use of the metaphor of the **"European house"**, this situation might be compared with a **condominium** in order to illustrate the different degrees of conditionality: while the highest (and abstract) level, principles and values, might be compared with the fact that all apartments in the condominium are equipped with heating, electricity and a common system for water supply and sewage, the decision on the layout of the single flats remains clearly with their owners (different possibilities in the usage of the single rooms, determining, e.g. the number and collocation of sockets and tubes), but has to be compatible with the other systems as well as with the general one (guarantee of interoperability and security, i.e. the concrete shape of sockets and tubes).

The method for overcoming the Sovereignty paradox as well as the No-blueprint paradox cannot be uniformity at the second level, i.e. regarding the fundamental decisions regarding the specific realization of the common abstract principles and values, as this would cancel diversity (making all flats alike; in addition, some solutions which are reasonable for large flats might not work for smaller ones, some owners are richer than others or simply have other priorities etc.). Thus, in terms of conditionality, rather than "European standards" European "adaptations" are needed. Instead of (fictitious) uniformity the different possible options in realizing the abstract fundamental principles have to be identified allowing for a conscious choice between them in order to find a suitable solution for the country in question. The method has to be comparative. There cannot be only one blueprint: only by drawing from comparison will it be possible to elaborate a range of alternative options (having future conformity with the *acquis communautaire* in mind). The EU should assist with comparative expertise in finding these options.

Having identified the substance, or at least different options, the question remains **how a legitimate decision can be taken on which option to choose**.

Of course, any legitimate decision has to be democratic. Again, the "ownership" debate has to be mentioned for the relationship between external and internal State builders (see Valery Perry's and Soeren Keil's contribution, 5). But within a consolidating democratic system often status quo-oriented political and societal elites dominate, while press and civil society are too weak for effectively exercising their function of integrating checks and balances. Voluntary change can be expected only if advantages outweigh disadvantages. Incentives will be perceived as such by politicians the more benefits can be expected for citizens. This has been effectively demonstrated by the visa-liberalization process which has triggered change, and – in the contrary sense – by police-reform and the attempts for constitutional reform in Bosnia (for the latter see Džihić and Wieser 2011, 1812–1818, and Venneri 2007). The costs of change have important consequences for the decisions on the realization of fundamental principles and values, for which often no immediate gain can be expected: these decisions cannot be left alone with the elites represented in the institutions, as this risks letting them fall into the "status quo trap". The repertoire of contention and parallel trajectories to international State-building in Bosnia is effectively illustrated by Outi Keranen's contribution; with the dramatically diminishing international interest in Bosnia, these risks have dramatically increased.

Direct intervention and coercion by the "International Community" as a means for overcoming obstruction (or alternative projects) by domestic politicians is no longer an option. The exceptional and transitional character of extraordinary measures, such as the Bonn Powers, has been clarified not least by the European Commission for Democracy through Law (Venice Commission 2005). Direct intervention and coercion have been substituted by indirect pressure (EU conditionality), but without changing the mainly intergovernmental approach in the relationship with the States: a sort of "path dependancy"?

In order to strengthen the democratic culture as well as to put pressure on politicians (by those represented), the citizens' perspective has to be included (Džihić and Wieser 2011, 1809) and the wider public has to become involved. The negative impact of the lack of public consultation and participation on democratic processes is illustrated by Risteska in her contribution: the example of Macedonia describes the one-sided nature of the accession process with the "fast-track" adoption of *acquis*-related legislation in order to guarantee formal compliance and a dialogue with political parties (i.e. elites) instead of an open policy-dialogue with non-State actors (Risteska, 18–20). Rather than relying on sanctions, incentives have to be created for open dialogue beyond institutions involving citizens.

A recent example illustrating the dilemmas of EU Member State-Building is Bosnia and Herzegovina and the difficulties in achieving a – limited – constitutional reform. While there is a clear obligation for the country to amend its Constitution since the ECtHR-judgment in the Sejdic-Finci-case of December (see Venice Commission 2008), nothing has happened for more than three years. Touching the Constitution means opening the Pandora's box which has been tapped by the Dayton Peace Agreement. What kind of State are we then talking about? It is evident that Bosnia's transition will not be concluded until it will be possible to exercise "local ownership" regarding its own Constitution. But can we expect, in the current situation, that politicians in Bosnia will discover and adopt a solution, if only sufficiently pressed or threatened (suspension of any progress and/or assistance as announced by the EU Commission in July 2012)? Or do we have to dictate the solution from the outside (bringing us back to the debate on Dayton II)? Is there a third way between the "wait and see" approach and a new form of a semi-protectorate?

It is necessary that the EU, without dictating one solution, clearly spells out what the different compatible options are from which to choose. It is also necessary that it contributes to (starting) a debate on these options. A constitutional compromise based on the objective of European integration might help to end the period of external imposition and guarantees. European integration as well as its domestic constitutional consequences should be added to the (Dayton) Constitution. Providing an answer to the question of "why do we stay together?",[2] such a constitutional objective might serve as the missing voluntary element which is the necessary basis for any democratic State and for a federal compact.

In fact, almost all EU Member States have amended their Constitutions, either on occasion of Treaty revisions or in view of their accession to the EU, in order to meet the requirements resulting from their integration into the EU legal system. While some of the necessary constitutional adaptations derive from concrete requirements of the *acquis communautaire* (and are thus specifically addressed in the accession negotiations, in the single chapters), other constitutional implications result from the general impact of EU membership on the domestic constitutional and legal system (see Woelk 2011). These include, above all, the constitutional basis for membership, but also its consequences, such as changes in the balances between domestic institutions (in particular between Executive and Parliament), changes in the internal distribution of competences as well as the participation in the EU decision making process and the implementation of EU law. In 2010, Croatia adopted a major constitutional amendment for the purpose of constitutional conformity with EU accession and integration; Chapter VIII (articles 143–146) introduced specific provisions on membership in the European Union in the Croatian Constitution (Narodne Novine 76/2010 of 16 June 2010).

This example underlines how a clear commitment to European integration can be positively framed in the Constitution. Commitment is rightly considered one of three pillars necessary for successful (EU Member) State-Building (Bieber 2011, 1798): the other two are the normative foundation of the State and its institutional capacity. While the latter has been at the focus of numerous "institution-building" projects, it is the normative foundation, the vision of the State and its acceptance by its citizens which needs to be addressed more by the EU. This is the "political" (or constitutional) "input dimension" of the good governance concept discussed by Risteska (using Börzel's analytical framework) as distinguished from the technical or "administrative" dimension, which is primarily output-oriented and still the main focus of the EU's attention.

In order to avoid new dependencies or, worse, new (*de facto-*) protectorates, EU Member State-Building in the context of consolidating democratic systems requires the EU to assume the role of an "interested moderator": it needs to develop perspectives, to suggest different (constitutional) options, to improve policymaking capacities and to guarantee public debate instead of only checking the fulfillment of "technical" conditions. Moreover, the combination of commitment and normative foundations are intrinsically linked with a more general cultural change to be brought about as the result of transition.

Cultural change, reconciliation and regional dimension

Cultural as well as structural changes are necessary for successful and sustainable implementation of reforms in practice. This conclusion by Marija Risteka in her analysis of the promotion of good governance by the EU in Macedonia is certainly true for reforms regarding technical and institutional issues. Unfortunately, Soeren Keil's observation seems correct that "the EU's limited impact on good governance in Macedonia, [i.e. in a comparatively less difficult environment, also] demonstrates the very limits of EU Member State Building". This shows that cultural change is necessary also on a more general level, as demonstrated by Bernhard Stahl's analysis of the relationship between Serbia (in its self-perception of a "sovereign nation State)" and the EU (as a "post-nation" polity), a constellation bringing us back to the sovereignty paradox. Historically, the building of the (Nation-) State and its integration are two distinct (and subsequent) processes which, in the Western Balkans, take place at the same time (Surroi 2011, 115). Bridging the divide between these opposing perceptions will succeed only if the focus is not only on the present and not only on the single State.

Including the past and the regional dimension is fundamental for the success of EU Member State-Building, for the normative foundations of the States as well as for their commitment to integrate together with others. The political use of (different) narratives for the purpose of political mobilization has been an important common feature throughout the region: Jelena Dzankić illustrates this with an analysis of the politicization of cleavages by opposing political elites in Montenegro's transition leading to the country's independence.

Until today, the "cultural deficit" in the transformation of the Western Balkan States includes the widely disregarded but important issue of **reconciliation**. Apart from the judicial persecution in war crime-trials – by the ICTY and more recently also by local judges – no serious attempt has been made in "coming to terms with the past". This is true also for reconciliation in the ample sense, i.e. relations between States and groups. It is indeed striking, but not surprising, that major steps regarding these relations have been made by Courts, such as the ICJ judgments on Srebrenica, Kosovo and the name-dispute between Greece and Macedonia or, in the case of the constitutional system of Bosnia by the Constitutional Court ("Constituent Peoples" in 2000) and by the ECtHR (Sejdic-Finci case in 2009).

But without clarifications and ample debate on the (recent) past, true and lasting democratization will be difficult. In its evolution after WW II the German case might be instructive for the establishment of a cultural change and democratization in a context conditioned by external values as well as driven by external powers – at least initially. Of course, Germany has not been contested in its statehood (after the decision on its division), and a generational change has been necessary, but consolidation of the German democracy could only be achieved on the basis of an ongoing debate on the Third Reich (uncomfortable for many). Again, in the Western Balkans the sovereignty paradox makes an encompassing discussion, analysis and elaboration of the past difficult, as these questions will not only and inevitably raise the question of guilt related to individual and collective action, but also touch the very (ideological and ethnic) foundations and myths of the new States requiring a differentiated approach rather than a national(istic) one. So far, the need for reconciliation has not been expressly acknowledged, addressed or encouraged by the EU. But it does not only regard the past: it is also fundamental for stability and the future, not least as a precondition for resolving existing conflicts among the States in the region as well as among the different groups within the States.

Finally, the **regional dimension**, which is both a problem and a chance at the same time.

The current "regatta approach", however, promising to produce incentives for voluntary implementation of reforms, seems to work only, if a country has become a candidate and if the accession-promise is credible and concrete (this could be observed in Croatia, and, at least to some extent, in Montenegro and Macedonia). Where the accession perspective is realistically more remote, as for the "unfinished States" (Bosnia, Kosovo and Serbia), the option of future parallel accession as well as greater emphasis on the regional dimension might be more productive ("at least on a smaller scale", Rupnik 2010, 9–10). For the EU, the "Cyprus lesson" makes it necessary to insist in future on the resolution of conflicts and controversial issues before accession. Besides the relations between Serbia, Kosovo, and BiH-RS, citizenship issues will also have to be considered more carefully, e.g. the status of Croats in BiH after Croatia's accession to the EU (considering the controversies with neighboring States regarding Hungarian or Romanian citizenship legislation). It is rightly predicted that dual citizenship will become a widespread phenomenon in the region (Štiks 2011, 134). Thus, it should be actively addressed (not only at a technical level).

The regional dimension also offers the chance for economies of scale in the development of the Western Balkans through network-building. Again, besides the institutional dimension, a citizens' perspective is useful for considering measures of complementary and supportive intervention. Like the networks in pre-war Yugoslavia, a generation of young civil servants and managers is currently building new cross-border networks, in particular due to common study experiences abroad. Supporting these spontaneous processes by creating additional occasions in the region, e.g. through a regional Academy for Public Administration, regional institutions for the training of police and judges as well as support for Universities or even a regional Erasmus-program for the exchange of students, would reinforce new personal relations across borders upon which a culture of cooperation can be built. It would also break up the self-centeredness of the single countries.

Taking the task seriously and talking straight

For more than a decade it has been repeated that **"the Hour of Europe"** has come (Rupnik 2011a). Looking into the mirror, the European Union should realize that "accession fatigue" and sinking popular support in the Western Balkans for integration require renewed European commitment and suggest a re-assessment of the current conditionality approach. The key features of a new strategy will have to include an incentives-based approach, consultation and assistance (without imposition) in constitutional issues, greater emphasis on involving citizens, and use of regional dimension in creating and supporting networks. As accession has already been promised to all States in the Western Balkans, at least as a future perspective, changing their status from "potential candidates" to candidates would be an important symbolic gesture: the political move of a visible renewed commitment by the EU would have the concrete and beneficial consequence of a serious structured framework for negotiation.

There are good reasons for taking the task of integrating the Western Balkans seriously, above all for the EU's credibility as an international actor as well as the costs of non-enlargement. In fact, the alternative to a renewed and serious engagement is a continuation of the current "limbo-situation" of quasi EU-protectorates: formally sovereign States which are conditioned in any substantial decision and dependent on EU assistance ("the choice facing the EU in the Balkans is between enlargement and Empire", (Rupnik 2011b, 30). Not only does such an approach contrast with the EU's own values, but it would be also far from effective: considering the limits of conditionality, it can be predicted that the EU would be able to exert, at maximum, only relative control on its periphery and the States would not advance in their democratic transition and culture.

However, even renewed engagement will not resolve a final paradox: time. "Good things come to those who wait" (Batt 2010, 5); a long-term approach is also suggested by Perry: rather than setting suggestive and symbolic dates for their accession, the States in the Western Balkans need a realistic time-frame based upon realistic expectations, on both sides. Time is needed, if the aim is not simply consolidation of post-conflict stability but creating sustainable (Member) States: any sustainable process of democratization and cultural change needs time. This is demonstrated by the current constitutional situation in Hungary and Romania as well as by the general gap in post-accession compliance records between strong formal, but weak practical compliance (Schimmelfennig and Trauner 2009). While Valery Perry and Soeren Keil's account of the OSCE's bottom-up approach to educational reform with a long-term perspective in Bosnia seems perfectly to summarize the elements of an inclusive and voluntary approach strengthening civil society, they also ask whether "bottom-up is enough", raising the further question of coordination between the EU and other organizations, and state that "the country's democratic consolidation – let alone reconciliation – will take some time" (Perry and Keil 17 and 19).

But time is a scarce resource for the Western Balkans. They have already lost a decade in the 1990s. Incentives for change depend on a credible perspective of accession as well as on concrete benefits for the population making European integration a real experience even before accession. The difficulties in keeping a positive momentum in the preparation for accession have led to the recent introduction of a "High Level Accession Dialogue – HLAD" between the EU Commission and Macedonia in 2012.[3] Again, this is an exercise involving mainly institutions and thus elites only. Therefore it will be necessary to think of further benefits similar to visa liberalization which provide immediate and tangible improvements in the everyday standards of living and employment prospects (Batt 2010, 5). Such improvements are useful for technical preparation, but even more so for triggering wide discussion and rallying popular support during the time necessary until accession.

Like looking into a mirror, the relation with the Western Balkans forces Europe to reflect over its own "values" and "standards". The degree of success of its attracting forces in the Western Balkans will thus be an important indicator for the state of the European model of pluralistic integration within the EU. This is currently demonstrated by the considerable stress on this model due to the economic and financial crisis: the question whether the current balance between sovereignty and integration is sustainable has thus to be answered not only by the Western Balkans but by the European Union as well.

As the International Commission for the Balkans, chaired by Giuliano Amato, put it already some years ago: "We expect Europe to live up to its promise", in the interest of the Western Balkans, but also in its own interest.

Notes

1. Serious concerns over democracy, the rule of law and the protection of human rights in Hungary have been expressed by European institutions after the adoption of a series of laws implementing Hungary's new Constitution, the first after the Communist era and in force since January 2012. Prime Minister Viktor Orban's party had won a two thirds majority in a parliamentary election in 2010 and immediately after rewrote the country's Constitution attracting widespread criticism for threatening the essentials of democracy. After ordering a change to the country's media law in 2011, the EU Commission in January 2012 began infringement procedures on laws concerning the retirement ages of judges, independence of the central bank and the independence of the data protection agency. In July, the EU Commission officially closed the infringement procedure over the independence of the central bank, after the Hungarian Parliament had passed amendments to its Central Bank Act. On 16 February 2012, the European Parliament passed a resolution urging Hungary to respect EU laws and values or risk having the EU assembly start a formal investigation into serious breaches of EU values, a never-before-used instrument in the EU Treaty. Based on a report commissioned to the civil liberties committee in the European Parliament, the Parliament will decide whether to activate Article 7 of the EU Treaty, with the ultimate sanction being loss of voting power for the Member State. On 18 July 2012, the EU Commission issued a report in which it questioned whether the Romanian government has the "understanding of the meaning of the rule of law in a pluralist democratic system." The report contained an 11-point-long to do list, including independence of the judiciary. Another special report on the Romanian situation will be drafted before the end of the year. Sources: EU Observer on Hungary <http://euobserver.com/political/115286 and on Romania <http://euobserver.com/political/117211. EU Commission – Press Release, *European Commission launches accelerated infringement proceedings against Hungary* (17 January 2012). http://europa.eu/rapid/pressReleasesAction.do?reference=IP/12/24. EU Commission, *Eleventh CVM Report on Romania* (18 July 2012). http://ec.europa.eu/cvm/docs/com_2012_410_en.pdf.
2. According to George Schoepflin, "States need a need a cohesive idea" (Schoepflin [1993] 1995) for justifying their existence; in his article, Schoepflin explains the break-up of Yugoslavia as a consequence of such an underlying vision of the common State getting gradually lost.

3. Introduced in March 2012 by Commissioner Füle, the High Level Accession Dialogue – HLAD shall "put the EU integration to the forefront of the domestic agenda and give it a new boost [...] by ensuring a structured, high level discussion on the main reform challenges and opportunities". The Dialogue "does not replace accession negotiations but it forms a bridge to them". See EU Commission Conclusions <http://ec.europa.eu/commission_2010-2014/fule/docs/news/20120315_conclusions.pdf. In June 2012, a High Level Dialogue on the Accession Process has also been launched with Bosnia and Herzegovina for explaining the requirements and the methodology of accession negotiations and concretely what is expected from Bosnia and Herzegovina in the EU accession process; see Joint Conclusions <http://europa.eu/rapid/pressReleasesAction.do?reference=MEMO/12/503&type=HTML.

References

Anastasakis, Othon. 2005. "The Europeanization of the Balkans." *Brown Journal of World Affairs* 12: 77–88.

Batt, Judy, ed. 2004. *The Western Balkans Moving On*. Institute for Security Studies: Chaillot Papers no. 70 (October). http://www.iss.europa.eu/publications/

Batt, Judy. 2010. *The EU and the Western Balkans: Preparing for the Long-Haul*. FRIDE Policy Brief, December: 1–5. http://www.fride.org/publication/840/the-eu-and-the-western-balkans:-preparing-for-the-long-haul

Bieber, Florian. 2011. "Building Impossible States? State-Building Strategies and EU Membership in the Western Balkans." *Europe-Asia Studies* 63 (10): 1783–1802.

Džihić, Vedran, and Angela Wieser. 2011. "Incentives for Democratisation? Effects of EU Conditionality on Democracy in Bosnia & Herzegovina." *Europe-Asia Studies* 63 (10): 1803–1825.

European Commission for Democracy through Law (Venice Commission). 2005. *Opinion on the Constitutional Situation of Bosnia and Herzegovina and the Powers of the High Representative*, CDL-AD (2005)004, 11 March 2005. www.venice.coe.int

European Commission for Democracy through Law (Venice Commission). 2008. Opinion no. 483/2008, 22 October 2008, *Amicus Curiae Brief in the Cases of Sejdić and Finci v. Bosnia and Herzegovina*. http://www.venice.coe.int

Haughton, Tim. 2007. "When Does the EU Make a Difference? Conditionality and the Accession Process in Central and Eastern Europe." *Political Studies Review* 5 (2): 233–246.

International Commission on the Balkans (chair Giuliano Amato). 2005. *The Balkans in Europe's Future*, April 2005. www.balkan-commission.org/activities/Report.pdf

Marko, Joseph. 2007. "Constitutions and Good Governance: Challenges for Post-Conflict Reconstruction and EU-Integration." In *Regional Cooperation, Peace Enforcement, and the Role of the Treaties in the Balkans*, edited by Stefano Bianchini, Joseph Marko, Nation R. Craig and Milica Uvalic, 65–78. Ravenna: Longo.

Mihaila, Roxana. 2012. "Europeanisation Faces Balkanisation: Political Conditionality and Democratisation – Croatia and Macedonia in Comparative Perspective." *European Perspectives – Journal on European Perspectives of the Western Balkans* 4 (1): 13–34. http://www.europeanperspectives.si

Pickering, Paula M. 2011. "The Constraints on European Institutions' Conditionality in the Western Balkans." *Europe-Asia Studies* 63: 1939–1944.

Pippan, Christian. 2004. "The Rocky Road to Europe: The EU's Stabilisation and Association Process for the Western Balkans and the Principle of Conditionality." *European Foreign Affairs Review* 9 (2): 219–245.

Privitera, Francesco. 2007. "Europe and the Balkans: A Mirror Image." In *Regional Cooperation, Peace Enforcement, and the Role of the Treaties in the Balkans*, edited by Stefano Bianchini, Joseph Marko, Nation R. Craig and Milica Uvalic, 153–160. Ravenna: Longo.

Rupnik, Jacques. 2010. "Reassessing European Challenges in the Balkans." *European Perspectives – Journal on European Perspectives of the Western Balkans* 2 (2): 7–12. Accessed October 2010. http://www.europeanperspectives.si

Rupnik, Jacques, ed. 2011a. *The Western Balkans and the EU: "The Hour of Europe."* Institute for Security Studies, Chaillot Papers 126 (6 June). http://www.iss.europa.eu/uploads/media/cp126-The_Western_Balkans_and_the_EU.pdf

Rupnik, Jacques. 2011b. "The Balkans as a European question." In *The Western Balkans and the EU: "The Hour of Europe"*, edited by Rupnik, Jacques. Institute for Security Studies, Chaillot Papers 126 (June): 17–30. http://www.iss.europa.eu/publications/

Schimmelfennig, Frank, and Florian Trauner, eds. 2009. "Post-accession compliance in the EU's new member states". *European Integration Online Papers (EIoP)* Special Issue 2(13). http://eiop.or.at/eiop/index.php/eiop/issue/view/22

Schoepflin, George. [1993] 1995. "The Rise and Fall of Yugoslavia." In *The Politics of Ethnic Conflict Regulation. Case Studies of Protracted Ethnic Conflicts*, edited by John McGarry and Brendan O'Leary, 172–203. London/New York.

Štiks, Igor. 2011. "The European Union and Citizenship Regimes in the Western Balkans." In *The Western Balkans and the EU: "The Hour of Europe"*, edited by Jacques Rupnik. Institute for Security Studies, Chaillot Papers 126 (June): 123–134. http://www.iss.europa.eu/publications/

Surroi, Veton. 2011. "The Unfinished State(s) in the Balkans and the EU: The Next Wave." In *The Western Balkans and the EU: "The Hour of Europe"*, edited by Jacques Rupnik. Institute for Security Studies, Chaillot Papers 126 (June): 111–120. http://www.iss.europa.eu/publications/

Toniatti, Roberto. 2010. "La transizione nei Balcani occidentali e il paradigma costituzionale europeo: il pluralismo delle fonti e delle identità." In *Il pluralismo nella transizione costituzionale dei Balcani: diritti e garanzie*, edited by Laura Montanari, Roberto Toniatti, and Jens Woelk, 337–405. Università degli Studi di Trento, Dipartimento di Scienze GiuridicheQuaderni del Dipartimento 92, Trento.

Venneri, Giulio. 2007. *Modelling States from Brussels? A Critical Assessment of the EU-Driven State-building of Bosnia and Herzegovina*. Paper. Cyprus Centre of European and International Affairs Nicosia. http://www.cceia-old.unic.ac.cy/pdf_files/Giulio%20Venneri%20Critical%20Assessment%20of%20the%20EU%20-Driven%20%20Statebuilding%20%202007-07%20%28December%29.pdf

Woelk, Jens. 2011. "Constitutional Challenges of EU Accession for South East European Applicant Countries: A Comparative Approach." Paper presented at the regional conference on Constitutional Challenges for South East Europe Applicant Countries, Skopje, 2 December. http://www.kas.de/wf/doc/kas_5123-1442-1-30.pdf?111117143038

Index

Tables are indicated in bold

ABR (anti-bureaucratic revolution) 72
Accession Partnership Agreement 96, 97
acquis communautaire of the EU 107, 108, 122n6, 130, 133, 134–5; and education 38, 48n13; non-compliance with 106, 109, 111; part of the accession process 1, 3, 90, 93, 96, 100
Ahtisaari, Martti 61, 68n4, 117, 120
Ahtisaari Plan, the 61, 63, 64, 117
Albania 10n5, 67–8, 78, 116; democratization and state-building in 55–8, 66; ethnic minorities 56–8, 60, 67, 68n1; Greek-Albanian relations 59–60, 66
Albanian Orthodox Church, the 59–60
Ashdown, Paddy 34

Bassuener, Kurt 34
Berlin Wall, the 53
BiH (Bosnia and Herzegovina) 136; curricular reform in schools 33, 36–44, 48n17, 49n22; post-conflict international state-building 12–20, 22, 23–4; resistance to external state-building 16–19, 21, 23 *see also* Bosnia; OSCE mission of international assistance to Euro-Atlantic integration in BiH
Bollano, Vasil 58
Bosnia 5, 7–9, 106, 116, 132, 133–4 *see also* BiH (Bosnia and Herzegovina); OSCE mission of international assistance to Euro-Atlantic integration in BiH
Bosniaks 49n22, 76 *see also* international statebuilding in post-conflict Bosnia and Herzegovina
Bosnian Croats 13, 19–22
Bosnian Serbs *see* international statebuilding in post-conflict Bosnia and Herzegovina
Brčko, status of 17–18, 40
Brda tribes of Montenegro 80
Brichambaut, Marc Perrin de 30

CARDS (Community Assistance for Reconstruction, Development, and Stabilization) 94–5
Catholic Church in Bosnia, the 20, 26n9
citizens and civil society involvement in statebuilding in Macedonia 97–9, 101
civic state, the 55, 61 *see also* state, the, new definitions of
cleavage in democracies, notion of 71, 77–8, 83, 84–5; religious cleavages 78–9, 83–4, 86n5
constitutional systems in Europe 129, 131, 134–5
Copenhagen Criteria, the 7, 108
CPC (Montenegrin Orthodox Church) 78–9, 84
Croatia 10, 19–20, 86n5; accession and EU relations 4–5, 13, 90, 108, 111, 135, 136; language curriculum in schools 42, 49n22; statebuilding agenda in 2, 5, 14–15
Croatian business interests in Bosnia 21–2
cultural change and EU governance 135–6
curricular reform in schools in BiH 39–42, 48n17, 49n22
Cyprus 105, 110, 111, 118, 120, 121

decentralization of the state 24, 63, 64, 94–5
democracy as statebuilding instrument 24
democratic structure consolidation 2
democratization and Europeanization 3–4 *see also* state-building
democratization and state-building in Albania and Kosovo 53–4, 58–61, 61–8; in Albania 55–8; in Kosovo 60–6
'democratization without state' process in Kosovo 60–1
Đilas, Milovan 73–4
direct intervention mechanisms 6–7
divides over statehood and identity in Montenegro 72, 78–84, 86n6
Djindjić, Zoran 113
Dodik, Milorad 18, 24, 37, 49n25

INDEX

DPA (Dayton Peace Accord) 15–16, 24, 25, 30–1, 47, 47n2; and RS (Republika Srpska) 14, 21
DPS (Democratic Party of Socialists), Montenegro 71, 72, 74, 75, 76–9, 81–2
Drljević, Sekula 81
DS (Democratic Party), Serbian 65, 113, 119
DSS (Serbian Democratic Party) 113, 114
Đukanović, Milo 73, 75, 79
Dutch refusals to sign the SAA 115, 118, 119

education reform in BiH 33, 36–44, 48n17, 49n22
EIDHR (European Instrument for Democracy and Human Rights) 95, 98
ESI (European Stability Initiative) 34
ethnic cleansing 21
ethnic influence on education reform 37–8, 40
ethnic minorities in Albania 56–8, 60, 67, 68n1
ethnic minorities in Bosnian education 41
ethnic-national cleavages in Montenegro 71, 72–6, **75**, 78–84
ethnic political parties, rise of 34, 35
ethno-cultural narratives and structural cleavages 72, 76–7, 82–3, 85
EU, the, and stabilization 106, 107, 112–21
EU accession policy 5–6, 18, 38, 58, 127–8, 136–8; the *acquis communautaire* 1, 3, 90, 93, 96, 100; strategic accession 106, 109, 110, 112–16 *see also* EU enlargement
EU enlargement 7, 105–7, 108–12, 128; through governance 89, 97; through Member State Building model 6–7, 128, 130, 132–3
EU financial support 6, 8
EU integration 2, 3–5, 7–8, 10, 29, 110; and the Western Balkans 67, 127–32
EU intervention in internal affairs 6–7, 8, 25, 64–5, 95, 134; through Member State building 129, 130–1 *see also* OSCE mission of international assistance to Euro-Atlantic integration in BiH
EU Member State Building 2, 4–10, 128–31, 132–8
EU-OSCE relations 46–7, 48n12
EU Police Mission, the 6

EULEX Mission, the 6, 64, 67, 118, 121
Euro-Atlantic integration 16, 29, 43, 47, 117
European Court of Human Rights 5
Europeanization 1–4, 106, 108, 109, 121, 128; in Macedonia 89–97, 99–101 *see also* EU Member State Building
external actors in Kosovo state building 64–5, 67

Finvest 22
frozen conflicts 47n2
functional cleavages 72, 73, 75–6
functional forms of ownership 33, 38, 39

German statehood 136
good governance and the EU 89, 90–5, 96–7, 135
"good will" paradox in the Western Balkans 131–2
Greece and Cypriot accession 110
Greek-Albanian relations 59–60, 66
Greek minority in Albania 56–8, 59, 66, 67, 68n1

HDZ (Croat party) 19, 20, 22, 111
HLAD (High Level Accession Dialogue) 138, 139n3
human rights discourses 23–4, 46
Hungary 138n1
HVIDRA (Association of Croatian Military Invalids of the Homeland War) 19, 20

ICJ (International Court of Justice) 65, 119–20, 121, 123n29, 136
ICTY (International Criminal Tribune for the former Yugoslavia) 106, 111, 114–16, 120
Index for Inclusion, the 41
international community, and statebuilding 14, 15–19, 22, 25
International Criminal Court, the 6
international statebuilding in post-conflict Bosnia and Herzegovina 12–16, 19–20, 22, 23–4; local resistance 16–19, 21, 23
IPA (Instrument for Pre-Accession) 96
ITA (Interim agreement on trade issues) 115, 118

JHA (Justice and Home Affairs) interventions 95
JSL (Joint Serbian List) 63

Karadžić, Radovan 115
Kosovo 6, 8, 18, 19, 37, 106, 116–20; democratization and state-building 53–4, 60–7
Kosovo-Albanians 117, 120
Kosovo Serbs 61–2, 65–7, 68n4
Koštunica, Vojislav 114, 117, 118

language as ethno-cultural cleavage 82–3, 86n5
law on referendum in Serbia 21
linguistic cleavages 78
local political elites and state-building 33, 34–5, 44, 47

INDEX

local resistance to international state-building 16–19, 21, 23, 26n6
Luka, Banja 18–19

Macedonia 6, 97–9, 101n4, 101n5, 135; and Europeanization 89–97, 99–101
Milošević, Slobodan 72, 112, 113–14
"mirror paradox" of the Western Balkans 132
Mladić, Ratko 114, 115, 119
mobilizing structures 14, 19–20, 24
modern state, the 106–7
mono-ethnic states 15
Montenegrin language, the 82–3
Montenegro 8, 37, 70–1, 81, 84–5; political polarization in **75**, 75–7, **77**
Mostar 16, 21
multi-ethnic state, the 61

national vetoes of DPA 16
nationalizing state, the 54–5
NATO bombing of Kosovo 18, 117–18
"no-blueprint" paradox in the Western Balkans 131, 133
"no damage" paradox in the Western Balkans 132
nomenklatura, former 108
non-saturated nation-state, the 112–13
norms and paths of transformation by CEE members post-1991 108–9
Northern Ireland 78
NPAA (National Program for the Approximation of Legislation) 99

OHR (Office of the High Representative) 14, 15, 17, 20, 23, 24; loss of credibility 16, 18–19, 25
Ohrid Framework Agreement, the 92–3
OMONIA (Democratic Union of the Greek Minority) 57, 58, 60
Orthodox Christianity 78–9
OSCE (Organisation for Security and Co-operation in Europe) 6, 9, 19, 29, 58, 129
OSCE mission of international assistance to Euro-Atlantic integration in BiH 29–32, 34–6, 45–7, 48n4; through educational reform 33, 36–44, 48n12, 48n13, 48n14
ownership of state-building projects 32–6, 43–4, 45

PBPNJ (Union of Human Rights Party) 57, 58
peacebuilding and political power 32–3
Petritsch, Wolfgang 34
PIC (Peace Implementation Council) 16, 31, 36
police reform and the SAA in Bosnia 18–19

policy development process in Macedonia 97–9, 101
political opportunity structures 14
political polarization in Montenegro **75**, 75–7, **77**
politicians' avoidance of responsiblities 34
Poplašen, Nikola 17, 18
post-modern state, the 107
PzP (Movement for Change), Montenegro 77

quadratic nexus, the, and external involvement in state-building 53, 54, 60, 66
see also democratization and state-building in Albania and Kosovo

Rambouillet accords, the 116
reconciliation and democratization 136
refugee returns 21, 22
regional co-operation 13
regional dimension to EU integration 136–7
Rehn, Olli 114, 117, 119
religious cleavages 78–9, 83–4, 86n5
religious influence in public education 49n20
Robbins, Gary 49n25
RS (Republika Srpska) 7–8, 14, 15, 16, 18, 38

SAA (Stabilization and Association Agreements) 4, 18; in Macedonia 92, 94; in post-conflict Serbia 114, 115, 117, 118–19, 120–1, 122
SAP (Stabilization and Association Process) 9, 92, 128
school civic bodies in BiH 39, 40–1
SEE (South-Eastern Enlargement) of the EU 108
self-rule funding scandal in Croatia 20
Serbia 6, 7, 9–10, 106–7, 109, 112–21, 122n1; Kosovo Serbs 61–2, 65–7, 68n4
Serbian nationalism in Montenegro 73–4, 77, 79
Serbian resistance to international community governance 16–19
SNP (Socialist People's Party), Montenegro 71, 75, 77
Solana, Javier 119
"sovereignty" paradox in the Western Balkans 131, 133
SPC (Serbian Orthodox Church) 78–9, 84, 113
SPS (Socialist Party of Serbia) 113, 114
SRS (Serbian Radical Party) 17, 113, 114
state, the, new definitions of 54–5, 61, 68, 106–7, 112–13, 135
state-building 3–5, 12, 21, 24, 92, 124; and the international community 14, 15–19, 22, 25 *see also* international statebuilding in post-conflict Bosnia and Herzegovina

INDEX

state identity and EU enlargement 105–10
state structures 1–2
strategic accessions to the EU 106, 109, 110, 112–16
structural cleavages 72, 73, 74–5
structural forms of ownership 33, 37, 38, 39
Switzerland 78
symbols and national identity 23, 80–1

Tadić, President Boris 6, 114, 115, 116, 117, 118, 119
transition theory 113, 122n11
triadic nexus, the, and the emergence of nationalism 54–5
tribalism and ethno-cultural cleavage in Montenegro 79–80

UNMIK (UN Interim Administration Mission in Kosovo) 60–1, 64, 65, 118

Venice Commission, the 5–6
Vujanović, Filip 82

Western Balkans, integration in the 128–38

Yannulatos, Anastasios 59
Yugoslavia 112, 138n2
Yugoslavian constitutional establishment 73–4

www.routledge.com/9780415623278

Related titles from Routledge

EU Conditionality in the Western Balkans

Edited by Florian Bieber

This volume examines how European institutions, the European Union in particular through its policy of conditionality, have shaped the post-conflict reconstruction of the Western Balkans. From state-building to democratization and environmental policies, this book explores whether and in what ways the EU has been successful in consolidating states and democracy in the Balkans.

This volume assesses the EU's struggle to transform the societies through conditionality and whether the offer of EU membership is enough to build stable democracies.

This book was published as a special issue of *Europe-Asia Studies*.

Florian Bieber is a Professor at the University of Graz, Austria and Director of the Centre for Southeast European Studies.

August 2012: 246 x 174: 184pp
Hb: 978-0-415-62327-8
£85 / $145

For more information and to order a copy visit
www.routledge.com/9780415623278

Available from all good bookshops

www.routledge.com/9780415638388

Related titles from Routledge

European Security Policy and Strategic Culture

Edited by Peter Schmidt and Benjamin Zyla

With the Lisbon Treaty in place and the European Union increasingly involved in international crisis management and stabilization operations in places near and far, this volume revisits the trajectory of a European strategic culture. Specifically, it studies the usefulness of its application in a variety of circumstances, including the EU's operations in Africa and the Balkans as well as joint operations with NATO and the United Nations.

The contributors find that strategic culture is a useful tool to explain and understand the EU's civilian *and* military operations, not in the sense of a 'cause', but as a European normative framework of preferences and constraints. Though at variance over the extent to which security and defence missions have demonstrated or promoted a shared strategic culture in Europe, the authors reveal a growing sense that a cohesive strategic culture is critical in the EU's ambition of being a global actor.

This book was published as a special issue of *Contemporary Security Policy*.

Peter Schmidt is Honorary Professor at the University of Mannheim and a former senior fellow of the Stiftung Wissenschaft und Politik in Berlin.

Benjamin Zyla is an Assistant Professor at the Graduate School of Public and International Affairs at the University of Ottawa.

January 2013: 234 x 156: 232pp
Hb: 978-0-415-63838-8
£85 / $145

For more information and to order a copy visit
www.routledge.com/9780415638388

Available from all good bookshops